THE NAMES AND TITLES OF JESUS

OTHER BOOKS BY THE SAME AUTHOR:

Rédemption Sacrificielle, Une enquête exégétique. Studia. Recherches de Philosophie et de Théologie publiées par les Facultés S.J. de Montréal, no. II, Desclée de Brouwer, 1961.
Un classement littéraire des Psaumes, Desclée de Brouwer, 1964.

THE NAMES
AND TITLES OF
𝕵𝖊𝖘𝖚𝖘

THEMES OF BIBLICAL THEOLOGY

BY

Leopold Sabourin, S.J.

Translated by Maurice Carroll

NEW YORK
THE MACMILLAN COMPANY

Library of Congress Catalog Card Number: 66–22534

FIRST AMERICAN PRINTING

Originally published in French as: *Les Noms et les Titres de Jésus: Thèmes de Théologie Biblique*, Les Editions de Brouwer S.A., Bruges, Paris, 1963.

Imprimi potest Montréal, le 4 août 1962
J. d'Auteuil Richard, S.J.
Provincial

Nihil obstat Edward J. Montano, S.T.D.
Censor Librorum

Imprimatur ✠ Terence J. Cooke, D.D., V.G.

The *nihil obstat* and *imprimatur* are official declarations that a book or pamphlet is free of doctrinal or moral error. No implication is contained therein that those who have granted the *nihil obstat* and *imprimatur* agree with the contents, opinions or statements expressed

68509

The Macmillan Company, New York
Collier-Macmillan Canada Ltd., Toronto, Ontario
Printed in the United States of America

CONTENTS

PART IV

SOTERIOLOGICAL TITLES

PART V

PROPERLY CHRISTOLOGICAL TITLES

FOREWORD

AT A critical moment in His career Jesus asked His disciples, "Who do men say that I am?" They answered, "Some say John the Baptist, others say Elijah, others say one of the prophets." Jesus then asked them, "Who do you say that I am?" Only Peter answered, "You are the Messiah," to which the text of Matthew adds, "the son of the living God" (Mark VIII: 27–33; Matt. XVI: 13–17; Luke IX: 18–22). This is the critical question for Christians: Who is Jesus? What are we to call Him? By what title or titles do we most fully and accurately identify His person and His mission? The history of Christian theology is full of statements which the Church had finally to judge inadequate or false. Such was the statement of Arius that Jesus is the created word of God; such was the statement of Nestorius that Jesus as man was not the natural son of God; such was the Modernist statement that the historical Jesus is not the Christ of faith. The church has had to search her belief and her traditions in order to protect the identity of Jesus from distortion; but the Church has never claimed that she has fully comprehended the reality of Jesus. She has never known Him with the clarity with which she expects to know Him in the eschatological vision. As long as she is the Church engaged in the world, she must continue to learn His reality more fully, for she learns her own identity only by understanding the reality of Jesus. The task is never finished, for each generation of the Church must achieve its own understanding of the reality of Him whose body she is.

In his confession Peter could say no more than that Jesus was the Messiah—accepting for the moment the commonly held opinion of interpreters that the phrase added in Matthew is an early expansion of the text of Mark. The brevity of Peter's confession is greatly expanded elsewhere in the New Testament. Father Sabourin has collected every phrase which can be called a title of Jesus. The number will astonish most readers. The titles disclose that the apostolic Church was already embarked on the search for a deeper understanding of the reality of Jesus. No one title can contain this reality, and the New Testament writers and their sources were aware of this. Many of the titles are still in common use in the Church; others have been abandoned. ☩Father Sabourin, like all biblical interpreters, is convinced that the Church today must keep in constant touch with the New Testament if she is to find her own formulation of who Jesus is and what He is. The New Testament is in this respect the unique source; it is the only collection of Christian documents whose understanding of Jesus arises from direct personal experience. Even those titles which are rarely or never used in our generation reveal aspects of the reality of Jesus which we shall miss without these titles.

The confession of Peter identifies Jesus as the Messiah. Messiah represents a Hebrew word which has come into English through Greek and Latin as Christ. Even in the New Testament one can discern the beginning of the development which issues in the use of the word Christ as a part of the personal name of Jesus rather than as a title. This is not an entirely felicitous development. For many modern Christians—a word which, to their surprise, could be rendered as Messianist—the name Christ has no more significance than the personal surnames which we bear ourselves. The linguist knows that the surname has a meaning, but most people either do not know the meaning of their own surname or never think of it as significant. It simply distinguishes them from people who bear other surnames, and could be replaced by a number with no loss of meaning. Yet when Peter called Jesus the Messiah, he used the most meaningful title that a Jew could employ. Like other titles, Messiah does not describe the reality of Jesus exhaustively; but it is the first step towards the understanding of the reality. Unless Jesus is understood as the Messiah of Israel, He is not understood at all.

It is part of the richness of Father Sabourin's treatment that each of the titles of Jesus is placed in its Old Testament background. Those who experienced the reality of the Incarnation knew no other way to describe their experience than to use biblical language. The Old Testament is the recital of the acts of God. The Incarnation is the climactic act of God, in history, the act in which the saving and the judging attributes of God are merged into unity. The disciples' use of biblical language was not a mere accident of cultural conditions. It was their faith and it is ours that the revelation of God to Israel and his inbreak into history in Israel were events without parallel. When Jesus is called "the son of God," the term "God" in the apostolic Church meant precisely the divine being, called Yahweh in the Old Testament, who revealed himself to Israel. The term does more than place Jesus on the divine level of existence; it places Him in relation to that divine being whom Israel had known from its origins.

The incarnation has its place in the course of sacred history; but the understanding of the Old Testament is itself transformed in the New Testament. If one reads Father Sabourin's treatment of the royal messianic titles, one will see to what an extent the sometimes political messianism of Judaism has been given a new dimension. Jesus fulfills the reality of the King Messiah without being a political king. A similar if less radical transformation can be observed in other titles. It is not only the King Messiah who receives a new dimension in the New Testament; Israel itself receives a new dimension, and learns its true reality in the revelation of God in Jesus. In the Christian faith historic Israel did not recognize this new dimension because it did not grasp the reality of Jesus. The Christian cannot pass judgment on Israel, as unfortunately he has so often done. He will do better to reflect on the fact that his own generation in the Church can likewise fail to recognize the reality of Jesus, and fail to recognize its own identity.

The first generation of the Church had the task of proclaiming Jesus to Gentiles who had no knowledge of the God of Israel or the history of Israel. The necessity of some adaptation was obvious, and the adaptation was made without fear, and even without any hesitation that has left any trace in the New Testament. The title "Son of Man," for instance, used in all four Gospels, does not appear in the epistles. It is altogether likely that this title, which is so distinctively Semitic that it is still obscure to us, was not meaningful for the Gentiles, and was replaced by other titles. Yet the Gospels suggest that this was Jesus' favorite designation of Himself. Certainly the apostolic preachers showed a boldness here which later Christians have often been afraid to imitate. Yet the apostolic preachers did not attempt to remove Jesus from the background of sacred history from which He emerged. They proclaimed the Messiah of Israel even to peoples who did not know what the word meant; and they were ready to take the trouble to explain Jesus in the only terms which they felt were adequate for the purpose. They invited people to believe in Jesus Messiah, not in some other savior figure, of which there was a sufficient number of examples in the Hellenistic-Roman world. Father Sabourin's study shows how abundantly the proclamation

of Jesus was enriched by quotations and allusions from the
Old Testament.

There was, of course, some degree of "Hellenization"
of the titles of Jesus in the early Church, and Father
Sabourin has pointed out this feature of the proclamation.
This was the first step in the unending process of understanding Jesus. Each generation and each culture must
interpret Jesus in its own terms. The danger of distortion
is great and obvious, and it would not be difficult to
enumerate a frightening number of examples. Not all of
the distortions are equally important. It is probably not
vital that most of the conventional representations of
Jesus in art not only have no assured likeness to his features,
but do not even suggest the man who appears in the Gospels.
It is not vital, but it is not trivial either. Any portrait of
Jesus must be idealized; in so far as the portrait represents
the ideal Jesus of the artist and of those for whom he
paints, it should at least suggest a Galilean villager rather
than a French nobleman or a matinee idol. Such defor-
mations are not found in the "Hellenization" of Jesus in
the New Testament. The general direction of the transformation is in greater emphasis on Jesus the risen Lord and
the son of God. Some scholars have affirmed that this is
deformation and not transformation; they forget that
the same Church which produced and read the epistles
also produced and read the Synoptic Gospels, from which
we learn all that we know of Jesus of Nazareth, the Galilean
villager who departed much less from His type than we are
inclined to think. But a proclamation of Jesus of Nazareth
which was not also a proclamation of the risen Messiah and
Lord would be a distortion of the reality also. The apostolic
Church wrought this transformation, its own growth in
understanding, with delicacy and assurance.

These are no more than a few hints of the lasting importance of the problems which Father Sabourin approaches
in this book. Nothing has been said of the solid learning and

technical competence with which he approaches the problems, or of the unusual clarity of his exposition. More and more readers of the Bible are now demanding works which go beyond the level of even the best popularization. It would be deceptive to say that Father Sabourin's book will be easy for all comers. It would be equally deceptive to say that the reward does not exceed the effort.

JOHN L. MCKENZIE, S.J.

INTRODUCTION

THE person of Jesus and His work constitute an inexhaustible research subject that can be approached from any number of viewpoints. For several reasons, however, the study of the names or the titles of Jesus is highly advisable. To be bound to a precise terminology at the outset is to gain an objective basis for a research that should not aim primarily at proving theses or confirming preconceived interpretations. Certainly the researcher's own elaboration is indispensable in biblical theology, for Scripture is the result of the collective effort of a host of authors or traditions whose mutual relations are more often juxtaposed than coordinated into a whole. The abiding presence of the Spirit, however, sees to the coherence, essential unity, and permanent value of their views.

New Testament usage of the names of Jesus, then, reveals the profound tendencies of primitive Christian tradition in reflecting the earliest theological thought on Christ. Several titles of Jesus are, in fact, veritable condensations of ancient Christological conceptions—some of them gained early popularity; others, reflecting an age or a milieu, soon fell into obscurity; all of them are invaluable as worthy witnesses to Christian thought in the Apostolic Age.

Anyone who appreciates the full significance the name held for the biblical mentality will understand that value. For a Semite, the name represents and embodies the man that it designates.[1] This concept is proved, above all, by the Name *par excellence*, the name of God, which sums up His attributes and power. When God wanted to manifest Himself to Jacob (Gen. XXV: 11) or to Moses (Exod. VI: 2), He conformed with that mentality and made His name known to them (Exod. III: 14; Ezek. XXXIX: 7).

The mentality in the New Testament is similar: graced with a new name, the risen Jesus inaugurates a new existence; with the divine name Κύριος, "Lord," He received transcendent power (Phil. II: 9f.; Heb. I: 4). At its "resurrection" Jerusalem, too, will be called "by a new name pronounced by the mouth of the Lord" (Isa. LXII: 2). To bear a name whose full import is known only by oneself is to be invested with limitless power. The divine Warrior, armed for the eschatological combat, bears "a name which no man knows except himself" (Apoc. XIX: 12). Conscious of the unique power of the divine Name, the first Christians called themselves "those who invoke the name of the Lord" (cf. Acts IX: 14, 21); from the name of the Lord or, more exactly, from Christ the Lord (cf. Phil. II: 11; Acts III: 16) they awaited the answer to their prayers with the same confidence as those under the old law who invoked the name of the Lord (Joel III: 5; cf. Rom. X: 13).

Throughout the Bible numerous persons have had significant names: "the man called his wife Eve because she was the mother of all the living" (Gen. III: 20); the future deliverer of the Hebrews received the name Moses from Pharaoh's daughter for, she said, "I drew him out of the water" (Exod. II: 10); Jacob's oracles about his sons' future and that of the tribes that will bear their names (Gen. XLIX), play cleverly on the sense of those names, associating a somewhat fortunate destiny with them and crowning patriarchal history with the news of the coming of a Messianic king (v. 10). By fulfilling his task of naming the animals (Gen. II: 20), Adam, in turn, shares in God's creative activity and affirms his superiority over irrational creatures, for knowing the name of a being is equivalent to having power over it (cf. Isa. XL: 26).

Several great figures among the chosen people even received names from God Himself defining their role at the time of the Preparation. At the age of ninety-nine the father of the faithful (cf. Rom. IV: 16) saw himself graced by God with a new name marking his destiny and mission: "You shall no longer be called Abram, but your name shall be Abraham; for I will make you the father of a multitude of nations" (Gen. XVII: 6). During a struggle, real or symbolic, with a supernatural being, Jacob, the father of a people, received the name Israel: "because you have contended with God and men, and have triumphed" (Gen. XXXII: 29).[2] Every name reveals the person or thing that it designates (cf. Isa. I: 26); it both commits to a path and dedicates to a destiny (cf. Hos. I: 4; Isa. VII: 14).

Our viewpoint is clarified by the present book's subtitle, *Themes of Biblical Theology*, which accounts for numerous omissions, as regards, for instance, scholastic terminology and the teachings of the Church's magisterium. In fact, biblical theology aims at teaching Christian reality *only* as it is expressed in the Bible. Therefore, it differs from exegesis by an effort at synthesis that tries to coordinate the elements dispersed throughout Scripture. Unlike speculative theology, it has no recourse to deductive reasoning; nor does it depend heavily on philosophical categories or on later developments of Revelation's data. Guided always by a tradition in accord with the analogy of faith, biblical theology teaches nothing incompatible with sure theological conclusions.

What should the book's actual title be? Should we talk of "names" or of "titles"? The formula that we have used excludes that choice and distinguishes the *names* of Jesus (Part I) from His *titles*. Occasionally, a "name," such as "Rabbi" or "Master," could as easily be placed among the "titles," but would be less easily assigned to a predetermined

category. The classification chosen also leads to discussion
on other counts; for example, we could not affirm that
titles such as "Bread of Life" or "Gate for Sheep" are clearly
Messianic. We shall concede also that "Son of Man" could
be classified either with the Messianic titles or with the
soteriological ones. As for the order of the titles within
each part, it is not purely arbitrary, but follows a certain
logic that is occasionally indicated.[3] We have grouped
under a single treatment closely related titles to facilitate
exposition.

Dealing with biblical theology necessitates many Scriptural references. To avoid padding we have chosen as our
guiding principle: Never more than two references to any
given subject. Yet we have not hesitated to quote lengthy
texts directly necessary for a given development. Almost
always their English translation is taken from the Confraternity of Christian Doctrine text with the kind
permission of the publishers.

The notes are few in number and contain only those
bibliographic directions judged indispensable. Two works,
however, deserve special mention: V. Taylor, *The Names
of Jesus* (London, 1954), and O. Cullmann, *The Christology
of the New Testament* (Philadelphia, 1959). We have
gratefully appreciated their treatment of the subject in
composing this work.

Taylor's inquiry will interest the reader looking for an
exhaustive coverage of the different uses of the various
titles of Jesus and for an authoritative analysis of the
principal texts together with conclusions on the history of
primitive Christology. Without diverting our attention
from the most important texts, we have tried to situate
them in the larger context of biblical revelation by also
examining the ideas of the Old Testament, which is
basically Christological in its orientation. As our subtitle
suggests, the book also treats the *biblical themes* related to
the names and titles of Jesus.

No less great is our debt to Cullmann's book, especially for his exposition of ten titles: Prophet, Servant, High Priest, Messiah, Son of Man, Lord, Saviour, Logos, Son of God, "God."

Numerous books and articles by Catholic authors have also competently explained some names of Jesus in a less systematic fashion.[4] For example, Monsignor Cerfaux's *Christ in the Theology of Saint Paul* (New York, 1959) has carefully analyzed the names "Son of God" and "Lord" and tried to determine the ideological contexts used for the different words in the formula "Our Lord Jesus Christ." We have reproduced in an Appendix (pp. 315–317) a list of names of the Saviour collected toward the end of the seventh century.[5]

Our treatments avoid technical discussions and those deep analyses that interest scholars alone. Directed to a cultivated public anxious to deepen its faith and eager to learn about the Christology of the New Testament, they also contain many developments on the Christian life. To treat of the titles of Jesus is to cover some important biblical themes. With that in mind, we hope that this work will offer subjects for further development or discussion on the intended level of biblical studies. To the authors whose works proved useful and to Father J. L. D'Aragon, who read the manuscript, we express our indebtedness.

NOTES ON THE INTRODUCTION

[1] "A name," Origen writes, "is a condensed expression representing the very nature of the thing named" (*De Oratione*, 24: *Patr. Graeca* II, c. 492). He next treats what has been called "the philosophy of the name" (cf. I. Hausherr, *Noms du Christ et voies d'oraison*, Rome, 1960, p. 27).

[2] The names *Abraham* and *Israel* are explained by Genesis according to an etymology which is popular and theological rather than real or scientific, as often in the Bible. The "priestly tradition" links to another episode the change of Jacob's name to that of Israel (Gen. XXXV: 10). This is but one out of many examples which illustrate the presence in the Pentateuch of various "traditions" occasionally mentioned in this book. This variety accounts for parallel narratives, stylistic variants, and other apparent incoherences of any given book.

³ For example: in Part III we distinguish the titles that are addressed to Jesus as "Leader" (10–14) from those that consider Him as "Life" (15–17) of the community. Elsewhere, as in Part IV, the more general titles are placed first, while in Part V the first three titles contain several common notions.

⁴ Several names or titles of Jesus are explained in most biblical dictionaries or encyclopedias. In his famous work *Los nombres de Cristo* (1st ed.), Fray Luis de León (†1591) reduces the names of Christ to ten: Shoot, Mirror, Way, Shepherd, Mountain, Father of the World to Come, Arm, King, Prince of Peace, and Bridegroom (cf. *Dict. de Théol Cath.*, vol. 9, I, c. 363). The recent edition of the *Obras Completas Castellanas* of Fray Luis de León (BAC, Madrid, 1951; cf. pp. 343–790) also includes a treatise on the following names: Son of God, Beloved, Jesus, Lamb. The names of Christ provide Fray Luis with a starting point for long theological dissertations. Among the older works may also be mentioned that of Ambrose Serle (1742–1812), *Horae solitariae . . . or, Essays upon some remarkable names and titles of Jesus Christ, occurring in the Old Testament and declarative of his essential divinity and gracious offices in the redemption of men . . .* , 3rd ed. (London, 1804), in two volumes, the second dealing with the names of the Holy Spirit. Closer to our times G. M. Roberti wrote his valuable *L'onomatologia del Divin Redentore* (Rome, 1960). J.-L. Leuba has also something to say about Christ's names in *L'Institution et l'Événement* (Neuchâtel, 1950). He divides them into two categories: some, like Son of David, King of the Jews, King of Israel, Christ, Son of God, are "institutional," while others, like Son of Man, Lord, Servant, are termed "spiritual." Even his distinctions do not seem to solve the difficulty of classifying certain titles whose meanings have progressed and changed with Christian reflection on Revelation. Some Semitic names later left out are explained by Père Daniélou's "Les titres du Fils de Dieu" in *Théologie du Judéo-Christianisme*, vol. I (Tournai, 1958), pp. 199–226. A popular exposition of the names of Jesus is offered by W. Barclay in *Jesus as They Saw Him* (SCM paperback, 1962). The chapters of the book, says the author, "began life as articles in the pages of the *British Weekly*, although many of them have been extensively revised and rewritten" (p. 7). Quite different in character is *Christologische Hoheitstitel, Ihre Geschichte im frühen Christentum* (Göttingen, 1963), in which F. Hahn presents a scholarly treatment of "Son of Man," "Lord," "Christ," "Son of David," "Son of God," adding an appendix on the "eschatological Prophet."

⁵ A Latin poet of the fifth century, Orientius, composed fifty poems on the names of Jesus: cf. L. Bellanger, *Le poème d'Orientius* (Paris, 1903) or *Patrologia Latina*, vol. 61, cc. 1003f.

I

THE NAMES OF JESUS

1

JESUS

THE proper name "Jesus" is the transcription of the Greek name ʼΙησοῦς, which itself is adapted from the Hebrew *Ieshoua*, a common Jewish name. Many biblical persons have borne this name: Joshua, son of Nun (Num. XIII: 3), and the high priest of the same name (Zech. III: 17); a priest (I Chron. XXIV: 11) and a Levite (II Chron. XXXI: 15), several Restoration pioneers (cf. Ezra II: 6; III: 9), the son of Sira (Sir. L: 27), an ancestor of Jesus Christ (Luke III: 29), and a fellow worker of St. Paul (Col. IV: 11). The name "Jesus," common enough in the first century A.D., later became uncommon for disparate reasons: Christian respect and Jewish scorn.[1]

"And when eight days were fulfilled for his circumcision, his name was called Jesus, the name given him by the angel before he was conceived in the womb" (Luke II: 21). This circumcision was symbolic of the complete stripping of His fleshly body that Christ was to accomplish by His death and resurrection (cf. Col. II: 11f.). To distinguish among people with the same name the Jews often added the father's name and even the mother's name: Simon, "son of Jona" (Matt. XVI: 17), Judas, "son of Simon" (John VI: 71). So too, the Gospel recalls that Jesus was "son of Mary" (Mark VI: 3). Even today Ethiopians (Semites like the Jews) adopt the father's first name as their second name.

He who came to accomplish all Promises and to be the culminating point of all salvation history received a name quite indicative of His work: *Jesus*. The angel Gabriel ("the man of God") appeared to a young Nazareth girl and said:[2] "*Rejoice*, full of grace, the Lord is with thee" (Luke I: 28). Astonished by the reference both to "Messianic joy" (cf. Zeph. III: 14–17; Joel II: 21–27) and to the *Emmanuel* prophecy (Isa. VII: 14), the humble virgin hears an explanation: "And the angel said to her: 'Do not be afraid, Mary, for thou hast found grace with God. Behold, thou shalt conceive in thy womb and shalt bring forth a son; and thou shalt call his name Jesus" (Luke I: 30f.).

Saint Matthew insists on the adoptive sonship of Jesus with relation to *Joseph*. Presenting Jesus as the Messiah and son of David, heralded by the prophets, he continues that insistence in his "list of generations" (Matt. I: 1–17). Nor does he fail to underline Joseph's role in giving Jesus His name: "Do not be afraid, Joseph, son of David, to take to thee Mary thy wife, for that which is begotten in her is of the Holy Spirit. And she shall bring forth a son, and thou shalt call his name Jesus; for he shall save his people from their sins" (Matt. I: 20f.). As the angel reminded Joseph, the Hebrew name Iehôshoua, or its shorter form, Ieshoua, means "Yahweh is salvation." The title "Saviour" belongs properly to Christ and is the reason why He was called Jesus at birth.

The origin of the name of Jesus is not therefore explained in the same way by Matthew and Luke. The Old Testament practice of having the father (Gen. IV: 26; V: 3) or the mother (Gen. IV: 1–25) name the firstborn remained in the New Testament. In the episodes of Jesus' infancy Matthew clearly sees the accomplishment of certain prophecies and so, before informing us that Joseph named Mary's son Jesus (Matt. I: 25), he cites the sign of the Lord: the virgin shall be with child, and bear a son, and shall name him Emmanuel (Isa. VII: 14; Matt: I: 23). If Jesus has not been called Emmanuel, His person and work, nonetheless, have fully realized the sense and import of that prophetic name. Since the Incarnation Jesus has been "God with us," as the angel declared to Mary: "The Lord is with thee" (Luke I: 28; cf. I: 35).

*
*   *

In the New Testament the name "Jesus" is especially used in writings that deal with the historical life of the Saviour: the Gospels, of course, but also the Acts of the Apostles, often recall that Jesus was "a man" of flesh and blood, who was caught up in contemporary history (cf. II: 22f., 32). Sometimes the local origin of the Incarnate Word is precisely stated, as in the phrases "Jesus of Nazareth" (Mark I: 24; XVIII: 37), "Jesus the Galilean" (Matt. XXVI: 69). The Book of Acts speaks of "the Nazarene sect" (XXIV: 5).

The name "Jesus" suggests the historic and earthly humanity of the Saviour, but not exclusively. In St. Paul, for example, the name appears a score of times, separated from the more common titles of Christ or Lord. Thus there is mention of "faith in Jesus" (Rom. III: 26), of "the life of Jesus" manifested in our bodies through suffering (II Cor. IV: 10f.). of the resurrection with Jesus (v. 14), of those who have fallen asleep with Jesus (I Thess. IV: 14). The Epistle to the Hebrews also uses the human name of Jesus widely, generally allotting it the prominent place in the sentence (cf. III: 1, XIII, 20). While the Apocalypse exalts the glorified Christ, it does not neglect Jesus' personal name (cf. I: 9; XIX, 10). The First Epistle of Saint John, too, mentions it, in relation with the Precious Blood (I: 7; cf. Heb. X: 10, 19).

The name Mary gave her child (Luke II: 27, 43) will also be used to designate the controversial healer (cf. John IX: 16; X: 19) who will sometimes stir Jerusalem's inhabitants: "And when he entered Jerusalem, all the city was thrown into commotion saying, 'Who is this?' But the crowds kept on saying, 'This is *Jesus*, the prophet from Nazareth of Galilee' " (Matt. XXI: 10f.). Saint John reports a scene that says a great deal about the mysterious prestige of Jesus. About to be arrested, he asks the Jews' emissaries: "Whom do you seek?" They reply: "Jesus of Nazareth." When, therefore, He said to them, "I am He," they *drew back* and fell to the ground (John XVIII: 6), like the enemies of the just man described in the Greek version of a psalm: "My enemies will *draw back* on the day that I shall call upon you, O Lord, certain that you are my God" (Ps. LVI: 10).

The *supernatural power* of the name of Jesus is frequently described in the Synoptics too: upon returning from a mission the seventy-two said to Jesus: "Lord, even the demons are subject to us in thy name" (Luke X: 17); those who believe in Jesus hear Him describe a whole series of future miracles to be performed in His name (XVI: 17f.). The rejected recall to no avail the prodigies they once accomplished in the name of Jesus (Matt. VII: 22f.). The power of that name even fomented rivalry: "John said to him, 'Master, we saw a man who was not one of our followers casting out devils in thy name, and we forbade him.' But Jesus said, 'Do not forbid him, because there is no one who shall work a miracle in my name, and forthwith be able to speak ill of me. For he who is not against you is for you.'" (Mark IX: 38ff.)

*
*   *

The death of Jesus did not suppress *the power of His name*. To the lame man begging alms at the gate called Beautiful, Peter declares: "Silver and gold I have none; but what I have, that I give thee. In the name of Jesus Christ of Nazareth, arise and walk" (Acts III: 6). Addressing the crowd, Peter associates *faith* with the power in the

name of Jesus: "And it is his name, by means of faith in
his name, that has made strong this man whom you behold
and recognize; moreover it is the faith that comes through
Jesus that has given him the perfect health you all see"
(III: 16). Summoned before the Sanhedrin to justify his
conduct, the apostle renders the same testimony: "In the
name of Jesus of Nazareth . . . even in this name does he
stand here before you, sound" (IV: 10ff.). This echoes the
psalmist's strophe: "O God, by your name save me, by
your power make me right" (LIV: 3).

Victims of persecution, the apostles implore God to
support their apostolate: "while thou stretchest forth thy
hand to cures and signs and wonders to be wrought by the
name of thy holy servant Jesus" (Acts IV: 30). Yet certain
moral conditions affect the invocation of His name, which
is not magical or automatically effective. Faith on the part
of the recipient is a requirement (Acts III: 16), and the
healer cannot work without mandate: in vain "certain of
the Jews, exorcists, also attempted to invoke the *name* of
the Lord Jesus over those who had evil spirits" (Acts XIX:
13). Besides, it is Jesus Himself who works the miracles, for
the name takes the place of the person: Peter says to the
paralytic of Lydda: "Aeneas, Jesus Christ heals thee"
(Acts IX: 34).

It is noteworthy that while, on earth, Jesus used to heal
and command spirits in His own name, the apostles would
later cure in the name of another. The visible prodigies He
worked symbolized also an invisible power—that, for instance,
to remit sins (Mark II: 1–12). When they baptized "in
the name of the Lord Jesus," the apostles showed that they
had understood (Acts VIII: 16; XIX: 5). Peter said to the
Jewish converts: "Repent and be baptized every one of you
in the name of Jesus Christ for the forgiveness of your sins;
and you will receive the gift of the Holy Spirit" (Acts II:
38; I Cor. VI: 11). Rather than the baptismal formula
(cf. Matt. XXVIII: 19), the expression "in the name of

Jesus" concerns the meaning of the rite itself: profession of faith in Christ and Christ's claim on those dedicated to Him.

NOTES ON 1

1 The "name of Jesus" has been studied thoroughly by J. Dupont in the Supplément to the *Dictionnaire de la Bible* (henceforth *DBS*), vol. VI, c. 514–41. In No. 369 of *Vie Spirituelle* (January 1952), devoted entirely to the *Name of Jesus*, there is a notable article that studies that name's use in the New Testament (pp. 5–18: C. Spicq) and in the Old Testament under such diverse forms as : Joshua, Hosea, Isaiah, Elisha, Jesus Ben Sirah (pp. 19–37: F. M. Lemoine). For "the mystery of the name Jesus" as it is prefigured in the Old Testament (especially by the name Joshua), see J. Daniélou, *From Shadows to Reality* (London, 1960), pp. 229–43. In a somewhat different area, cf. J. E. Ménard, *Les élucubrations de l'Evangelium Veritatis sur le "Nom,"* in *Studia Montis Regii*, 1962, pp. 185–214.

2 The translation (our own) of the Greek χαῖρε as "rejoice" is based on the interpretation of the Greek Fathers of the Church and is proposed by modern exegetes. Cf. an article by Père Lyonnet in *Ami du Clergé* (1956), pp. 39ff., and R. Laurentin's *Structure et Théologie de Luc I–II* (Paris, 1957), pp. 64–71. There is no general consensus, however, among scholars, on the matter: cf. A. Strobel, *"Der Gruss an Maria"* (Luke I: 28) in *Zeitschrift für die Neutestamentliche Wissenschaft* (1962), pp. 86–110.

2

SON OF JOSEPH, SON OF MARY

WITH the exception of some intimates, the contemporaries of Jesus knew nothing about His virginal birth. Even the Gospel texts reflect popular tradition by frequently naming Jesus "son of Joseph" (Luke IV: 22; John I: 45; VI: 42). The two genealogies, however, make certain distinctions: "And Jacob begot Joseph, the husband of Mary, and of her was born Jesus who is called Christ" (Matt. I: 16); "And Jesus himself, when he began his work, was about thirty years of age being—as was supposed—the son of Joseph . . ." (Luke III: 23). Because of the supposed paternity of Joseph, Luke can speak of the "parents" of Jesus (II: 27) and of "his father and mother" (II: 33). The very variety of expressions formulated for the family relations of Jesus testifies to the truth of the Incarnation and the fidelity of the evangelists to their sources.

The people of Nazareth were astonished by the wisdom of one of their number: "Is not this the carpenter, the son of Mary?" (Mark VI: 3). It seems that the original text of Mark was more closely related to Matthew XIII: 55: "Is not this the carpenter's son? Is not his mother called Mary?" The evangelists, then, willingly associate the son and the mother. In the lodging at Bethlehem the Magi saw "the child with Mary his mother." (Matt. II: 11). To "Mary, the mother of Jesus," Simeon addresses his prophecy (Luke II: 34). Near the cross, John tells us, stood Mary, the mother of Jesus (XIX: 25-27) when Jesus said to the apostle who represented us all: "Behold thy mother." The disciples who had gathered together in the Cenacle to pray with Mary, the mother of Jesus, and with His brethren, understood this (Acts I: 14). Following biblical and Semitic usage, (cf. Gen. xiii: 8) the term "brethren of Jesus" (cf. Matt. XII: 46) does not refer to sons of Mary but rather to cousins or close relatives of Jesus.

The Gospels, then, speak about Mary soberly. Jesus left His Church the joy of discovering the glories of Mary, mother of all the saved upon Calvary. Mary's role as mediatrix was to be gradually attested by a cult that fulfills Scripture's words: "All generations shall call me blessed" (Luke I: 48).

Christian piety has multiplied words to describe the salvific role of the mother of God and of men. Of all the titles in her litanies, *Ark of the Covenant* is one of the most biblical. To the virgin's objection the angel answers: "The Holy Spirit shall come upon thee, and the power of the Most High shall *overshadow* thee" (Luke I: 35), a quite obvious allusion to the luminous cloud which attested the presence of God in the Tent (Exod. XL: 34f.) and on the propitiatory, above the *ark of the covenant* (I Sam. IV: 4; Ps. LXXIX: 2). Yahweh lived *in the midst* of Israel (cf. Deut. VI: 15, VII: 21); Luke underlines God's descent *into the womb* of the Virgin (I: 31; II: 21), the daughter of Sion (cf. Zeph. 14–17; III: Isa. XII: 6).[1]

The presence of God in the midst of His people is one of the major Old Testament themes. Even the Visitation episode subtly exploits the *typology of the Ark of the Covenant*, Yahweh's mobile sanctuary. "The highly stylized account is filled with traits that lead us back, reference by reference, to the account of David's transfer of the ark to Jerusalem."[2] Luke I: 39–44 compared to II Sam. VI: 2–11 displays several parallels (more evident in the original): the same region concerned, the country of Juda; the same manifestations, the joy of the people of Jerusalem, Elizabeth's joy, the joyous leaps of David and John the Baptist, the cries of the people and of Elizabeth. "The ark going toward Jerusalem—and such is also Mary's direction—is conducted *into the house* of Obededom (II Sam. VI: 10) and Mary goes *into the house* of Zachary (Luke I: 40). In both houses the presence of the ark and of Mary are mutual sources of blessing. On the arrival of the ark David had exclaimed: "How can it be that the ark of the Lord comes to me?" (II Sam. VI: 9). Elizabeth, too, uttered a cry of wonder at Mary's arrival: "And how have I deserved that the mother of my Lord should come to me?" (Luke I: 43). Shortly afterward the parallelism between "the ark of the Lord" and "the mother of the Lord" reappears: "The ark of the Lord stayed with Obededom for three months" (II Sam. VI: 11); "Mary remained with Elizabeth about three months" (Luke I: 56). In Messianic times, Jeremiah explains, the ark of the covenant will no longer be missed, another will not be built, nor will there be any memory of it (III: 16). Although Jerusalem will doubtlessly be called "the throne of the Lord" (III: 17), a new ark of the covenant, a thousand times more marvelous than the first, will be the world's guarantee of God's abiding presence (cf. John I: 14).

While Mary did enjoy privileges due the divine and virginal maternity, she was, nonetheless, made not by a miracle-working God but by a God "who so loved the world that he gave his only begotten son" (John III: 16; cf. Rom. VIII: 32). In Mary it is not these prodigies we admire but her faith and total commitment to realizing the salvific plan. Before everything else in this "handmaid of the Lord" (Luke I: 38), Elizabeth will praise the faith: "And blessed is she who has believed, because the things promised her by the Lord shall be accomplished" (Luke I: 45). Mother according to the flesh, Mary was also mother according to the faith. To understand this we need only reflect on the spiritual paternity of Abraham, who also will beget a son according to the promise: "Is anything too wonderful for the Lord?" (Gen. XVIII: 14; Luke I: 37).

Mary's maternity is more than an event in her personal history; it constitutes an irreplaceable link in salvation history: humanity's welcome to God who descends upon this earth. And so Mary is the perfect redeemed one, the finest fruit of her divine Son's redemption. Through faith man receives the justification offered him; through Mary God is linked to man. The child Jesus was not an imaginary child. From Mary He received a definite body, and, in a certain sense, a definite soul, for it is the quality of bodies that makes souls differ at the dawn of existence. The soul of Jesus easily dominated that perfect body received from Mary. The Son of Man resembled His mother not only in physical features but also in His intellectual and religious physiognomy. Although there can be no end to describing all that Jesus received from His mother, it is, however, little compared to all that the mother received from the Son.

NOTES ON 2

[1] This verse, Isa. XII: 6, is thus correctly translated by the *Bible de la Pléiade* "Exulte et crie de joie, *habitante de Sion*, car grand est au milieu de toi le Saint d'Israël."

[2] René Laurentin, *Structure et Théologie de Luc I–II*, pp. 79f. On the subject of the literary genre of Luke I–II, Laurentin concludes: "From the analyses presented in the preceding chapter, it is clear that one of the most characteristic procedures of Luke I–II consists in narrating Christ's infancy by alluding to the Scriptures (the midrashic procedure). Reflection on the Scriptures, not storytelling, is the essence of the midrashic genre that draws upon all their nuances to incorporate new facts into the great Revelation. In Luke the genre is applied to history (cf. pp. 93, 96f.). In yet another work, *Court traité de théologie mariale* (Paris, 1953), Laurentin writes (p. 113): "A Marian bibliography would contain almost 100,000 titles. Rigorous selection must be employed." Laurentin makes just such a selection. Of interest, too, are C. Spicq's *Ce que Jésus doit à sa mère selon la théologie biblique et d'après les théologiens mediévaux* (Montréal–Paris, 1959), 55 pp.; Karl Rahner's *Mary, Mother of the Lord* (New York, 1963); Romano Guardini's *La Mère du Seigneur* (Paris, 1954). Guardini draws attention to the gulf separating the two notions of procreatrix and mother; then he adds: "Mary could become mother of that unique Son only on condition of assuming maternity in the personal sense." A footnote clarifies: "Perhaps it is that fundamental point

that separates Catholics and Protestants on their ideas of Mary. Protestants seem to consider Mary only as the mother of the man Jesus in the purely physical sense and to exclude both her role as mother of the Incarnate Son of God and the personal relationship that unites her to the Redeemer. What follows from these views would react against the very person of Christ. The definitions of the Council of Ephesus refer as often to Mary as to Christ (pp. 29ff.).

3

THE MASTER

STANDING before Pilate, Jesus solemnly proclaimed that He had come into the world "to bear witness to the truth" (John XVIII: 37). Many Gospel texts show that during His public ministry people often addressed Jesus by calling him: "Master!"

Two evangelists, Mark and John, are witnesses to the frequent usage of *Rabbi*, that reverential title accorded doctors of the Law. On the mount of the Transfiguration, where Jesus appeared as a new Moses, Peter addressed Jesus, saying "Rabbi, it is good for us to be here" (Mark IX: 5). Enlightened from above, the guileless Nathanael (probably the Bartholemew of the Synoptics) declared the Messianic sonship of Jesus :"Rabbi, thou art the Son of God, thou art King of Israel" (John I: 49). In the passages proper to his Gospel, Matthew designates the Master by the name Rabbi only once: "And Judas who betrayed him answered and said, "Is it I, Rabbi?" (Matt. XXVI: 25). The term Rabbi, Hebrew or Aramaic, literally means "my great one." *Rabboni*, an intensive form of the title, figures in two exclamations recorded in the Gospels, one uttered by Bartimeus, the blind man (Mark X: 51), the other by Mary Magdalene (John XX: 16).

An eyewitness account brings us to the meeting of Jesus with His first disciples. Of John and Andrew, His followers,

Jesus asks simply: "What is it you seek?" They say to him: "Rabbi [which interpreted means 'Master'], where dwellest thou?" (John I: 38). John also informs us that the Greek word διδάσκαλος, frequent in the Synoptics (Matt., Mark, Luke), translates the original word *Rabbi*. The same explanation accompanies the use of *Rabboni* (John XX: 16). In the proper sense, διδάσκαλος means "teacher." Finding the term inadequate for the Saviour, Luke often preferred the expression 'επιστάτης, "master" (literally, "president"), as when he reports the disciples' cry for help to the Saviour asleep in the boat. "Master, we are perishing" (VIII: 24.). John usually retains the original word *Rabbi* and thus escapes the problem of translating.

The use of *Rabbi* and its translated form, Taylor notes, clearly illustrates the destiny of several names or titles of Jesus. Little by little, the early or primitive expression proved inadequate for designating the person of Jesus as it became better known. And for that reason, the use of *Rabbi* is limited to the Gospels, those faithful witnesses of the first human reactions before the mystery of Jesus. The title *Rabbi* was spontaneously conferred upon Jesus, although He had not gone through rabbinic schools: "And the Jews marveled, saying: 'How does this man come by learning since he has not studied?' Jesus answered them, and said: 'My teaching is not my own, but his who sent me' " (John VII: 15f.). Soon, however, other titles would be judged more suitable for designating Him who came not only to teach but also to *be* "the Way, the Truth, and the Life" (John XIV: 6).

The French word *Maître*, with its various implications, still enjoys a certain popularity in designating Jesus.[1] In the fullest sense, there is only one Master, God, or the One whom He has placed over all things: "But do not you be yourselves called 'Rabbi,' for one is your Master, and all you are brothers" (Matt. XXIII: 8).

In fact, the Fourth Gospel presents Jesus as *Divine Wisdom* come upon earth to teach men and to be the life of the disciples. Under such conditions the title *Rabbi* was destined to have a short career.

NOTES ON 3

[1] The word "Master" often serves as an inadequate translation of Κύριος, "Lord" (cf. p. 257).

II

SIMPLE MESSIANIC TITLES

MESSIANISM

JESUS received several titles as the one who realized in His own person and work the hopes long identified with the Old Testament expectation of the Messiah. Some of them are collective or communal in scope and will be examined only after the simple titles, associated with the Messiah as an individual; others, such as "Servant" and "Son of Man" could be appropriately listed among the Messianic titles, but they are assigned to another, more proper, category.

Messianism is a very complex notion and must now be examined. Bent toward the future, the Messianic idea was, A. Gelin says, "the longing for a definitive era coinciding with the movement of faith itself."[1] And so the Messiah belongs also to eschatology, being a figure of the last days. In an acceptable sense the word "eschatology" may allude either to the end of the world or to an important turning point in human history that somehow inaugurates a new era. Only by God's transcendent intervention does such an event happen: God's relation to history is conceived as a series of interventions that make its sweep unpredictable.[2] An important current of biblical tradition assigns a decisive role to the Messiah in the unfolding of the most crucial turning points of world history.

"Messianism without a Messiah": such a phrase is sometimes used to describe a biblical tradition that concentrates on a basic expectation, that of the coming of *God Himself* to establish His rule and to ensure effective recognition of His royalty. God did come in the past: He delivered the Israelites from bondage in Egypt; He will come again to chastise the nations (Isa. XXXII: 28), to re-establish Sion (Isa. LII: 8), to judge the earth (Ps. XCV: 13), or to save it (Wis. XVI: 7). This theme of God's coming, therefore, constituted an obscure searching toward the mystery of the Incarnation.

Now Messianic expectation followed a trend perceptible in the first texts: the proto-evangelium (Gen. III: 15), the promises to the patriarchs (cf. Gen. XII: 3; Rom. IV: 13), and the commitments to the Covenant (cf. Exod. XIX: 5f.). Derived from a Hebrew word meaning "to anoint" or to "rub with oil," the term "Messiah" is usually applied to *the king* and to the ritual of his investiture (cf. I Kings I: 34). High priests (cf. Exod. XXX: 30) and even simple priests (cf. Lev. VIII: 30; X: 7) were also anointed, although prophets were not.[3] All three groups of leaders (king, prophet, priest) enjoyed Messianic preferment in view of the roles they would play as founders of the Covenant.

With the settlement in Canaan hopes focused on the person of the king who, according to the biblical conception, embodies the whole people and appears as its natural mediator. In time the royal line will prove disappointing and drive the people to "Messianism without a Messiah," the theme of Yahweh-King, found in Deutero-Isaiah (cf. XLIII: 15; LII: 7f.),[4] and in several Psalms (cf. XCII: 1; XCV: 10; XCVII: 6; XCVIII: 1). With the monarchy's disappearance and the collapse of national hopes came a new source of Messianic promise: the *Servant of Yahweh* now embodies the vocation of the "Remnant" of Israel (cf. p. 135) called to self-sacrifice for the salvation of the world (cf. Isa. LIII). The Servant figure is linked to prophetic Messianism and to the *Son of Man*, whose transcendence is still greater. As for Ezekiel, he favored a postexilic theocracy closely related to priesthood (chs. XL–XLVIII). Thus was strengthened the concept of priestly Messianism, mentioned by a few texts: Num. XXV: 12f.; Jer. XXXIII: 14–26; Zech. VI: 11f.; Sir. XLV: 25. Among the "soteriological titles" will be examined that of *High Priest*, together with the noble figure of Melchizedek.

Apologetics in the past strained its ingenuity by trying to draw "a premature portrait of the future" with details taken out of their Old Testament context. Today we prefer to read in the Messianic idea the continuity of God's intervention.[5] In the Old Testament the chosen people was restored by victories over the enemy; in the New Testament all mankind is invited to become a chosen people. God's intervention in Israel showed His concern, prefiguring and even inaugurating the fulfillment of His universal, salvific plan. Israel's history is a sacred history. Because Messianic longing often saw future spiritual realities in a material form, it could hardly be clearly expressed, and only gradually was it freed from its all too human features. Seen in the light of the New Testament, Messianism appears to be ancient history's most advanced expression of its inclination toward Christ and the Communion of Saints.

As the Christian era dawned, the longing for the Messiah was intensified, as it appears, for instance, in the apocryphal *Psalms of Solomon*. The inspiring ideas of Psalm XVII center on the following theme: "See, O Lord, and raise up for them their King, David's son, in an age you, O Lord, know, so that he may rule over Israel, your servant, and gird him with strength to crush the unjust rulers." It is the accomplishment of this hope that rejoiced old Simeon, who "awaited the consolation of Israel" and who had been promised "that he should not see death before he had seen the Christ of the Lord" (Luke II: 25f.).

NOTES ON MESSIANISM

[1] *The God of Israel, The God of Christians* (New York, 1961), p. 199.
[2] A. Gelin, "Messianisme" in *DBS*, vol. V, c. 1165f. Cf. also *L'Attente du Messie* (Bruges, 1954); *La Venue du Messie. Messianisme et eschatologie* (Bruges, 1962), works written in collaboration.

[3] R. de Vaux, *Ancient Israel: Its Life and Institutions* (New York, 1961) p. 400. "In all probability, the custom of anointing the high priest was already practiced from the end of the Persian period, though the first written evidence we can date with certainty comes much later." Earlier he had recalled that all the texts concerning *priestly anointing* were postexilic redactions. "It is therefore possible that, after the disappearance of the monarchy, the royal anointing was transferred to the high priest as head of the people and later extended to all the priests" (p. 105). I Kings XIX: 16 is often cited to prove that some prophets were anointed. But it seems that here the term "anointing" is due to the context and is inexactly applied to the "consecration" of the prophet to God, as in Isaiah LXI: 1 (cf. Ps. CIV: 15).

[4] The *Deutero-Isaiah* or the "Book of the Consolation of Israel" comprises chapters XL–LV of Isaiah, and is the work of an anonymous author of the end of the Exile, a disciple of Isaiah and a great prophet too. Chapters LV–LXVI are also some three centuries later than the eighth-century prophet although they do not present the same unity of composition as chapters XL–LV.

[5] J. Daniélou detects, in Israel's expectation, two parallel trends: one concerns the *divine actions*, the glory of which will, at the end of time, make the former ones look pale; the other awaits the eschatological advent of figures which will reflect, at a higher level, those of the past. Prophecy is, in fact, not seldom the foreseeing of the recurrence of past events (cf. *Approches du Christ*, Paris, 1960, pp. 94f.).

4

HE-WHO-COMES

THE notion of a "Messianism without a Messiah," of a coming of God Himself, is the best introduction to this title, for the formula *God-Who-Comes* certainly is behind the Messianic name "He-Who-Comes," as the New Testament shows. Dominated by the intervention of God in past, present, and future history, Old Testament theology is a sacred drama stretching from the beginnings to the end of the world's history. The chief actor in this drama wears many faces.

According to one image that describes the theophany on Sinai (cf. Exod. XIX: 16–25) the *God-Who-Comes* comes forward as the "Lord of the Storm" (cf. Nah. I: 2–6). Elsewhere, the eschatological God shows Himself under the appearances of a "warrior" (Isa. XLII: 13), but more often He "visits" earth through destructive armies (Isa. V: 26–30). The *God-Who-Comes* is also portrayed as "a judge," as for example in this royal psalm cited by I Chronicles XVI in association with the Levites' service of the ark, "Yahweh's resting place":

> *Let the plains be joyful and*
> *all that is in them*
> *Then shall all the trees of the*
> *forest exult*
> *before the Lord, for he comes;*
> *for he comes to rule the earth.*

> *He shall rule the world with justice*
> *and the people with his constancy.*
> (Ps. XCV; 12f.; cf. Joel IV: lf.)

Other liturgical acts proclaimed God as a "monarch" whose dominion grows strong over all peoples (cf. Ps. XLVI). This conviction already appeared in a strophe of the paschal song known as "the song of the sea": "The Lord shall reign forever and ever" (Exod. XV: 18). And Isaiah trembled when he recalled his prophetic experience: "My eyes have seen the King, the Lord of hosts" (VI: 5).

Yet the *God-Who-Comes* is not only a terrifying God. In Old Testament texts He is often given the quality of "father": "O Lord, hold not back, for you are our father . . . you, Lord, are our father; our redeemer you are named forever" (Isa. LXIII: 15f.; cf. also Isa. LXIV: 7; Deut. XXXII: 6; Jer. III: 19; XXXI: 9; Mal. II: 10; Ps. LXVII: 6; LXXXVIII: 27; Tob. XIII: 1, 4; Sir. XXIII: 1, 4; Wis. II: 16; XIV: 3). So, too, *Abiel* (cf. I Sam. IX: 1) is composed of *abi*, "my father," and of *el*, "God." The eschatological God displays even maternal feelings: in the new Jerusalem Yahweh says "as a mother comforts her son, so will I comfort you" (Isa. LXVI: 13).

In the Old Testament, then, and even in the New, the drama of the last days is described in images which set the whole creation in motion (cf. Amos VIII: 19; Matt. XXIV: 29). "The fact that *God will come* is the only permanent element in Old Testament eschatology, all the colorings that describe His return are but secondary and impermanent elements."[1]

When the fullness of time came, God sent His Son (Gal. IV: 4; cf. Eph. I: 10) to proclaim the approach of the Kingdom of God (Mark I: 15; cf. Dan. VII: 22), which would be restored, independently of Jewish national hopes (cf. Acts I: 6–8). Still other testimonials show that at the time of the New Testament redaction, *Messianic times were identified with eschatological times*. Of the medicinal punishments inflicted on the young Israelite people St. Paul said: "Now all these things happened to them as a type and they were written for our correction, upon whom the final age of the world has come" (I Cor. X: 11). The prologue to the Epistle to the Hebrews adds that God, "last of all in these days" spoke to us through His own Son Christ (I: 2), who, manifesting Himself once and for all "at the end of the ages, has appeared for the destruction of sin by the sacrifice of himself." (Heb. IX: 26; cf. I Pet. I: 20).

Of course, Messianic times do not coincide with the end of the world, but their arrival marks *the end of a world*, therefore an eschatological intervention by God. God once came in the Incarnation (cf. John I: 14); He will come again in the Judgment confided to the Son of Man (John V: 22, 27). For many Jews the expectation of the *God-Who-Comes* coincided with that of the Messiah. Thus, John the Baptist sent to ask of Jesus: "Art thou he who is to come [ὁ ερχόμενος] or shall we look for another?" (Luke VII: 19).[2] The Greek term signifying "he who is to come" is found again in the Fourth Gospel: in the mouth of John the Baptist twice (I: 15, 27); in this statement of Lazarus' sister Martha: "Yes, Lord, I believe that thou art the Christ, the Son of God, who hast come into the world" (II, 27); in the people's thoughts: "This is indeed the Prophet who is to come into the world" (VI: 14; cf. Deut. X: 18).

At the Messianic entry of Jesus into Jerusalem, the crowd shouted to Him: "Hosanna! Blessed is he who comes in the name of the Lord!" (Mark XI: 9). In Luke this exclamation from Psalm CXVII (v. 26) appears in Jesus' own mouth: "Behold, your house is left to you. And I say to you, you shall not see me until the time comes when you shall say, 'Blessed is he who comes in the name of the Lord!'" (XIII: 35). In all likelihood, this prophecy refers to the definitive *parousia* of Jesus (cf. I Cor. IV: 5; XI: 26). A similar association is found in the Epistle to the Hebrews,

where Habakkuk's prophecy with the Septuagint application to the Messiah is quoted: "For again a while, a very
short while, *He-Who-Comes* will arrive and will not delay"
(Heb. X: 37).

The Apocalypse also takes up the *God-Who-Comes*
motif in a primitive liturgical doxology; "He is, He was,
He is coming" (I: 4, 8; IV: 8). By these frequent New
Testament reminders of the closeness of the End all the
faithful were kept on the alert and saw in every catastrophe
an announcement of the final eschatological drama. For
each individual too, *He-Who-Comes* must be the host
expected at any hour: "Watch, therefore, for you do not
know at what hour your Lord is to come" (Matt. XXIV: 42).

Besides these texts that explicitly mention the Messianic
title *He-Who-Comes*, there are a great many biblical
passages that present the various mysteries of Jesus' life
and work as a *coming*. In His eschatological discourse
Jesus announces that after the cosmic cataclysms "they will
see the Son of Man coming upon the clouds of heaven with
great power and majesty" (Matt. XXIV: 30; cf. Dan. VII:
13). According to Mark, at Judgment the Son of Man "will
come with the holy angels in the glory of his Father"
(VIII: 38), a text probably inspired by a saying in Zachariah:
"Then, the Lord, thy God, *shall come*, and all his *holy ones*
with him" (XIV: 5).

Even though Genesis (XLIX: 10) is not to be read any
longer as a direct prophecy of the Messiah's coming
(Shiloh),[3] its words may be applied to David, as empire-
builder and type of the Messiah. As we have already seen,
several statements by John the Baptist refer to the Messianic
coming. When the Precursor stated that "he who is coming
after me is mightier than I" (Matt. III: 11), he was thinking
perhaps of Isaiah's words: "Here *comes* with power the Lord
God, who rules by his strong arm" (XL: 10), a text next to the
explicit reference: "A voice cries out. In the desert prepare
the way of the Lord" (XL: 3; Matt. III: 3). Allusions to the

fire (Matt. III: 10–12) recall the purifying activity of the Angel of the Covenant described in Malachi (III: 2f.):

> *Lo, I am sending my messenger*
> *to prepare the way before me;*
> *And suddenly there will come*
> *to the temple, the Lord whom*
> *you seek,*
> *And the messenger of the*
> *covenant whom you desire.*
> *Yes, he is coming, says the*
> *Lord of hosts.*
> (Mal. III: 1; cf. Matt. XI: 10.)

The title *He-Who-Comes* characterizes, then, the principal actor in the great eschatological drama of the kingdom that exists already and is yet to come (cf. Luke XVII: 20f.; Matt. VI: 10). We have only to observe the frequent use of the verb *to come* throughout the New Testament to realize how great a part the *coming of the Messiah* plays in the saving plan of God. To some extent all salvation history is dominated by the expectation of the Incarnation and the wait for the Last Judgment—the two great "days of the Lord." With the creation of man that expectation came into being. Was not Adam himself, in St. Paul's words, *"the figure of him who was to come"* (Rom. V: 14)?

NOTES ON 4

[1] G. Pidoux, "Le Dieu qui vient, Espérance d'Israël," in the collection *Cahiers théologiques de l'actualité protestante*, no. 17 (Neuchâtel, 1942), p. 53. A chapter of this work is entitled: "Les visages du Dieu qui vient." Let us also mention the specialized study of S. Mowinckel, *He that Cometh* (Oxford, 1956). J. Dupont dedicated several pages to the title "Celui qui vient" in his article *L'ambassade de Jean-Baptiste*, in *Nouvelle Revue Théologique* (1961), pp. 814–21. At the end of a development on "Messianism without a Messiah" (the theme of Yahweh-King), A. Gelin writes: "It is surprising, Podechard liked to say, that, given the important place the preaching of the reign of God holds in the Gospel, even today more importance is given to the announcement of the Messiah-King than to the announcement of the kingdom of God. Surprising, too, that, given Jesus Christ is God and that in him God came upon earth, we fail to find in him the accomplishment of the promises which announced

the coming of Yahweh upon earth to establish his reign there" (*DBS*, vol. V, c. 1192). It has been observed by some authors that it is only in more recent texts that God is *invoked* as "Father" in the Old Testament (cf. R. Le Déaut, *La Nuit Pascale*, Rome, 1963, p. 87, n. 47).

[2] Cf. J. Dupont, "Art Thou He Who Is to Come?" *Theology Digest* (1964), pp. 42–47.

[3] W. L. Moran proposes to translate thus (Gen. XLIX: 10b): "Until tribute is brought to him, and his is the obedience of the peoples" (in *Biblica*, 1958, pp. 405–25).

5

THE CHRIST

STRICTLY speaking, the term *Messiah* is equivalent to "Christ" because the Hebrew word *māshiaḥ* or "Anointed [of the Lord]" is translated by the Greek Χριστός. Only twice in the entire New Testament does the Greek transcription Μεσσίας appear—in the Fourth Gospel, where John often cites a Hebrew word and then explains it. Andrew said to Simon, his brother: "We have found the Messiah (which interpreted is the Christ)" (John I: 41); the Samaritan woman said to Jesus: "I know that the Messiah is coming (who is called Christ), and when he comes, he will tell us all things" (John IV: 25).

In Mark and in Acts, the title *Christ* is most often used to designate Jesus as the Messiah. Interestingly enough, in Mark the expression is used only by others and never by Jesus of Himself: to the Master's question: "Who am I?" Peter answers: "Thou art the Christ" (VIII: 29). To Jesus on the cross the scribes address this challenge: "Let the Christ, the King of Israel, come down now from the cross ..." (XV: 32).

The other Gospels use the term *Christ* in the sense of Messiah even more than Mark does, and almost always in reporting sayings of others than Christ: John the Baptist reminds his disciples: "I am not the Christ but have been sent before him" (John III: 28). The Jews of Jerusalem affirm somewhat haughtily: "Yet we know where this man is from; but when the Christ comes, no one will know

where he is from" (John VII: 27; cf. vv. 31, 41f.). Martha,
however, expressed her faith thus: "Yes, Lord, I believe
that thou art the Christ, the Son of God, who hast come
into the world" (John XI: 27). On the feast of the Dedication
the Jews surrounded Jesus and asked: "How long dost
thou keep us in suspense? If thou art *the Christ*, tell us
openly" (John X: 24). The "Messianic secret" somewhat
stressed by Mark (cf. I: 34; IV: 12) seems to be echoed in
that question. According to John, however, the "Messianity" of Jesus, hidden from unbelievers (cf. XII: 39f.), is
revealed only to believers (cf. I: 41, 45).

Did Jesus call Himself Christ? The Gospel texts that
would answer "yes" are not very firm. Thus, for instance,
in Mark (IX: 41), it is probable that the text originally read:
"for whoever gives you a cup of water to drink because you
are *mine* . . . ," following the sense of Matthew (X: 42).
Even in the phrase, "for one only is your Master, the
Christ" (Matt. XXIII: 10),[1] "the Christ" seems to be the
evangelist's comment. In this passage from the priestly
prayer the term "Christ" certainly comes from John: "Now
this is everlasting life, that they may know thee, the only
true God, and him whom thou hast sent, Jesus *Christ*"
(XVII: 3). Even Jesus declared Himself to be the Messiah
only with reserve,[2] for this title could be understood in a
political and national sense, far removed from the profound
religious and biblical meaning that suited the expected
Sent of God.

Already at the time of the temptations in the desert,
Jesus had firmly committed Himself by rejecting a soft,
luxurious Messianism (temptation of the loaves; cf. Ezek.
XLVII; Ps. LXXI: 16), a miraculous one (temptation of the
pinnacle or of the gratuitous sign; cf. Sir. XXXVI: 5), and
a domineering one (temptation on the mountain; cf. Isa.
LX; Zech. XIV; Ps. II), in favor of a humble and religious
Messianism.[3]

Later on, John tells us, the Jews also tried to compromise

Jesus: "If thou art the Christ, tell us openly" (X: 24.). The answer of Jesus reaffirms His previous statements on His title as Sent from God. Once again, He refuses to proclaim Himself *Messiah* publicly, because of the possible implications of the term. Nevertheless, Jesus was certainly conscious of being the Messiah and He said so at the right moment: Jesus replied to the Samaritan woman who had stated her belief in the imminent coming of "the Christ": "I who speak with thee am he" (John IV: 26).

By retaining the Messianic sense of the title "Christ," the Book of Acts reflects at a later date the Gospel tradition. Paul used the Scriptures in his discussions with the Jews, "explaining and showing that *the Christ* had to suffer and rise from the dead, and that this is *the Christ*, even Jesus, whom I preach to you" (XVII: 3). "Paul was wholly occupied with the word, emphatically assuring the Jews that Jesus is the Christ" (XVIII: 5).[4] Out of twenty-five uses in the Acts, only twice does the composition of the *personal name* Jesus Christ (IX: 34; X: 36) appear. Two of the Gospels begin with a similar usage: "The beginning of the Gospel of *Jesus Christ*, the Son of God" (Mark I: 1); "The book of the origin of Jesus Christ, the Son of David, the son of Abraham" (Matt. I: 1).

This usage, unusual in the writings of a historical nature, became popular when the inspired authors began to grow more interested in that reflective, theological knowledge of Jesus, Christology. Thus in Paul's writings the archaic formula "Jesus the Christ" was supplanted by the complete title "Our Lord Jesus Christ" then used in the Christian communities. More than a title, the word "Christ" has taken on the value of a proper name in this passage: "For such do not serve Christ our Lord (Κύριος), but their own bellies (Rom. XVI: 18). Traces of the original meaning *Messiah* remain in a few texts—in Romans (IX: 5), for example, where Paul recalls that "from the Israelite race is *the Christ* according to the flesh." Furthermore, the

formula "Christ Jesus," often used by Paul (cf. Rom. VI:
3, 11, 23), shows that he never forgot the etymology of
"Christ." The expression "the Christ" recalls especially the
Messianic aspect of the person of Jesus, while the simple
"Christ" tends to become a personal name. Both can still
claim to be translations from the Gospels: "Jacob begot
Joseph, the husband of Mary, and of her was born Jesus who
is called *Christ*" (Matt. I: 16); "And it had been revealed
to him by the Holy Spirit that he should not see death
before he had seen *the Christ* of the Lord" (Luke II: 26).

Other writings of the New Testament manifest this
transformation of the word "Christ" into a personal name.
In fact, the growing influence of *worship*, which led to the
fixing of a certain number of names, must have been
partly responsible for the trend. The gradual recognition of
Jesus' greatness and of the depth of His being called for
new formulas. Jesus was, indeed, the promised Messiah and
was called such in polemics with the Jews. But He was
more than that, and Greek-speaking communities, less
aware of the Messianic tradition, hastened the adoption of
"Jesus Christ" as the name for the glorious, risen Saviour.
The tendency to make "Christ" a proper name clearly
indicates that the primitive community rejected, as did
Jesus Himself, the ideas of a political or national Messiah.
In "Christ" and "Christians" the community recognized
the new Israel in which all the hopes of the ancient one
were being accomplished to an unbelievable degree.

As the transcendence of Christ was exalted, the danger
grew of forgetting about the historic Jesus. Toward the end
of the first century John closes his Gospel with a truth that
he had underscored throughout: these signs have been told
"that you may believe that Jesus is the Christ, the Son of
God, and that believing you may have life in his name"
(XX: 30).[5] A similar concern leads him to suggest that
several deeds of the public ministry announced rites of the
Christian liturgy: the marriage at Cana, the cleansing of

the Temple, the healing of the paralytic and of the man born blind, the multiplication of the loaves, the washing of the feet, the piercing with the lance.[6]

Monseigneur Cerfaux finds the word "Christ" suitable to describe the person who begins his career in eternity and continues it in the Church. It has a greater extension than the name "Jesus," related to the mortal life of the Saviour, and also a wider meaning than the name "Lord," used for the Risen One present in the community. He then concludes: "Paul sees a difference between Jesus Christ and Christ Jesus. When we say 'Jesus Christ,' our thought starts with the idea of that man Jesus, whom God raised from the dead and in whom he has caused us to recognize the dignity and the role of 'Christ,' the messianic saviour. On the other hand, when we say 'Christ Jesus,' our thoughts start with the idea of the pre-existent Christ, who was manifested in the man Jesus of Nazareth."[7]

NOTES ON 5

[1] This saying possibly contains an allusion to the unlimited prestige of the Doctor of Justice in the Qumrân sect (cf. *Nouvelle Revue Théologique*, 1960, p. 1051).

[2] To the question of Caiphas, "Art thou the Christ?" Jesus answered, indeed, according to Mark (XIV: 61), "I am." It is, however, permissible to read in the original text "Thou said it . . . " instead of "I am" (cf. Matt. XXVI: 64; Mark. XV: 2). Thus, Jesus would have answered, "Thou said it; as for me I declare it: you shall see the Son of Man sitting at the right hand of the Power and coming with the clouds of heaven." Against the political role of a King-Messiah Jesus reaffirms the transcendent and salvific mission of the Son of Man. Cf. O. Cullmann, *The Christology of the New Testament*, pp. 119–22; V. Taylor, *The Gospel According to St. Mark*, p. 568; X. Léon-Dufour in *DBS*, vol. VI, c. 1465.

[3] A Gelin, art. "Messianisme," *DBS*, vol. V, c. 1206. Cf. C. Larcher, *L'actualité chrétienne de l'Ancien Testament, d'après le Nouveau Testament* (Paris, 1962), pp. 82–119: "Only at the end of His earthly career did He [Jesus] freely give Himself over to an undeniable messianic ovation (the entry into Jerusalem on Palm Sunday)" (p. 114).

[4] In the Acts there is often question of "preaching in the name of Jesus" (cf. IV: 18; V: 40; IX: 27). J. Dupont believes that the preaching is probably designed to show that Jesus is the Messiah or the Christ (cf. *DBS*, vol. VI, c. 526). Other authors believe that the sense of "Messiah" can be given to the word "Christ" in these Pauline texts: Rom. X: 6f.; I Cor. I: 23; X: 4; XV: 22;

II Cor. I: 5; IV: 4; V: 10; Eph. V: 25; Col. I: 24. Cf. also I Pet. I: 11; I John II: 22; V: 1; Apoc. XI: 15; XII: 10.

5 The demonstrative in the expression *"this* Jesus" (cf. Acts I: 11; II: 36; V: 30; IX: 17), J. Guillet says, "almost always translates the fundamental Christian affirmation, the continuity between the person who appeared in flesh and the divine being who is confessed in faith" (*Vocabulaire de théologie biblique*, Paris, 1962, c. 488).

6 Cf. O. Cullmann, *Early Christian Worship* (London, 1953), pp. 37–119; B. Vawter, "Johannine Sacramentary," in *Theology Digest* (1964), pp. 11–16; D. M. Stanley, "Liturgical Influences on the Formation of the Gospels" in the *Catholic Biblical Quarterly* (1959), pp. 24–38; P. E. Brown, "The Johannine Sacramentary Reconsidered," in *Theological Studies* (1962), pp. 183–206.

7 L. Cerfaux, *Christ in the Theology of Saint Paul* (New York, 1959), p. 508; cf. p. 488; see p. 261, n. 11.

6

THE DAVIDIC KING

THE New Testament frequently associates the person of Jesus with the dynasty of David, with nuances that we must now examine. That association should not surprise us, for before the Exile the king was the privileged inheritor of the Messianic hope in Israel.

THE MESSIAH, SON OF DAVID

The Bible often calls the king "the Anointed of God" (cf. I Sam. XXVI: 9, 11, 23) or equivalently "the Christ of God." As a candidate for the dignity of Messiah, each king in David's line is called on to embody the ideal Israelite monarch. "In the Old Testament perspective the reign of the Kingdom of God would be established in this world and temporal blessings accompany and attest spiritual values. The monarchy was infused with grace; its status was raised; its role was central in the smooth functioning of the Covenant and became one of the basic factors in the perspective of salvation."[1] Consequently the enthronement of a Davidic king meant his divine adoption (cf. Ps. II: 6–8).

Thus, the great Messianic texts are associated with royal figures: the oracle of Balaam (Num. XXIV: 17); the prophecy of Nathan (II Sam. VII: 1–16); the sign of the Emmanuel (Isa. VII: 14); the advent of the just king (Isa. XI: 1–9) and of the Bethlemite Messiah (Mic. V: 1); the Messianic eruption of 520, evoked by Haggai (II: 23) and

Zechariah (VI: 9–14), where a scribe substituted the name of Joshua, the high priest, for that of the Davidic Zorobabel (v. 11); and finally, the enthusiastic poem of Zechariah's disciple, describing the arrival of the humble and peaceful king (Zech. IX: 9; cf. Matt. XXI: 5).

For a long time, faith in the Messiah was associated with Israel's national restoration, which affected the literary presentation of the hope in the establishment of Yahweh's universal reign. It is to a root sprung from Jesse's stock (Isa. XI: 1), to one of David's line, that would be entrusted the human task of a restoration modeled on the successes of the Davidic era (Ezek. XXXVII: 22–24). With those considerations in mind, the importance of royal Messianism is less surprising.

Royal anointing existed outside of Israel. The fable of Yotam (Judg. IX: 7–15) attests that the rite was known in Canaan before the Israelite monarchy was established. The order given to Elias to go and "anoint Hazael as king of Aram" (I Kings XIX: 15) is also cited. While Egypt's high officials were anointed upon assuming their positions, the Pharaoh himself was not. Hittite kings were consecrated with "the holy oil of royalty." In Israel, royal anointing is a religious rite expressing the will of God: "Samuel took the phial of oil and poured it over Saul's head, then he embraced him and said: 'Is it not the Lord who hath anointed thee as leader of his people Israel?'" (I Sam. X: 1). The rite also conferred a grace, *the coming of the Spirit*, as in David's case: "The spirit of the Lord took possession of David from that day on." (I Sam. XVI: 13; cf. X: 10).

The New Testament associates with emphasis anointing and the bestowing of the Spirit: at His baptism Jesus is *anointed "with the Holy Spirit and with power"* (Acts X: 38; cf. Isa. LXI: 1);[2] all Christians (cf. I John II: 20), especially the Apostles (II Cor. I: 21f.) receive an anointing that stamps the Holy Spirit upon them in varying degrees (Eph. IV: 30). The importance of the king in ancient Israel is almost always associated with the sovereignty of the Lord (cf. Ps. II: 2; XX: 7), whose royalty is never forgotten by the psalmists (Ps. XLVI; 3: XCII: 1) or by the prophets (Isa. XXXIII: 22; Jer. X: 10).

Several New Testament titles remind us that Jesus was considered Messianic king, the offspring of David. The first title to be examined is the principal one: *Son of David*. The Synoptic Gospels report that, as Jesus passed by, the blind man Bartimeus cried out: "Son of David, have mercy on me!" (Mark X: 47). Mark, and Luke with him, have reported only one other instance (Mark XII: 35–37) when the title was applied to Jesus. Matthew, on the contrary, records additional examples: the two blind men (IX: 27), crowds (XII: 23; XXI: 9), the Canaanite woman (XV: 22) and the children in the Temple (XXI: 15)—all proclaim the Davidic lineage of Jesus. From the very beginning of his Gospel Matthew had shown some interest in the title: "Genealogy of Jesus Christ, *Son of David*, son of Abraham" (I: 1; cf. Luke III: 31).

Both the family of Jesus and the primitive Church believed in the Davidic origin of the Saviour. On several occasions in his Infancy account (I: 27; II: 4; cf. Matt. I: 20), Luke attests to and reflects the longing for a Davidic king (I: 32, 69; II: 11). Concerned with legal descendance, the two genealogies list Joseph's ancestors. By consistently affirming the virginal birth, Matthew and Luke suggest that Mary also was of Davidic lineage. This hypothesis can be traced from an ancient textual variant: "Because *they* [Joseph and Mary] *were* of the house and line of David (Luke II: 4). Besides adoption, it was a new attempt to reconcile the Davidic ancestry of Jesus with the virginal birth. That ancestry is clearly affirmed by St. Paul when he speaks of the Son of God, born "to the flesh, of the offspring of David" (Rom. I: 3), in a context connected with a primitive confession of faith.

A question arises: Did Jesus call Himself "Son of David"?

There is only one text that could supply an answer: "And while Jesus was teaching in the temple, he addressed them saying, 'How do the Scribes say that the Christ is the *Son of David*? For David himself says, by the Holy Spirit, The Lord said to my Lord: Sit thou at my right hand, till I make thy enemies thy footstool. David himself, therefore, calls him 'Lord'; how, then, is he his son?' " (Mark XII: 35–37; Ps. CIX: 1). At first sight, Jesus seems to be rejecting every Davidic affiliation. In fact, what He repudiates is the determining value of fleshly ancestry. If the Christ is Saviour, it is indeed by His divine origin (cf. John I: 13),[3] rather than by his Davidic origin. True sonship and true parentage in the kingdom of God are other than those of flesh, as Jesus said on another occasion (Mark III: 31–35). So too, St. Paul will tell the Jews that the true sons of Abraham are those who live by faith (Gal. III: 7). In the enigma he proposes from the statement of Psalm CIX, Jesus does not intend to deny His Davidic ancestry. He simply denies being a political Messiah-King, for His kingdom is not of this world (John XVIII: 36). The real Messiah is greater than the one expected. Probably for that reason the title "Son of David" was not retained for long in the Christian Church. Once again the Gospels testify to a primitive tradition and thereby proclaim their historical worth.

CHRIST-KING

To the title "Son of David" that of "King" is fittingly joined. Jesus was called "King of the Jews" on many occasions, usually in scorn, at His trial and during Pilate's questioning: "We have found this man perverting our nation, and forbidding the payment of taxes to Caesar, and saying that he is Christ a king" (Luke XXIII: 2; cf. Mark XV: 2–12). With words and gestures the governor's soldiers struck the "King of the Jews," and crowned Him with

thorns (Mark XV: 16–19; John XIX: 2f.). The enemies of
the Crucified mocked him, saying: "Let the Christ, the
King of Israel, come down now from the cross, that we may
see and believe!" (Mark XV: 32). But at the last moment
the good thief will ask to be received into the kingdom of one
whose heavenly dignity he discerned (Luke XXIII: 42).
Previously Jesus had answered "yes" to the question of
Pilate: "Thou art then a king?" (John XVIII: 37).

Earlier, at the triumphal entry into Jerusalem, the crowd
in its eagerness to honor Jesus had acclaimed Him King:
"Blessed is he who comes as a king, in the name of the
Lord! Peace in heaven and glory in the highest!" (Luke
XIX: 38; cf. II: 14). In Matthew (XXI: 5) and John (XII: 15)
the influence of Zecharias (IX: 9) is more apparent:
"Rejoice heartily, O daughter Sion, shout for joy, O
daughter Jerusalem. See, your king shall come to you; a just
saviour is he, meek and riding on an ass, on a colt, the foal of
an ass." To prevent His disciples from trying to proclaim
Him king as the crowd urged them, Jesus had to force them
to leave the scene of triumph that followed the multiplication of the loaves (Mark VI: 45). For them, Cullmann
observes, there was obviously a great difference between
being one of the intimates of a powerful Messiah-King and
being the disciples of a man condemned to death (cf. Matt.
XX: 21).

The primitive Christian community manifested only
mild interest in the title "King" as applied to Jesus. St. Paul
does not even mention it, perhaps out of deference to
sensitive Empire authorities. Later on, during the persecu-
tions, Jesus' royalty will be insisted upon by the Johannine
writings. According to the Fourth Gospel, Nathanael, upon
recognizing Christ's supernatural knowledge, exclaimed,
"Rabbi, thou art the Son of God, thou art King of Israel"
(I: 48). The multiplication of the loaves will later incite the
crowd to proclaim its benefactor *king* (VI: 15). The Apocalypse does not hesitate to call Jesus "the ruler of the kings

of the earth" (I: 5), the "King of kings" (XVII: 14; cf. XIX: 16). Only that book also ascribes these titles to Christ: the *Lion of the Tribe of Juda* (V: 5; cf. Gen. XLIX: 9), the *Root and Offspring of David* (XXII: 16; cf. Isa. XI: 1; Rom. XV: 12), *He Who Has the Key of David* (III: 7). Derived from Isaiah (XXII: 22), this last version of the royal title teaches that all authority to admit or to exclude from the city of David, the New Jerusalem, rests with Christ. Earlier, the Seer had learned from *He-Who-Lives*: "I was dead and behold I am living forevermore, and I have the keys of death and of hell" (Apoc. I: 18). By His death and resurrection Jesus cleared a passageway that leads from this world to the next (cf. Heb. X: 20).

MORNING STAR

A last royal title applied to Jesus, the *Star*, will now require some consideration. It is mentioned at the end of the Apocalypse: "I, Jesus, have sent my angel to you to publish these revelations concerning the churches. I am the root and the offspring of David, *the radiant morning star*" (XXII: 16; cf. II: 28). The well-known passage from the prophecy of Balaam comes to mind (Num. XXIV: 17):

> *I see him, though not now;*
> *I behold him, though not near:*
> *A star shall advance from Jacob,*
> *and a staff shall rise from Israel.*

So too, *the sign of the star* in Matthew (II: 2, 9f.) would testify to the coming of the Messiah-King.[4] In Mesopotamia the star was the sign of a king being made divine: "Where is he that is born king of the Jews? For we have seen his star in the East and have come to worship him" (Matt. II: 2). A late Midrash recounts that, on the day Abraham was born (cf. Matt. I: 1), the astrologers (or "Magi") notified King Nimrod that he should seize the child, for an evil omen had foretold his birth: they had seen a star rising in the heavens and devouring four other stars. Such hypothetical parallels cannot be used to relegate the star's appearance over Bethlehem to the realm of pure symbol. Yet we should recall that a sign more eloquent than a royal star could hardly be found to accompany the coming of a king (cf. Matt. II: 2) who would be "the light of the world" (John I: 4–9; VIII: 12). Using literary allusions, the evangelists freely grafted on historical facts a theological enrichment derived from their inspired meditation of Scripture.

The Second Epistle of Peter heralded the *eschatological* coming of Christ as the rising of "the morning star." After pausing to recall that fleeting anticipation of the glory of the Son of Man, the mysterious Transfiguration, the text continues:

And we have the word of prophecy, surer still, to which you do well to attend, as to a lamp shining in a dark place, until the day dawns and the morning star *rises in your hearts.* (II Pet. I: 19.)

The star or morning star was a *symbol of primacy* already familiar to the authors of the Bible; it is used, for example, in Sirah to exalt the high priest Simon (L: 6) and in Isaiah to describe the pride of the pagan tyrant (XIV: 12).[5]

The coming of the Davidic Messiah-King also answered a *longing* whose echoes can be found in first century B.C. writings. In one of the apocryphal Solomonic Psalms we read: "See, Lord, and raise up for them their King, David's son, in the time that thou knowest, O God, so that he may reign over Israel, thy servant" (XVII: 23). Much earlier, the *inspired* psalmist had foreseen the investiture of the Messiah-King by God Himself: "I myself have set up my king on Sion, my holy mountain" (Ps. II: 6). Royal Messianism, then, found its fulfillment in Jesus. Several elements of Nathan's prophecy (II Sam. VII: 12–16) are taken up in the annunciation made to Mary (Luke I: 32f.). It is noteworthy that the angel's message places divine

sonship before royalty: "He shall be great, and shall be
called the Son of the Most High; and the Lord God will
give him the throne of David his father." Was not this to
suggest that Jesus would be a Messianic king because He
is by nature the very Son of God?

By making Melchisedec, the mysterious "king of Salem,"
a "type" for Jesus Christ, the Epistle to the Hebrews (VII)
freed Messianic royalty from its national and earthly bonds,
and sought to give it a priestly significance (cf. Ps. CIX), for
according to the "cultural legend" of the Jerusalem sanctuary, Melchisedec came to Abraham bearing bread and wine
(Gen. XIV: 18). Christ is "King of Justice" and "King of
Peace" (Heb. VII: 2) to such an eminent degree that human
understanding cannot grasp all the rich nuances those
names contain.[6]

NOTES ON 6

[1] A. Gelin in *The God of Israel, the God of Christians* (New York, 1961), p. 203.
On the same subject, see "Le Messie, Fils de David," *Évangile*, no. 24; also
J. M. Gibbs, "Purpose and Pattern in Matthew's Use of the Title Son of
David," *New Test. Stud.* X (1964), pp. 446–64. Père de Vaux has treated
"Israelite Royalty" in *Ancient Israel: Its Life and Institutions* (London, 1961),
pp. 100–14. L. Ligier discovers deep significance in the citation of Psalm
VIII in Matthew (XXI: 16): "This psalm, whose meaning we know (cf. "Son
of Man") here reveals its full scope. Jesus, new David and new man, enters
into possession of the sanctuary in the name of the new creation" (*Péché
d'Adam et péché du monde*, vol. II, p. 64). "The evidence for this statement
overflows on the preceding events, revealing a resemblance between the
coming of Jesus and the restoration of the Davidic dynasty overthrown by
Absalom. Certainly, neither the facts, nor their order, nor the composition
of the account, exhibit a rigorous symmetry, but there is, nonetheless, a
similarity filled with contrasts, an analogy both in situations and in description, a clear recurrence of themes that underline the presence of a new David."
Specific references of unequal value are then proposed (pp. 64–67). Diverse
aspects of the theme "Christ-King" are given in *Lumière et Vie*, no. 57 (1962).

[2] Cf. Luke IV: 18; Acts X: 37f. According to Père de la Potterie, "the true
and, in a certain sense, the only context in which the New Testament speaks
of Christ's anointing, is that of Baptism" ("L'onction du Christ," in *Nouv.
Rev. Th.*, 1958, p. 250). This anointing is of the prophetic type, but Acts
IV: 27 connects it with the mission of the Suffering Servant, which Jesus
received at baptism. An anointing of the royal type, recalled by Hebrews
(I: 9) and associated with the Ascension, belongs to a citation of Psalms
(XLIV: 7f.), introduced to stress the supremacy of Christ. De la Potterie

observes that the New Testament places no other link between the theme of *anointing* and the name "Christ," and has no concern for the word's etymology (p. 251). At His baptism the anointing marked for Christ the inauguration of His public ministry: "Anointing calls up the idea of a consecration that sets one aside in God's service and promises divine gifts: that is why the Messiah is said to be anointed by the Lord (Isa. LXI: 1)" (J. Bonsirven, *Épîtres de saint Jean*, Paris, 1953, pp. 142f.).

[3] Even if the plural reading ("who were born": more probable) is adopted, the reference is still relevant, because our sonship is bound to that of the Saviour. *Bible de Jérusalem* has the singular.

[4] We have mentioned before (pp. 10f.) the influence of the *midrashic genre* on the redaction of Luke I–II. In Matthew's Infancy account, too, there is great care to associate historical interest with religious reflection in order to discover in Scripture the pattern as well as the uniformity of God's activity. Cf. M. Bourke, "The Literary Genus of Matthew I–II," in *Catholic Biblical Quarterly* (1960), pp. 160–75. J. Daniélou recalls that "in certain Eastern traditions *Balaam* was identified with Zoroaster, founder of the *magi*. The consequence was that Balaam himself was regarded as a magus. At once we see a new relationship between the prophecy in Numbers (XXIV: 17) and Matthew (II: 2). It is no longer the star alone which is *common to both*, but also the fact that each is concerned with *magi*, that is to say, Iranian priests" (*Primitive Christian Symbols*, Baltimore, 1964, p. 112). After research on the original context of the *Messianic star*, Daniélou concludes: "Thus the references to the star in the New Testament and Judaeo-Christian writings are seen to be closely connected with the battle fought against magian influence by missionaries, men who had come to Christianity from Essenism, in Syria and particularly at Damascus" (p. 121). Curiously enough, the name Balaam appears in the context of the citation on *"the morning star"* (cf. Apoc. II: 14; II Pet. II: 15). Syria was probably the place where Matthew's Gospel originated and so the interest he had in the Magi would reflect the attempt made in Syria to neutralize the star-worship fostered by the Magi. In Matthew the Messianic king is not the star, but the star leads the Magi to the true God who is revealed in the epiphany of Bethlehem. Largely unsuccessful attempts have been made to connect the visit of the Magi to Jesus with that of the Queen of Sheba to King Solomon (cf. *CBQ*, 1961, pp. 51–54). On Matthew (I–II) see also S. Muñoz Iglesias, "Literary Genre of the Infancy Gospel in St. Matthew," *Theol. Digest* (1961), pp. 15–20.

[5] The expressions "Star of the Morning, son of the Dawn" (Isa. XIV: 12) are found in a context that shows "points of contact with Phoenician mythology" (*Biblical Journal*), which we now understand better thanks to the Ugaritic texts of Ras Shamra (cf. p. 206, n. 2).

[6] The Apocalypse (XX: 4–6) says of the *martyrs* that after having been "beheaded because of the witness to Jesus and because of the word of God": "And they came to life and *reigned with Christ a thousand years*. This is the first resurrection. The rest of the dead did not come to life till the thousand years were finished. Blessed and holy is he who has part in the first resurrection! Over these the second death has no power; but they will be priests of God and Christ, and will *reign with him a thousand years*." Literal millenarianism is generally abandoned today and the Church has also disavowed that interpretation that would have Christ return to earth to rule there in the company of His faithful for a thousand years. Another traditional interpretation, dating back to Augustine, sees the *millennium* as comprising the Church's

rule between Christ's resurrection and *parousia*. A third interpretation suggests: "The resurrection of the martyrs symbolizes the Church's renewal after the persecution in Rome, just as the resurrection of the dry bones in Ezekiel (XXXVII: 1ff.) symbolizes Israel's renewal after the Diaspora" (M. E. Boismard, *L'Apocalypse*, Paris, 1950, p. 79; cf. A. Feuillet, in *DBS*, vol. VI, c. 1399). On the relationship between the title Κύριος and the royal dignity of Jesus, cf. pp. 257ff.

7

THE PROPHET

THE Messiah is one "Anointed." Since the prophets did not receive anointing, the word "prophet" seems out of place among the Messianic titles. Beyond the etymological or formal meaning, however, the term "Messiah" can be used to designate the person the Bible calls "He-Who-Is-to-Come," as previously explained. In these words, John describes the populace's reaction to the multiplication of the loaves: "When the people, therefore, had seen the sign which Jesus had worked, they said, 'This is indeed the Prophet who is to come into the world'" (VI: 14). A simple answer cannot be given to the question: Was Jesus a prophet? Capable of several meanings, this title is, in fact, applied both to John the Baptist and to the Saviour.

PROPHETISM

The prophetic role was gradually defined and purified in the religion of Israel. The books of Samuel and of Kings mention confraternities of prophets (cf. I Sam. X: 5; II Kings II: 3) and describe the strange conduct of these ecstatics, subject to collective trances (I Kings XXII: 10), not rarely communicated to onlookers (I Sam. X: 10; XIX: 20–24). Certain kings, like Achab, gladly surrounded themselves with these professional prophets, ready to pronounce favorable oracles.

The *true* prophets of Israel are of another stamp. Gifted

with a personal, irresistible vocation (Jer. I: 4–10), they cannot silence the divine message entrusted to their interpretation (Amos III: 8; Jer. XX: 7–10). Different from divination, which transmits isolated revelations, true prophecy becomes preaching: it interprets events, makes God's will and plan known, foretells, if need be, the executing of divine judgments.

From the long prophetic file certain impressive figures emerge: Moses, Samuel, Nathan, Elias, Eliseus, and the authors of our prophetic books. Last of these books was Daniel, completed by the middle of the second century B.C. when the appeal to oracles of the past (cf. Dan. IX: 6–10) seemed to admit that prophetic inspiration had ceased. According to Joel (III: 1f.), the return of the prophetic spirit was to accompany the coming of the Day of Yahweh, whose dawn was one with the appearance of Messianic times (cf. Acts II: 17–21). A half century after the Book of Daniel, I Maccabees deplores the disappearance of the prophetic charism (IX: 27; cf. Ps. LXXIII: 9) and foresees "the coming of a prophet" (IV: 46; XIV: 41). The Rule of the community of the New Covenant of Qumrân exhorted its members to hold fast to the Law, "until the arrival of a prophet and of the Messiases of Aaron and of Israel."[1]

THE WAITING FOR A PROPHET

According to Jewish expectations, a *definite* prophet was to come back at the end of time (eschatological return). Had Moses not said to Israel: "A prophet like me will the Lord, your God, raise up for you from among your own kinsmen; to him you shall listen" (Deut XVIII: 15)? In some articles the return of Moses himself was awaited, but attention was early fixed on Elias, probably because he had been taken up without passing through death (cf. II Kings II: 1–13). At the Transfiguration those two prophets will know a temporary return (cf. Mark IX: 4). The belief in the return of the *same* prophet survives in the expectation of Christ's *parousia*.

The New Testament presents *John the Baptist* as a prophet, as a new Elias, in his role as precursor of God Himself (cf. Luke I: 17, 76; Mal. 3, 23f.), or even more often in his mission as forerunner of the Messiah. To the question of the disciples, "Why then do the Scribes say that Elias must come first?" Jesus answered: "Elias indeed is to come and will restore all things. But I say to you that Elias has come already, and they did not know him, but did to him whatever they wished. So also shall the Son of Man suffer at their hands." Then the disciples understood that his words referred to John the Baptist (Matt. XVII: 11–13; cf. XI: 14). *Because* of his mission the Precursor suffered; the Suffering Servant, like Jesus, accomplished his mission *by* suffering. From some angles the diverse Messianic or Christological conceptions have no doubt reacted one upon the other.

In the Fourth Gospel there are traces of a polemic directed against a sect which exaggerated the importance of the Baptist's role to the detriment of that of the true Messiah (cf. John I: 8; III: 28–30). The affirmation that Jesus has pre-existed (John I: 15) has demolished the principal argument of these heretics: John the Baptist preceded Jesus; therefore he is greater (cf. Matt. III: 11). Considering John as the eschatological prophet, the sect of the Baptist was later to answer affirmatively a question already asked during the Precursor's lifetime: "Might he not be the Christ?" (Luke III: 15). John the Baptist, however, merely defined his role by citing Isaiah: "A voice cries out: In the desert prepare the way of the Lord" (XL: 3; cf. John I: 23; Matt. XI: 10).

JESUS, THE PROPHET

The Gospel texts that apply the title of prophet to Jesus belong to two categories. According to some, Jesus was a prophet among several. The resurrection of the young man of Naim, for example, produced this effect: "But fear seized upon all, and they began to glorify God, saying: A *great prophet* has risen among us, and God has visited his people" (Luke VII: 16; cf. XXIV: 19). The enemies of Jesus were afraid to seize him, because the crowds "regarded him as *a prophet*" (Matt. XXI: 46). Jesus seems to accept this popular conviction, when He says to the people of Nazareth, who received Him coldly: "A prophet is not without honor except in his own country, and among his own kindred, and in his own house" (Mark VI: 4).[2] He refuses to change His plans in the face of Herod's threats: "Nevertheless I must go my way for it cannot be that a prophet perish outside Jerusalem" (Luke XIII: 33).

Other circles wondered whether Jesus was the *eschatological prophet*, the one whose return would accompany the last times, the Messianic times. Some thought, for example, that he was Elias come back to life (cf. Mark VI: 15; VIII: 28). The acclamation on Palm Sunday probably must be interpreted in the same way and be read: "This is Jesus, *the prophet*, from Nazareth of Galilee" (Matt. XXI: 11). This coincides with the clear expression of popular belief, already quoted: "This is indeed the Prophet who is to come into the world" (John VI: 14). That statement, then, attests a tradition that would consider "the Prophet" as a title of the Messiah, of "He-Who-Comes."

Luke is responsible for the clearest comparisons of Jesus with the eschatological Elias. Poorly received at Nazareth, Jesus justifies His universal mission by an appeal to the examples of Elias and Eliseus (cf. Luke IV: 24–27). Only Luke reports the resurrection of the son of the widow of Naim (VII: 11–17), in an account which recalls a similar miracle worked by Elias for the son of the widow of Sarepta (cf. I Kings XVII: 17–24). The urgency of an immediate response to the Master's call is illustrated in Luke (IX: 61f.), as in the case of Eliseus (I Kings XIX: 19–21), by the example of the plowman. Even the words about fire falling from heaven to earth (cf. Luke XI: 54; XII: 49) could be connected to Elias' great deed on Mount Carmel (cf. I Kings XVIII: 38).

Reporting the discourses of Peter and Stephen, the book of Acts (cf. III: 22; VII: 37), attests that Jesus is the prophet who, like Moses, was going to arise at a time fixed by God (Deut. XVIII: 15; cf. John I: 45). On the other hand, in a heretical branch of ancient Judaeo-Christianity there will be an exaggerated interest given Jesus, the *Prophet*. It considered His coming as a definitive reincarnation of the true Prophet who had already appeared in several persons, from Henoch to Moses. This conception will find its termination in the religion of Islam.

During His public ministry Jesus behaved as a prophet on several occasions.[3] He spoke in the name of God, made His will known, announced His judgments, and predicted, in particular, the future destinies of the kingdom (cf. Matt. XXIV–XXV). At His baptism Jesus enjoyed an inaugural vision; at every moment His interior glance penetrated the mysteries of the other world (cf. Luke X: 18, 21) and the secret of hearts (cf. John IV: 19). He predicted His own passion and resurrection; had recourse, as did the prophets, to symbolic actions to transmit His message (Matt. XXI: 18–22; cf. Luke XIII: 6–9) and manifested a deep understanding of the Scriptures (cf. Matt. XXII: 40). On two points, in particular, Father de Grandmaison wrote, "Jesus enters a terrain reserved to God alone: the pardon of sins and the intimate knowledge of the heart." John the Baptist recognized the prophetic dignity of Jesus: "For he whom God has sent speaks the words of God, for not by measure does God give the Spirit" (John III: 34; cf. Luke XXIV: 19).

Several features of the Prophet of the last times can fit the person of Jesus: authority and definitive character of His preaching, predominant role of the Word (cf. Heb. I: 1f.), perspective of an eschatological return, absence of a political program, interest in the preparation for the imminent reign of God, acceptance of suffering, thaumaturgical gifts (cf. John IX: 9, 17), submission to the Spirit (cf. Luke IV: 1; X: 21), and knowledge of the "signs of the times" (Matt. XVI: 2f.).

Other aspects of the conception of the eschatological Prophet are difficult to include in an authentic Christology. To be aware of that, it is enough to recall some central elements of the mission of Jesus. He came to obtain the remission of sins by His death and resurrection; His work, unlike that of the prophets, is not achieved with His coming, but survives into the present and opens out into the future; His role is not restricted to preparing the kingdom but aims at establishing it first on earth, in the Church. To the formula of the prophetic oracles, "thus says Yahweh," Jesus prefers another, which reveals the authority of the Man-God: "Amen, amen, I say to you." If the idea of pre-existence, inseparable from the person of the Incarnate Word, is added, one easily understands that as an expression of faith in Christ, the notion of Prophet had to be abandoned. This remark should not turn us aside from the following truth: the figure and the role of the Prophet allow us to understand better certain mysteries about the person and work of the Saviour, especially those dealing with His intimate communion with God the Father.

NOTES ON 7

[1] *Manual of Discipline*, IX: 11. In this text the coming of the prophet is distinguished from that of the two Messiahs, one royal and one priestly. On "prophetic Messianism" there is the article of J. Giblet in *L'attente du Messie*, pp. 85–130. On the two Messiahs, cf. A. S. Van der Woude, "Le Maître de Justice et les deux Messies de la communauté de Qumrân" in *La secte de Qumrân et les origines du christianisme* (Bruges, 1959), pp. 121–34.

[2] The question "What is the homeland of Jesus?" and the relation between Mark (VI: 4) and other texts is discussed by J. Willemse, "La Patrie de Jésus selon Saint Jean IV, 44," *New Test. Stud.* XI (1964–65), pp. 349–64. In John (IV: 44) "his own country" is Jerusalem, where the Father of Jesus resides (cf. John II: 16; Luke II: 49). "His own" received Him not (John I: 11) refers mainly to the Jerusalemites.

[3] Jesus' prophetic action is described at length in F. Gils, *Jésus prophète d'après les Évangiles Synoptiques* (Louvain, 1957), pp. 48–166. In our treatment of the matter we are especially indebted to O. Cullmann, *The Christology of the New Testament*, pp. 13–50. The periodical *Évangile* devoted two issues (nos. 3 and 4) to the theme "Prophets of the Bible and Christ."

8

THE JUST ONE AND THE HOLY ONE

THESE two "Messianic" epithets are found in Peter's address to the Jews, as recorded in the book of Acts: "But you disowned the Holy and Just One, and asked that a murderer should be granted to you; but the author of life you killed, whom God has raised up from the dead; whereof we are witnesses" (III: 14f.). The resurrection constitutes divine sanction of the attribution to Jesus of the double title. An ancient hymn inserted in the First Epistle to Timothy affirms that Jesus Christ "was justified in the Spirit" (III: 16). This difficult passage also must, it seems, be referred to the resurrection, in which the Spirit animated the body of Jesus and transformed it into a "spiritual" body (cf. I Cor. XV: 44). The body of Jesus, in its mortality, represented sinful humanity (cf. Rom. VIII: 3).

Because of the frequent recourse of the book of Acts to the typology of Moses and of the Servant of God, it seems that in the text (III: 14), the words "Just" and "Holy" represent honorary titles addressed to Jesus, as "a prophet saving his people with a powerful justice."[1] The same inspired book applies the Messianic title of "Just" to Jesus in two other texts. Stephen fulminates against the conduct of the Jewish persecutors: "Which of the prophets have not your fathers persecuted? And they killed those who foretold the coming of the Just One, of whom you have now been the betrayers and murderers" (Acts VII: 52; cf. Matt. XXIII: 35ff.). A very different context provides the second example. Ananias says to Saul, the convert who will be called Paul: "The God of our fathers has appointed thee beforehand to learn his will and to see the Just One and to hear a voice from his mouth" (Acts XXII: 14).

Retracing previous uses of "Just" to designate the Messiah is an uncertain and difficult task. In his last words David had affirmed that the ideal king would "govern men with justice" (II Sam. XXIII: 3; cf. Ps. LXXI: 3). It is by justice that a king reigns, adds Isaiah (XXXII: 1), whose "Emmanuel book" assured us that the Messiah was going to establish and strengthen his royalty "in right and Justice" (IX: 6; cf. Zech. IX: 9). In an oracle which underlines Messianic universalism, Yahweh is called "just God and Saviour" (Isa. XLV: 21). To the same Deutero-Isaiah context belongs the description of the Suffering Servant who gives up his life in expiation to *justify* multitudes (Isa. LIII: 10f.). A variant from the book of Henoch, an apocryphal, probably pre-Christian, apocalypse, describes the expected Messiah as the Just One who will manifest Himself before the elect (XXXVIII: 2).

This precise *Messianic sense* of "Just" is nowhere else met in the New Testament (except perhaps in I John II: 1). The message of Pilate's wife (Matt. XXVII: 19) and the centurion's testimony (Luke XXIII: 47; cf. Wis. II: 18) underline rather the legal innocence of Jesus, while a passage from the First Epistle of Peter sees in him the suffering Just One: "Because Christ also died once for sins, the Just for the unjust, that he might bring us to God. Put to death indeed in the flesh, he was brought to life in the spirit" (III: 18; cf. Matt. XXIII: 35).

We have seen how Acts III: 14 applies the Messianic epithet "holy" (ἅγιος) to Jesus. This book also calls the Saviour the "holy servant" of God (IV: 27, 30), in a context that evokes at one and the same time the royal sonship (cf. v. 26 and Ps. II: 1f.) and the Messianic anointing of the new Servant, accomplished at the Baptism. The Greek term

παῖς can mean "son" or "servant." John recalled to the
recipients of his First Epistle: "But you have an anointing
from the *Holy One*" (II: 20). To the angel of the Church
at Philadelphia he wrote: "Thus says the *holy one*, the
true one, he who has the key of David, he who opens and
no one shuts, and who shuts and no one opens" (Apoc.
III: 7).

Another Greek word, ὅσιος, also meaning "holy," is
used by Acts to designate the Saviour in relation to His
resurrection: "Thou wilt not let thy *Holy* One see corrup-
tion" (II: 27; cf. XIII: 35). The text is quoted from Psalms
(XVI: 10), which, in the Greek version, marks a doctrinal
progress that stresses the Messianic sense and affirms belief
in the resurrection. The Hebrew text merely reassures the
just man before an imminent peril: God will not let his
friend go down into the pit. The formula "the holy [man]
of God" is used in the Old Testament to define certain
persons, like Aaron (Ps. CVI: 16) and Eliseus (II Kings
IV: 9).

Twice Jesus is called "holy of God" in the Gospels: by the
demoniac (Mark I: 24; Luke IV: 34) and by Peter after the
multiplication of the loaves (John VI: 69; cf. Acts III: 14).
Père Lagrange believes that this title expresses the super-
eminent dignity of Jesus. Sanctity would be a characteristic
of the Messianic times announced (cf. Dan. VII: 27), and
how could it be otherwise than that "the head of that new
order would be the holy one of God *par excellence*"?
Already, at the Annunciation, the Virgin had learned that
"The Holy One to be born shall be called the Son of God"
(Luke I: 35). The angel Gabriel, very much earlier, had
explained a Messianic prophecy to Daniel, in circumstances
similar to the announcement to Zachary (cf. Luke I:
10–13 and Dan. IX: 20–23). The final element of that
explanation spoke of the anointing of the *Holy of Holies*
(Dan. IX: 24), a clarification that can be possibly understood
of the High Priest, promoted no doubt to the Messianic

dignity. The frequent association in the Bible of these three concepts, "sanctity," "anointing," and "Spirit," leads to the identification of "Holy One" with "bearer of the Spirit." In the same perspective the title "Holy One" can be found suited to Jesus by virtue of His dignity as High Priest.

The application of the title "Holy" to Jesus no doubt constitutes another example of the tendency of the New Testament to designate Jesus by divine titles. The Jews freely called God "the Holy One" (cf. Heb. III: 3; Isa. XL: 25).[2] As designations of the Messiah, we must conclude, the epithets "Just" and "Holy" constitute formulas explicitly Christian, born of a need to express evident features of Jesus' personality.

Those unsatisfied by this brief coverage of the title "Holy One of God" can complete their information by examining the section on the title "Son of God," for these two designations in the New Testament are close from more than one viewpoint. Confronted with Jesus, the unclean spirits cried out: "I know who thou art: the *Holy One of God*" (Mark I: 24) or instead "Thou art the *Son of God*" (Mark III: 11; V: 7). These questionable testimonies can be confirmed by the message to Mary: "The *Holy One* to be born shall be called the *Son of God*" (Luke I: 35) or by the relation that Christ Himself established between "the one whom the Father has *sanctified*" (Greek) and "the Son of God" (John X: 36). In the fullest sense, it must be observed, the divine sonship of Jesus is quite another thing than Messianic sanctity.

NOTES ON 8

[1] A. Descamps, *Les Justes et la Justice dans les évangiles et le christianisme primitif hormis la doctrine proprement paulinienne* (Louvain, 1950), p. 79.

[2] Cf. A. Lefèvre, "Holy Is the Lord," in *The God of Israel, the God of Christians*, pp. 65–75. Also Hos. XI: 9; Isa. VI: 1–13; Exod. XXXVI: 21–23; Luke I: 49.

III

COMMUNAL MESSIANIC TITLES

9

"I AM THE WAY, THE TRUTH, THE LIFE"

THIS complex title (John XIV: 6) is a good introduction to a
section devoted to names that relate Jesus to the community:
He is the Way that leads it to God, because He is the Truth
that lights it and the Life that nourishes it. "No one comes
to the Father but through me," adds Jesus (John XIV: 6).
He is the Way toward the Father, for He makes the Father
known and communicates His life to men. This triple title
expresses in a compact way all the mediating and salvific
power of Jesus. It reflects clearly the theological interests
of St. John and his way of expressing them. Here would be
the place to describe the Johannine characteristics, if there
were not so many remarkable treatments readily available.[1]

Few New Testament books, in fact, present as many
peculiar features as does the Fourth Gospel. Already, about
the year 200, Clement of Alexandria called this work "the
spiritual Gospel." Fruit of a long maturation, it testifies to
a deeper penetration into the meaning of the words and
actions of Christ, who had once predicted such an eventual-
ity: "But the Advocate, the Holy Spirit whom the Father
will send in my name, he will teach you all things, and
bring to your mind whatever I have said to you" (John
XIV: 26); "But when he, the Spirit of truth, has come, he
will teach you all the truth" (John XVI: 13). The Fourth
Gospel has been slowly ripened in the meditation of a
disciple "saturated with divine revelation," according to a
saying of Saint Jerome.

The person of Jesus plays so central a role in the religious thought of John that it tends to assume the entirety. That explains why the Fourth Gospel is *Christocentric* in the extreme. The "kingdom" of the Synoptics, for example, is relegated to the background by the radiant figure of the King; the Vineyard is no longer the field of the Gospel laborers (cf. Matt. XX: 1f.), but Christ Himself and all His disciples incorporated in Him; the Light is more than a ray illuminating the faces of Christians (cf. Matt. V: 14), it shines forth in the very person of Christ, who says: "I am the light of the world" (John VIII: 12). John seldom analyzes; he contemplates—and it is the fullness of the mystery of Jesus that he contemplates. Beyond the visible and changing world His glance penetrates to the supernatural world, dominated by the figure of Christ, whose eternal, hieratic features often glimpse through the Evangelist's remarkable serenity of thought and language. John's work is a testimony of faith, of a faith whose object is rooted in historic truth: the Christ living in His Church and the historic Jesus whom John knew are one and the same:

Many other signs[2] also Jesus worked in the sight of his disciples, which are not written in this book. But these are written that you may believe that Jesus is the Christ, the Son of God, and that believing you may have life in his name.

(John XX: 30f.)[3]

"I AM THE TRUTH"

The Johannine Christ often has recourse to the formula "I am" to attribute metaphorical or symbolic titles to Himself: "I am the bread of life" (John VI: 35); "I am the light of the world" (VIII: 12); "I am the door of the sheep" (X: 7); "I am the good shepherd" (X: 11); "I am the resurrection" (XI: 25); "I am the way . . ." (XIV: 6); "I am the vine" (XV: 1). In the Old Testament "I am" is a formula peculiar to Yahweh, *who reveals Himself* and who commands.[4] Of the original phrase, "I am who am" (Exod. III: 14), often only the first part has been retained: "I am" (cf. Deut. XXXII: 39; Isa. XLIII: 10 [Greek]), as in God's command to Moses: "This is what you shall tell the Israelites: *I am* sent me to you" (Exod. III: 14). Probably inspired by that usage, Jesus said to the Jews: "When you have lifted up the Son of Man,[5] then you will know that *I am* he" (John VIII: 28; cf. XIII: 19). That word foretells that, by glorifying the Son, God is going to ratify His right to the name of God and to its inherent glory (cf. Isa. XLII: 8; LII: 6). To the same group of listeners Jesus also said: "For if you do not believe that *I am* he, you will die in your sins" (John VIII: 24). In the immediate context He had declared to them: "You know neither me nor my Father. If you knew me, you would know my Father also" (VIII: 19).

In the mouth of Christ the formula "I am" implies pre-existence and divine knowledge, as can be inferred from two other sayings of Jesus, one addressed to the Jews: "Amen, amen, I say to you, before Abraham came to be, *I am*" (John VIII: 58); the other to the disciples: "I tell you now that when it has come to pass you may believe that I am He" (XIII: 19). Is Jesus here not speaking as God, who said over and over again through the mouth of Ezekiel: "You shall know that I am the Lord" (Ezek. XI: 10; XII: 20)? The Johannine uses of "I am" can be associated with the emphatic "I" of Wisdom (Prov. VIII: 12–21), comparable to certain formulas of mystery cults. The other Gospels attributed to Jesus a strong personality that is expressed by an insistent "I," but not by the Johannine "I am." The "I say to you" that fill the first discourse in Matthew (V: 22–44) can be cited as examples of Synoptic usage.

Detailed explanation of the titles "the Way" and "the Life" is given in the later sections devoted to "the Door" and "the Bread of Life." Several aspects of the title "the

Truth" belong equally to the symbol of "the Light." Did
not the Psalmist write: "Oh send out *thy light and thy
truth;* let them lead me, let them bring me to thy holy will
and to thy dwelling! (Ps. XLII: 3)?[6] In John, too, the two
notions are linked: "For everyone who does evil hates the
light and does not come to the light . . . but he who does
the *truth* comes to the light" (John III: 20; cf. I John I: 6).
To do the truth is to walk in the light, for what appears in
the open is true. This, however, is not the principal
meaning of the idea of truth.

According to Platonic philosophy, the true is what
corresponds to the real or to the subsistent idea which fixes
the nature of the real, in contrast to changing contingen-
cies. The *biblical* notion of truth implies the idea of stability
and constancy, founded on fidelity in accomplishing a plan.
In this sense, God alone is the absolute True, for whatever
He has resolved to do, He can accomplish. The truth of God
is particularly manifest in His faithfulness in keeping the
Covenant (Deut. VII: 9); it is also present in the words
of God (II Sam. VII: 28), in His judgments (Ps. XVIII:
10), in His works (Ps. CX: 7), in His commandments (Ps.
CXVIII: 86). In sapiential and apocalyptic literature,
"truth" becomes in some texts synonymous with "revealed
doctrine," a sense which will be taken up by the New
Testament.

In a series of characteristic uses the Fourth Gospel gives
the following interpretation to the epithet "true": the true
is what is authentic and fully realizes the notion of a thing.
In this sense, the adjective "true" describes the light (I: 9),
the worshippers (IV: 23), the bread of heaven (VI: 32),
the vine (XV: 1), God Himself (XVII: 3). John the Baptist
was perhaps a light (cf. V: 35) but not the true light (I: 9).
The flesh of Jesus is a "true nourishment" (VI: 55), in
contrast with perishable food.

According to its properly Johannine meaning, truth
(ἀλήθεια) designates the Christian revelation brought by

Jesus (John I: 17; VIII: 32) to demonstrate God's faithfulness in fulfilling His promises. Jesus Himself is the truth
(John XIV: 6) or "full of grace and of truth" (I: 14; cf.
Exod. XXXIV: 6), as the Incarnate Word (I: 14) who reveals
the Father to us (I: 18). In the Apocalypse Jesus is also
called the True One (III: 7; cf. XIX: 11), the Amen, the
faithful and *true* Witness, the Beginning of the creation of
God (III: 14), because in Him are all God's promises
accomplished.

To the Jews Jesus had said: "You are seeking to kill me,
one who has spoken *the truth* to you which I have heard
from God (John VIII: 40); to Pilate, who could save or
crucify Him, He said: "I have come into the world to bear
witness to *the truth*" (XVIII: 37). Such witness He will
render less by words than by His sacrifice, in which was
expressed the truth or faithfulness of God's promise to save
the world. Pilate did not wait for an answer to his question:
"What is truth?" (John XVIII: 38), for being of this "world"
he was not one of those whom Jesus described when He
said, "he who does the truth comes to the light" (III: 21).

In the New Testament as in the Old, "truth" also often
means moral rectitude. "To do the truth" is to perform
one's deeds in God (John III: 21). "To be in truth" (I John
III: 19) or "to live in truth" (II John IV: 3; John IIIf.),
according to John, is to observe the commandment of God:
"To believe in the name of His Son Jesus Christ and to love
one another" (I John III: 23) is, finally, to attach oneself to
Him who said: "I am the Way, the Truth, and the Life"
(John XIV: 6).

"Truth in the Christian sense is not, then, the immense
domain of the real to be conquered by an effort of thought.
Rather it is the revelation of the Father made present in
Christ and enlightened by the Spirit, a revelation that we
must welcome in faith. Only when we have done so will it
transform our lives, and through it, as the liturgy asks, will
we manifest in our deeds the light of truth."[7]

NOTES ON 9

[1] Cf. J. M. Lagrange, "Gospel According to Saint John" in *The Gospel of Jesus Christ* (Baltimore, 1939), Introduction; D. Mollat and F. M. Braun, *L'Évangile et les Épîtres de saint Jean (BJ,* Paris, 1953); J. Huby and X. Léon-Dufour, *L'Évangile et les Évangiles* (Paris, 1954), pp. 214–96; R. Schnackenburg, *New Testament Theology To-day* (New York, 1963), pp. 90–106. Among non-Catholic commentaries on John are prominent those of C. H. Dodd and C. K. Barrett.

[2] On the concept of "sign" (σημεῖον) so frequent in the Fourth Gospel (cf. II: 23; IV: 54; VI: 2; XI: 47; XII: 18), cf. D. Mollat in *Sacra Pagina* (International Biblical Congress of 1958), vol. II, pp. 209–18. The σημεῖον, a divine sign, not only "guarantees and authenticates this mission (of the One Sent), but also manifests it; it expresses the supernatural reality that Jesus is going to reveal and communicate to men" (p. 212). Between the "signs" of the Fourth Gospel and those of the Exodus (cf. pp. 214f., and *Recueil Lucien Cerfaux,* vol. II, pp. 44–46) a relationship does exist. The Johannine σημεῖα are *meaningful* events: words and deeds in Jesus' life carrying a symbolic element useful for instructing the Messianic community (that inaugurates eschatology) in its ritual.

[3] Cf. F. Mussner, "Historical Jesus and Christ of Faith," *Theology Digest* (1964), pp. 21–26.

[4] Referring to E. Schweizer's work *Ego Eimi* (Göttingen, 1939), L. Cerfaux describes the formula ἐγώ εἰμι as a "theme of revelation" (*Recueil Lucien Cerfaux,* vol. II, p. 21). Cf. J. Galot's article "Je Suis," in *Revue du Clergé Africain,* 1959, pp. 124–44. "The Christ of Saint John," writes C. Spicq, "is essentially a Revealer who transmits and shows the Father in his person" (*Dieu et l'homme,* Paris, 1961, p. 95). Often considered as a borrowing from Hellenism or the oriental religions, where gods, sovereigns, and prophets often reveal their dignity with ἐγώ εἰμι and a modifier, the Johannine formula was used to be understood by the milieu it addressed: "the cosmopolitan society of a great hellenistic city such as Ephesus under the Roman Empire" (C. H. Dodd, *The Interpretation of the Fourth Gospel,* Cambridge, 1953, p. 9). But A. Feuillet is correct to recall how greatly these "autodoxologies" of the oriental gods differ in meaning from the Johannine revelations, which are related to the statements of biblical Wisdom (cf. "Les thèmes bibliques majeurs du discours sur le pain de vie," in *NRT,* 1960, pp. 924f.).

[5] Cf. p. 207, n. 7, and p. 6 (John XVIII: 6).

[6] Revised Standard Version.

[7] I. de la Potterie, in *Vocabulaire de théologie biblique,* c. 1098; N. Lazure, *Les valeurs morales de la theologie johannique* (Paris, 1965), pp. 70–92.

10

THE GOOD SHEPHERD

THE symbolic discourse[1] of the Good Shepherd (John X) develops and applies to Jesus a theme well attested in the New Testament and deeply rooted in the Old Testament, where Psalm XXIII perfectly embodies the theme: "The Lord is my shepherd." A choice of texts will show what biblical and Messianic hopes are evoked by this saying of the Johannine Christ: "I am the good shepherd" (John X: 11).

The function of pasturing assumed a character of nobility in ancient times. At Sumer, as at Babylon, the figure of the shepherd was associated with royal titles. Two thousand years before Christ, the Egyptian sage Ipuwer predicted that an ideal king would deliver his country from its miseries: "They will say of him: This is the Shepherd of all men. Evil is not in his heart. His sheep are few and he spends his day taking care of them."[2]

Kind toward the nomadic civilization, the Yahwist tradition is suspicious of urban settlements. It praises Abel's conduct (Gen. IV: 2), yet blames the builders of Babel (Gen. XI: 1–9). Yahweh is God of the patriarchs, those free-wandering sheiks, owners of great flocks. Nomadic life lends itself more to colloquy with God by reason of its inevitable renouncements and its direct contact with nature's marvels.

Another great shepherd of sheep, Moses (Exod. III: 1), receives the difficult mission of shepherding men (cf. Isa. LXIII: 11; Ps. LXXVI: 21). The people he has made one,

he will lead it, in God's name (Ps. LXXVII: 52) for forty
years from the Nile to the Jordan, but will not see it
settle in Canaan. The sojourn in the desert, where Israel
lived with pure faith in God, will be steadfastly quoted as
the ideal epoch in the history of God's people. The New
Testament, in particular St. Paul (cf. I Cor. X: 1–13),
sees "in the assembly [ἐκκλησία] in the wilderness"
(Acts VII: 38) a figure of the Christian community, having
Christ as its leader, nourishment, and life.

On his deathbed Jacob blessed Joseph and his sons: "May
the God in whose presence my Fathers Abraham and Isaac
lived, the God who has been *my shepherd* all my life until
this day, the angel who has delivered me from all evil,
bless the boys . . ." (Gen. XLVIII: 15f.). The mention of
the Angel, a term for God in His sensible manifestation
(cf. Gen. XVI: 7), assigns the text to the Elohist tradition,
which tends to underscore the transcendence of God.
In the text cited, the Elohist works a theological transposition that will later be adopted: God Himself is called
Shepherd. The theme has ties throughout the entire Old
Testament, particularly in the prophets (cf. Isa. XL: 11;
Mic. VII: 14) and in the Psalms (cf. XXII and LXXIX: 2).

The priestly tradition frequently exalts the role of the
priesthood. This preoccupation appears in a text which
mentions the *imposition of the hands* on bestowal of the
office of shepherd on Joshua, on the eve of the entrance
into the promised land:

Then Moses said to the Lord, "May the Lord, the God of the
spirits of all mankind, set over the community a man who shall
act as their leader in all things, to guide them in all their actions;
that the Lord's community may not be like sheep without a
shepherd." And the Lord replied to Moses, "Take Josue, son
of Nun, a man of spirit, and lay your hand upon him . . . and as
he directs, Josue, all the Israelites with him, and the community
as a whole shall perform all their actions." (Num. XXVII: 15f., 21.)

This bestowal of powers entails several elements which

will be integrated into the double image of the Fourth Gospel: the Good Shepherd and the Door of the Sheep (X: 1–6).

To the shepherd David, who knew how to defend his sheep against the lion and the bear (cf. I Sam. XVII: 34), Yahweh had said: "Thou art the one who will pasture my people Israel" (II Sam. V: 2; cf. Ps. LXXVIII: 70f.). A prophet characterized the evil wrought by certain negligent kings, particularly Ahab. "I have seen all Israel scattered on the mountains, like a flock without a shepherd" (I Kings XXII: 17). The fall of Samaria in 721 would be followed, according to an oracle of Micah, by a reunion of the two kingdoms, divided by the schism that followed Solomon's death. This return to unity appears, in the prophet's vision (Mic. II: 12f.), as a gathering of sheep under the crook of a single shepherd. In a more distant future will arise the Messiah-King, the true shepherd. He will be born in Bethlehem, as David, the ancestor of the Messianic line: "He shall stand firm and shepherd his flock by the strength of the Lord, in the majestic name of the Lord, his God" (Mic. V: 3).

The return to Jerusalem of the exiles from Babylon marks the beginning of the great gathering which is to characterize the formation of the Messianic people. In those days "I will appoint over you shepherds after my own heart, who will shepherd you wisely and prudently" (Jer. III: 15). God Himself will be the supreme Shepherd: "He who scattered Israel now gathers them together, he guards them as a shepherd his flock" (Jer. XXXI: 10). The allegory of the shepherd and his flock forms the principal theme of Chapter XXIII of the collection of the prophecies of Jeremiah. Through his Messiah-King, the Davidic shepherd, God is going to repair the damage done by bad shepherds:

I myself will gather the remnant of my flock from all the lands to which I have driven them and bring them back to their

meadow; there they shall increase and multiply . . . Behold, the
days are coming, says the Lord, when I will raise up a righteous
shoot to David; as king he shall reign and govern wisely, he
shall do what is just and right in the land." (Jer. XXIII: 3, 5.)

Chapter XXXIV of Ezekiel resumes the same theme: the
contrast between the conduct of bad shepherds and that of
the true Shepherd. In it are found several features which
appear also in the parable of the Good Shepherd. It is said
of the Shepherd-King:

I will appoint one shepherd over them to pasture them, my
servant David; he shall pasture them and be their shepherd.
I, the Lord, will be their God, and my servant David shall be
prince among them. I, the Lord, have spoken. (Ezek. XXXIV:
23 f.)

The conclusion of the Gospel parable, "there will be one
flock, one shepherd," apparently draws from that chapter
in Ezekiel which predicts the reunion of the kingdoms of
Juda and Israel: "My servant David shall be prince over
them, and there shall be one shepherd for them all"
(Ezek. XXXVII: 24). On the other hand, the parable of
Jesus reflects Jeremiah's universal perspectives (cf. III: 17),
which were somewhat neglected by Ezekiel.

References to the shepherd themes abound in the Old
Testament. Let us mention by way of conclusion the "book
of the shepherds" (Zech. XI: 4–17), added at the end of the
fourth century to the writings of the Prophet Zechariah.
This shepherd allegory belongs to a literary unit from which
the New Testament has drawn Messianic oracles: the advent
of the Messiah-King (IX: 9; cf. Matt. XXI: 5); the price of
the Just One (XI: 12f.; Matt. XXVII: 9f.); the Pierced One
(XII: 10; cf. John XIX; 37); the dispersed flock: "Strike the
shepherd that the sheep may be dispersed, and I will turn
my hand against the little ones" (XIII: 7; cf. Matt. XXVI:
31). The purifying ordeal (cf. Ps. XLIII: 12; LXXIII: 1)
will, in fact, precede the formation of the new sheepfold

(Isa. XL: 10f.). To "those clothed in white robes," "those who have come out of the great tribulation," that is, from Nero's persecution, a great promise is made. "The Lamb who is in the midst of the throne will shepherd them and will guide them to the fountains of the waters of life" (Apoc. VII: 17; Isa. XLIX: 10).

Several texts from the Synoptic Gospels implicitly apply the title of Shepherd to Jesus. First, there is Mark's reflection on the multiplication of the loaves: Jesus "saw a large crowd, and had compassion on them, because they were like sheep without a shepherd. And he began to teach them many things" (VI: 34; Matt. IX: 36). Then, Luke records Jesus' reassuring words to the disciples: "Do not be afraid, little flock, for it has pleased your Father to give you the kingdom" (XII: 32; cf. Dan. VII: 27). Finally Matthew notes that Jesus first refused the pleading of the Canaanite woman by saying: "I was not sent except to the lost sheep of the house of Israel" (XV: 24). The Infancy accounts had already associated the coming of Jesus with the life of the shepherds (Luke II: 8; Matt. II: 6). The parable of the lost sheep (Luke XV: 4–7) and the imagery in the description of the Last Judgment (Matt. XXV: 31–36) are also inspired by shepherd life and are dependent on Chapter XXXIV of Ezekiel, from a literary viewpoint.

The Fourth Gospel willingly presents Christ as the one fulfilling all types: new Jacob (I: 51; cf. IV: 12), new Temple (II: 19) with fruitful side (XIX: 34; cf. Ezek. XLVII: 1), new Moses (III: 14; cf. VI: 31f.), true light of the world (I: 9; cf. VIII: 12) and source of living waters (VII: 37f.; cf. Jer. II: 13), true Shepherd (X: 1–16), and true vine (XV: 1).

The symbolic discourse of the Good Shepherd (John X: 1–16) mingles parabolical traits with allegorical applications. Other elements harm the clarity of the narrative: the Good Shepherd is opposed to thieves and hirelings; furthermore. He is called the Door of the Sheep, a new comparison in an already complex context. The point of the comparison is easily isolated: Jesus is the Good Shepherd, a theme probably suggested by the conduct of the synagogue leaders toward the man born blind (John IX). The Good Shepherd of the parable differs from all other "shepherds" in His extreme devotion: *"He lays down his life* for his sheep" (v. 11), according to the literal translation of the text, which alludes to the sacrifice of the Suffering Servant (Isa. LIII: 10). For John, the death and glorification of Jesus bring life to men.

The parable adds that the sheep know the Good Shepherd and are known to Him. In Johannine theology, in fact, knowledge plays an important role: knowing is almost synonymous with believing (cf. VI: 69). From a biblical point of view, true knowledge is experimental and depends on love: "Now this is everlasting life, that they may know thee, the only true God, and him whom thou hast sent, Jesus Christ" (John XVII: 3).

Jesus Christ is the unique Shepherd of men (John X: 16), "the great Shepherd of sheep" (Heb. XIII: 20), "the Prince of the shepherds" (I Pet. V: 4). Peter will write to a group of converts: "For you were as sheep going astray, but now you have returned to the shepherd and guardian of your souls" (I Pet. II: 25). Before His departure Jesus confided to Peter the charge of being on earth the visible representative of the true Shepherd of the sheep (John XXI: 15–17). One of his chief concerns is to guard the unity of the flock that Jesus' death had reunited, according to Caiphas' prediction: "This, however, he said not of himself; but being high priest that year, he prophesied that Jesus was to die for the nation; and not only for the nation, but that he might gather into one the children of God who were scattered abroad" (John XI: 51f.).

The figure of the Good Shepherd is a comfort for every man, for every believer in a superterrestrial being who directs human destinies. It is clothed with diverse features according to religious beliefs and according to conditions of life. It is an answer both to the sighs of the unfortunate and to the rapture of the blessed:

> *The Lord is my shepherd, I shall not want.*
> *In verdant pastures he gives me repose;*
> *Beside restful waters he leads me, he*
> *refreshes my soul.*
> *He guides me in right paths for his name's*
> *sake.*
> *Even though I walk in the dark valley*
> *I fear no evil; for you are at my side*
> *With your rod and your staff that give me*
> *courage.*
> *You spread the table before me in the*
> *sight of my foes;*
> *You anoint my head with oil; my cup over-*
> *flows.*
> *Only goodness and kindness follow me all*
> *the days of my life;*
> *And I shall dwell in the house of the*
> *Lord for years to come.* (Ps. XXIII.)

NOTES ON 10

[1] Jesus' discourse on the Good Shepherd is both parable and allegory. C. K. Barrett calls it a "symbolic discourse" (*The Gospel According to St. John*, London, 1955, p. 304; cf. p. 307). The Johannine parable παροιμία (John X: 6; XVI: 25, 29; cf. II Pet. II: 22) would have a similar sense: "a symbolical saying requiring interpretation" (Hoskyns-Davey, *The Fourth Gospel*, London, 1954, p. 369). On this subject see L. Cerfaux, "Le thème littéraire para-bolique dans l'Évangile de saint Jean," in *Recueil Lucien Cerfaux*, vol. II, pp. 17–26. St. John's symbolic language corresponds to the mysterious proposal of the kingdom's secrets and their subsequent public proposal. In John Jesus first reveals Himself to the Apostles and then more clearly so.

[2] Cf. "Le Seigneur est mon berger" in *Évangile*, no. 28, p. 74. Since Manethon (third century) the name *Hyksôs* has been given the sense of "shepherds" or "Shepherd-Kings"; it really means "princes of foreign lands" (cf. G. Posener, *Dictionnaire de la civilisation égyptienne*, Paris, 1959, p. 136).

11

THE DOOR, THE WAY

THE parable of the Good Shepherd associates the image of the door with the figure of the shepherd. Jesus is the Door that gives access to the sheep (John X: 7), for He is the "great pastor of the sheep" (Heb. XIII: 20), who appoints the legitimate pastors of the flock. Jesus is also the Door that *leads the sheep* (John X: 9) into the fold, into the Kingdom of God, at first the Church, then eternal life. The "thieves" and "pillagers" (X: 8), who have not come through the Door, are false Messiahs and pseudo-Saviours (cf. Matt. VII: 15); the Pharisees in particular, often blamed by Jesus (cf. Matt. XXIII: 1–36; Mark VI: 34). In the Old Testament already, the double simile of Shepherd and Door figures in one text, that of Micah mentioned above:

I will gather you, O Jacob, each and every one, I will assemble all the remnant of Israel; I will group them like a flock in the fold, like a herd in the midst of its corral; they shall not be thrown in panic by men. (II: 12f.)

The image of the door can recall several contexts. In the mind of the ancients, heaven is an enclosure located above the earth. Access to it is through doors (cf. Ps. LXXVII: 23) or a door, the same one that gave passage to the Redeemer on His way down and the one that introduced the redeemed above. High mountains facilitated these comings and goings. In the plains storied towers were built as a substitute for mountains, such unfinished ziggurats, visible in

Babylon, probably suggested the story of the Tower of Babel (Gen. XI: 1–9). To the same imagery belongs the ladder of angels in Jacob's dream (Gen. XXVIII: 12), to which refers the prophecy of Jesus to His Apostles: "You shall see heaven opened, and the angels of God ascending and descending upon the Son of Man" (John I: 51). In that episode of the itinerant patriarch, the place of the theophany is called "gate of heaven" (Gen. XXVIII: 17). The Seer of the Apocalypse writes: "After this I looked, and behold, *a door* standing open in heaven, and the former voice, which I had heard as of a trumpet speaking with me, said, Come up hither, and I will show thee the things that must come to pass hereafter" (IV: 1). At another theophany, that of Jesus' baptism, the heavens opened (Mark I: 10), as if to answer the prophetic prayer: "Oh, that you would rend the heavens and come down" (Isa. LXIII: 19).

Two verses of Psalm CXVII, the last of the Hallel psalms (CXII–CXVII), recited on great Jewish feasts, are applied to Jesus in the New Testament: "The stone which the builders rejected has become the cornerstone" (v. 22; cf. Mark XII: 10); "Blessed is he who comes in the name of the Lord" (v. 26; cf. Mark: XI; 10). When He said "I am the Door" (John X: 9), the Saviour had perhaps in mind another verse of that psalm: "This gate is the Lord's; the just shall enter it" (v. 20). In the perspective of John, in fact, Jesus is the true temple of God (cf. II: 19).[1]

*

*   *

The preceding observations equally suit the title "the Way" included in the famous Johannine saying: "I am the Way, the Truth and the Life" (John XIV: 6). According to the immediate context, "the Way" clearly constitutes the central title; in fact it is stated as an answer to Thomas' question: "Lord, we do not know where thou art going

and how can we know the way?" (XIV: 5). Let us paraphrase again: Jesus is the Way that leads the community
to God, because He is the Truth that lightens it and the
Life that nourishes it.[2]

The association of these three titles, Way, Truth, Life,
could have been suggested by many Old Testament
passages, especially by some Psalms: "The way of truth I
have chosen" (CXVIII: 30; cf. XXIV: 10); "You will show
me the path of life" (XV: 11; cf. Prov. VI: 23). The
Epistle to the Hebrews will call the way traced by Jesus
toward the heavenly sanctuary "a living way". No one
comes to the Father but through me" (John XIV: 6). Jesus
is then the unique way that leads to the Father, as He is the
only Door that leads the sheep to the fold. The Fourth
Gospel had already said: The Son of Man is the ladder that
links heaven and earth (I: 51); or again, "No one has
ascended into heaven except him who has descended from
heaven: the Son of Man who is in heaven" (III: 13; cf. Bar.
III: 29). Jesus can be the Way, because He is the Pontiff in
whom God and man unite.[3]

God had led His people on the roads of the Exodus,
through tortuous and difficult paths, into the desert and as
far as the Promised Land. Under His leadership once more
(cf. Isa. XL–LV), a new desert crossing led Israel back from
the land of exile into Palestine. The Gospel of the Public
Life opens with this appeal: "Make ready the *way* of the
Lord, make straight his paths" (Luke III: 4). A new Moses,
Christ is the leader who is to guide the sons of God toward
their salvation (Heb. II: 10). And so He invites men to
follow Him (Mark VIII: 34). Luke presents His return to
the Father as a going up to Jerusalem (cf. IX: 51), which
through death would lead Him to glory (XXIV: 26). On the
eve of His exodus Jesus keeps repeating to His disciples that
He is *going* to the Father (John XIII: 1; XIV: 12).

In Christ raised on the Cross, St. Paul declares, Jews and
Gentiles have been reconciled: "Through him we both have

access in one Spirit to the Father" (Eph. II: 14–18). Jesus went to the Father through the crucifixion and resurrection. In Him, Christians die and rise, as the Apostle explicitly teaches (cf. Rom. VI: 8; VIII: 11). Thus, by following Jesus, the first Christians thought that they belonged to the *Way* which leads to the Father (Acts IX: 2, XXII: 4). In two Gospels Jesus calls "narrow" the *door* that leads to life. It is difficult to enter through it (Luke XIII: 24). In Matthew's account, the *way*, beyond the door, is also narrow, and difficult to find (VII: 14). For the first Evangelist, before the End there is the life in the Church, requiring a continuous moral effort. Matthew joins two similes, that of the door and that of the way, as he joins elsewhere two parables, that of the marriage feast and that of the wedding garment (XX: 1–14).[4] It is not enough to get in the Church. One must add good conduct to faith. The true believer will succeed, for Jesus said: "I am the door. If anyone enter by me he shall be safe, and shall go in and out, and shall find pastures" (John XI: 9).[5]

NOTES ON 11

[1] See p. 127.

[2] Explanations of the titles "the Truth" and "the Life" are given on pp. 62f.

[3] It is known that at the origin of the Latin word *pontifex* ("bridge builder") there are Indo-European expressions meaning "way": thus πάτος, "step," "walk," hence "beaten road" (cf. A. Ernout and A. Meillet *Dictionnaire étymologique de la langue latine*, p. 751).

[4] Cf. R. Swaeles, "L'orientation ecclésiastique de la parabole du festin nuptial en Mt., XXII, 1–14," *Ephem. Theol. Lovan.* (1960), pp. 655–84.

[5] On the way similar matter is differently treated in John and in the Synoptics, see p. 60, p. 105, n. 2., p. 114, n. 1.

12

THE LIGHT OF THE WORLD

Two sayings of Jesus were pronounced in one and the same circumstance: "If anyone thirst, let him come to me and drink, he who believes in me; as the Scripture says, from within Him there shall flow rivers of living water" (John VII: 37f.). "I am the light of the world. He who follows me does not walk in darkness, but will have the light of life" (John VIII: 12). They appear, in fact, in two consecutive discourses, one on living water, the other on light.[1]

Both sayings seem connected with the context of the Jewish Feast of Tabernacles or Tents, also called the Feast of the Harvest (cf. Exod. XXIII: 16), "the feast" (I Kings VIII: 2), or "the feast of the Lord" (Lev. XXIII: 39). In New Testament times, according to the Mishnaic treatise *Sukka*, every morning, for eight days, the priests solemnly went to draw water at the pool of Siloe and brought it in a golden vase to the Temple. At night the Temple area called "the porch of women" was lighted. This double ceremony would have furnished Jesus the opportunity to reveal Himself both as the source of living waters and as the light of the world.

Biblical uses of the theme of light in a religious sense are quite numerous. Beginning with the priestly account of creation (Gen. I: 3f.), they fall into two categories: some are related to various descriptions of Messianic times; others present the just man's moral conduct as walking in the light.

MESSIANIC LIGHT

The eschatology of the Messianic kingdom contains a decisive split between the impious, destined for "exterior darkness" (Matt. VIII: 12; XXII: 13), and the just, who "will shine as the sun in the kingdom of their Father" (Matt. XIII: 43). Already Daniel had associated the *condition of the elect* with the splendor of the light: "The wise shall shine brightly like the splendor of the firmament, and those who lead the many to justice shall be like the stars forever" (XII: 3). St. Paul used to invite Christians to thank the Father, "who has made us worthy to share the lot of the saints in light, and who has rescued us from the power of darkness and transferred us into the kingdom of his beloved Son, in whom we have our redemption, the remission of our sins" (Col. I: 12f.). Apocalyptic circles at the time of Jesus shared similar views, as is apparent from the following passage of the Book of Henoch:

And I will bring forth in shining light those who have loved My holy name, and I will seat each on the throne of his honour. And they shall be *resplendent* for times without number; for righteousness is the judgement of God; for to the faithful He will give faithfulness in the habitation of the upright paths. And they shall see those who were born in darkness led into darkness, while the righteous shall be *resplendent*. And the sinners shall cry aloud and see them *resplendent*, and they indeed will go where days and seasons are prescribed for them. (CVIII: 12–15.)[2]

In Messianic times the Holy City will shine forth with light; all nations will run toward it: such is Isaiah's comforting vision (LX: 1–3), which Saint John's Apocalypse has taken up (XXI: 23f.), and applied to all the inhabitants of the heavenly Jerusalem (XXII: 5).

But the principal source of light will be the *Messiah Himself*. To the *Suffering Servant* it was declared:

I, the Lord, have called you for the victory of justice, I have grasped you by the hand; I formed you, and set you as a covenant of the people, a light for the nations. (Isa. XLII: 6f.)

I will make you a light to the nations, that my salvation may reach to the ends of the earth. (XLIX: 6.)

As will be seen below, Jesus personifies the mysterious figure of the Servant in His life and in His work. Zachary had foreseen it, for he recognized in his son John the Forerunner of the "rising sun," destined to light "those who sit in darkness and in the shadow of death" (Luke I: 78f.). In the return of Jesus to Galilee, Matthew discerned the accomplishment of Isaiah's prophecy (IX: 1): "The people who walked in darkness have seen a great light; upon those who dwelt in the land of gloom a light has shone" (Matt. IV: 16). St. Paul had received directly from Jesus the mission to go to the pagan nations "to open their eyes that they may turn from darkness to light and from the dominion of Satan to God . . ." (Acts XXVI: 18). Established to be "the light of nations" (Acts XIII: 47), the Apostle is, in fact, only the herald of the true Messianic light; according to the prophecy "of the prophets and of Moses," after having suffered, Christ would effectually awake first from among the dead and "would announce the light to the people and to the pagan nations" (Acts XXVI: 23). The light that He brings is that of Messianic salvation.

*

*   *

In the Fourth Gospel, Jesus *is* the light of the world: "I am the light of the world. He who follows me does not walk in the darkness, but will have the light of life" (John VIII: 12). The context of the Feast of Tabernacles, as we have already said, could have determined the circumstance of that declaration, the substance of which will be repeated later on: "I have come a light into the world, that whoever believes in me may not remain in the darkness" (John XII: 46). The mention of "the light of life" and the promise made to the believer that he will escape the darkness lead us to suppose that, like Matthew (IV: 16), John sees in Jesus' coming the fulfillment of Isaiah's prophecy: "The people who walked in darkness have seen a great light; upon those who dwelt in the land of gloom a light has shone" (IX: 1).

As long as I am in the world I am the light of the world (John IX: 5). This saying also belongs to a *Messianic* context, for it was pronounced at the healing of the man born blind (John IX: 1–41), an episode which symbolized, for John, the victory of light over darkness. We can also recognize in it a characteristic of the Servant's mission, mentioned in a text cited above (Isa. XLII: 6f.). The refusal which the Jews oppose to Jesus' miracle furnishes the occasion for another teaching: "For judgment have I come into the world, that they who do not see may see, and they who see may become blind" (John IX: 39). The healing of the man born blind becomes a judgment, because it takes place on the Sabbath. The blind man recovers his sight, but formalism blinds the Pharisees, of whom it could be said what Paul says of every Jew, that he boasted of being "the guide of the blind, the light of him who walks in darkness" (Rom. II: 19; cf. Matt. XV: 14). The Jews' negative reaction to the miracle illustrated only one aspect of the far greater drama already present in John's Prologue: "And the light shines in the darkness; and the darkness grasped it not" (John I: 5). The connection between this drama and the idea of judgment will be explained to Nicodemus:

Now this is the judgment: The light has come into the world, yet men have loved the darkness rather than the light, for their works were evil. For everyone who does evil hates the light, and does not come to the light, that his deeds may not be exposed. But he who does the truth comes to the light that his deeds may be made manifest, for they have been performed in God.

(John III: 19–21.)

On two occasions (John I: 9; I John II: 8) John adds a clarification whose precise meaning is not easy to grasp:

Christ is the *true* light. The light that is Christ is *true* on several scores: this light transcends earthly light as spirit, matter; it reduces the light of the Law to mere shadow; this light alone completely verifies the notion of light. In John's Prologue the Word (the *Logos*) is declared to be the light, while John the Baptist is witness to the light. Finally, Christ is the true light, because He fulfills the prophecies, because he brings salvation.

*

*   *

Messianic light is also a *divine light*, the true light *par excellence*. Of this Logos-Light John had declared: "And the Word was God" (John I: 1). According to a procedure dear to the primitive Church, a *divine* attribute is applied to Christ, for light, in the Bible, is constantly associated with the *presence of God*. After the Exodus a luminous column lighted by night the march of the Hebrews across the desert (Exod. XIII: 21f.: Yahwist tradition). During the theophany on Sinai "the mount was all wrapped in smoke, for the Lord came down upon it in fire" (Exod. XIX: 18). The "glory of the Lord" in the priestly tradition is described as "a consuming fire" (Exod. XXIV: 17; cf. Deut. IV: 24), or even as a dazzling light that will shine on the face of Moses (Exod. XXXIV: 29; cf. II Cor. III: 7). The hymn of Creation represents God "robed in light as with a cloak" (Ps. CIII: 2). The first creature made by Yahweh (Prov. VIII: 22–31), "the refulgence of eternal light" (Wis. VII: 26), Wisdom, is conceived as a human being very close to God and surpassing light in beauty.

Divine light is a *good* for man that guides and saves him, a truly lasting column leading him across the desert to the Promised Land of Blessedness. "The Lord is my light and my salvation. Whom should I fear?" (Ps. XXVI: 1; cf. Mic. VII: 8). "For with you [God] is the fountain of life, and in your light we see light" (Ps. XXXV: 10). Associating "life" and "light," this passage could have suggested the Prologue's affirmation: "The life was the light of men" (John I: 4).[3]

WALK IN THE LIGHT

"I am the light of the world. He who follows me does not walk in the darkness, but will have the light of life" (John VIII: 12). Here, as in the Prologue, the themes of light and life are joined together as a certain indication of the continuity that links the discourse on the light to the preceding one on living water (VII: 37f.). Far more important, however, is the new idea introduced: to walk after Jesus is to leave darkness behind and to enjoy the light of *life*. This development clearly illustrates a peculiarity of John's writings: his language reflects the biblical milieu and assimilates formulas common to primitive Christianity, while his thought transforms this traditional source into a new synthesis focused on the person of Jesus. Thus both the Old Testament and the primitive community made special use of the current metaphor "light," but, in a special sense, to characterize a manner of living. For John, however, Christ is the light.

In the former economy, light and darkness recall the different paths of the just man and the wicked man:

> *But the path of the just is like shining*
> *light,*
> *that grows in brilliance till perfect day.*
> *The way of the wicked is like darkness;*
> *they know not on what they stumble.*
> (Prov. IV: 18f.)

The light is a *path* or *way* that the wicked have not followed: "We, then, have strayed from the way of truth, and the light of justice did not shine for us, and the sun did not rise for us" (Wis. V: 6). The Book of Proverbs condemns sinners who "leave the straight paths to walk in ways of darkness" (II: 13). To follow the way of light is to observe the Law, "for the bidding is a lamp and the teaching a light, and a way to life are the reproofs of discipline" (Prov. VI: 23). The just man tells his God: "A lamp to my feet is your word, a light to my path" (Ps. CXVIII: 105; cf. John I: 1, 4).[4] The Book of Wisdom speaks of "the imperishable light of the Law" (XVIII: 4). To this current of ideas also belongs Peter's exhortation to his readers: you do well to attend to "the word of prophecy," or Scripture, "as to a lamp shining in a dark place" (II Pet. I: 19).

In the language of the first Christian communities the light usually symbolized the *Christian life*. Even Paul's First Epistle already affirms that Christians are "all children of the light" (I Thess. V: 5). In fact, upon becoming God's people they were called out of darkness into the wondrous light of God (I Pet. II: 9f.). Darkness they were, now they have become "light in the Lord." They must therefore act as "children of the light" (Eph. V: 8), having laid aside "the works of darkness" to put on "the armor of light," the equipment of virtue (Rom. XIII: 12). On another occasion St. Paul asks:

For what has justice in common with iniquity? Or what fellowship has light with darkness? What harmony is there between Christ and Belial? Or what part has the believer with the unbeliever? And what agreement has the temple of God with idols? (II Cor. VI: 14f.)

These formulas recall the language of the Qumrân writings which associate the enemies of the chosen people with "the party of Belial," and in particular, an Essene work called *The Combat of the Sons of Light and of the Sons of Darkness*. The central theme of John's Gospel will also be concerned with the conflict of light and darkness.[5]

In a passage proper to Luke, the Evangelist can be seen

to be "Paul's interpreter," when he reports this saying of Jesus in connection with the parable of the unjust steward: "The children of this world, in relation to their generation, are more prudent than the children of light" (Luke XVI: 8). The Sermon on the Mount recalls the duties that accompany the honor of being a child of light:

You are the light of the world. A city set on a mountain cannot be hidden—Neither do men light a lamp and put it under the measure, but upon the lampstand, so as to give light to all in the house. Even so let your light shine before men, in order that they may see your good works and give glory to your Father in heaven. (Matt. V: 14–16.)

Saint Paul will make a similar recommendation to the Philippians: act as "children of God without blemish in the midst of a depraved and perverse generation [cf. Deut. XXXII: 5]. For among these you shine like stars in the world holding fast the word of life" (II: 15f.).

For John, to be a child of light is to adhere in faith to Christ, the light of the world, who states:

Yet a little while the light is among you. Walk while you have the light, that darkness may not overtake you. He who walks in darkness does not know where he goes. While you have the light believe in the light, that you may become sons of light.

(John XII: 35f.)

This adhesion in faith is conditioned by moral conduct; the presence of light reveals the heart's recesses: "Men have loved the darkness rather than the light, for their works were evil" (John III: 19). John's First Epistle establishes *fraternal charity* as the criterion of a life submitted to light (II: 9–11). All the commandments lead back to a single one, that of love, which leads on to holiness. Long ago, God had proclaimed in Leviticus: "Be holy, for I, the Lord, your God, am holy" (XIX: 2; cf. I Pet. I: 16). To walk in the light and to love one's brothers is to imitate God who is both light (I John I: 5) and love (IV: 8).

A PERSONAL CONFLICT

The conflict between light and darkness (cf. I Cor. VI: 14f.) is especially stressed in John's writings. Because the presence of Jesus is a judgment, every man is committed to the conflict that opposed once in Palestine the two chief antagonists, Jesus and Satan. With His death Jesus freed men from Satan's tyranny: while Christ was *lifted up* on the cross and glorified (John XVII: 1), "the prince of the world is *cast down*" (John XII: 31f.). After He had detected *Satan*'s presence at the outset of the Passion (John XIII: 27), Jesus revealed the judgment of the prince of this world (John XVI: 11): "When, therefore, he had received the morsel, he went out quickly. *Now it was night*" (John XIII: 30). This Johannine statement is based on Jesus' reflection: "Now is your hour and the reign of darkness" (Luke XXII: 53). Beyond the Jews who want to kill Jesus (John VIII: 40), John sees, in fact, their instigator, Satan, "a murderer from the beginning" (VIII: 44), for he is the same one who drove Adam and Eve to revolt against God and brought fraternal hatred into the world, as it appeared in the murder of Abel (cf. I John III: 12, 15).

That world[6] ruled over by Satan is the lower, carnal world fundamentally opposed to the higher, celestial world from which the Son of Man came and to which He returns (John XIII: 1). In that sense, neither Jesus Himself (John VIII: 23), nor His kingdom (XVIII: 36), nor His disciples (XV: 19) are of that world whose very appearance betrays hatred for God (XV: 18–27) and seems to evoke the definitive state of reprobation. Under one of its aspects,[7] in fact, the Johannine world is described as positively hostile to God by its adherence to darkness and its resistance to the light. That attitude creates a dramatic conflict between Christ-light and world-darkness that will be resolved only by a judgment (κρίσις: cf. XII: 31). The presence of Jesus, then, constrains men to make a decision: those who prefer darkness to light, by refusing to believe, will die in their sins (John VIII: 24), citizens of that world for which Jesus does not pray (XVII: 9). John's First Epistle even forbids true disciples to love the world with its covetousness and pride (II: 15–17). Yet the world also designates the human race that God and Christ's love totally embrace: "For God so loved the world that he gave his only begotten Son, that those who believe in him may not perish, but may have life everlasting" (John III: 16; cf. I John IV: 9).

Christians by their vocation are engaged in that struggle that pits the two great antagonists, the King of Light[8] and the Prince of Darkness, against each other. Their victory is guaranteed by Him who could say: "I am the light of the world. He who follows me does not walk in darkness, but will have the light of life" (John VIII: 12); "But take courage, I have overcome the world" (John XVI: 33). The proto-evangelium had predicted that long conflict and its outcome (Gen. III: 15), which Paul interprets: "But the God of peace will speedily crush Satan *under your feet.* The grace of our Lord Jesus Christ be with you" (Rom. XVI: 20). Light will also accompany Christians into the future world, for "God is light" (I John I: 5), "Father of Lights" (Jas. I: 17; I Pet. II: 9) and He "dwells in light inaccessible" (I Tim. VI: 16), which lights up the New Jerusalem (Apoc. XXI: 23; cf. Isa. LX: 20):

And there shall be no more any accursed thing; but the throne of God and of the Lamb shall be in it, and his servants shall serve him. And they shall see his face and his name shall be on their foreheads. And night shall be no more; and they shall have no need of light of lamp, or light of sun, for the Lord God will shed light upon them; and they shall reign forever and ever. (Apoc. XXII: 3–5.)

NOTES ON 12

[1] The episode of the woman taken in adultery (John VII: 53 to VIII: 11) is an inspired, historical account, but not a Johannine one; it was inserted in its present location in several late manuscripts.

² Translation of R. H. Charles, *The Apocrypha and Pseudepigrapha of the Old Testament* (Oxford, 1913), vol. II, p. 281.

³ Clement of Alexandria (cf. *Protreptica*, IX, 84) seems to have known a primitive hymn that was longer than the one represented by the fragments of Eph. V: 14. Here is the complete text from M. E. Boismard in *Quatre hymnes baptismales dans la Première Épitre de Pierre* (Paris, 1961), p. 12:

Awake, sleeper,   The sun of the resurrection,
And arise from among the dead,   The one begotten before dawn,
And Christ will enlighten thee.   Whose rays give life.

⁴ This description of the Law as "a light on the way" can be related to an Exodus theme: "The Lord preceded them, in the daytime by means of a column of cloud to show them the way, and at night by means of a column of fire to give them light . . ." (XIII: 21). The Law was, in fact, considered as an embodiment of Wisdom (Sir. XXIV: 23) that proclaims: "In the highest heavens did I dwell (κατεσκήνωσα: cf. John I: 14; Joel IV: 17, 21; Zech. II: 14), my throne on a pillar of cloud" (Sir. XXIV: 4). Become the Law, this Wisdom came down from the clouds (Bar. III: 29; cf. Exod. XXXIII: 9), "has appeared on earth, and moved among men" (Bar. III: 38). Cf. also p. 129, n. 7.

⁵ The Qumrân texts favor the thesis that claims Judaism as the original milieu of the Fourth Gospel. This makes less probable any direct influence of extra-biblical literature on John. On this subject, see: F. M. Braun, "L'arrière-fond du quatrième Évangile," in "*L'Évangile de Jean*, pp. 179–96; cf. *Revue Thomiste* (1960), pp. 209–24; G. Quispel, "*L'Évangile de Jean et la Gnose*," and J. Coppens, "Le Don de l'Esprit d'après les textes de Qumrân et le Quatrième Évangile," respectively pp. 197–208 and pp. 209–24 in *L'Évangile de Jean*.

⁶ On "the sin of the world," cf. M. E. Boismard, "Jésus Sauveur, d'après saint Jean," in *Lumière et Vie*, no. 15, pp. 105–10.

⁷ In Saint John's writings *kosmos* sometimes means the physical universe (cf. John XI: 9; XVII: 5, 24; XXI: 25), but in most cases the term designates the human universe, either historical humanity, fallen and to be redeemed (III: 16f.; IV: 42), or humanity which refuses God offering Himself in Christ (I: 10; XIV: 17; XVII: 25). The enemy whom Jesus came to conquer is prince of this world (XII: 31; XIV: 30; XVI: 11). Those who choose to remain in his power and prefer darkness to light change salvation in condemnation (cf. C. K. Barrett, *The Gospel According to St. John*, p. 135). Jesus did not come to condemn the world (III: 17; XII: 47), even though His presence does, in fact, condemn the unbelievers (II: 19; IX: 39). This opposition between Jesus and the unbelievers is also found between the believers and the world, between those born of the Spirit and those born from the flesh (cf. John I: 12f.; III: 6). It must be noted, however, that Christianity does not definitely condemn the flesh, as does Platonism. The sacrificial return of Jesus to His Father took place in two stages: death to the flesh and to sin (cf. Rom. VI: 10; VIII: 3), corporal resurrection, under the Spirit's power (cf. Rom. VIII: 11; I Cor. XV: 44). On the Pauline notions of "flesh" (σάρξ) and of "body" (σῶμα), as referred to Redemption, see: L. Sabourin, *Rédemption Sacrificielle* (Bruges, 1961), pp. 369–71.

⁸ G. M. Roberti reminds us, following St. Augustine (*De Gen. ad litt.*, IV, 28), that Christ is Light in the proper sense, whereas He is called "the Stone" in a metaphorical sense only (*L'onomatologia del Divin Redentore*, p. 238).

13

THE BRIDEGROOM

SEVERAL New Testament texts, even parables, call Jesus the *Bridegroom* in relation no doubt to the Messianic community considered as the *Bride*. Among the "community" titles that of *Bridegroom* holds a special place, for it is particularly apt in expressing the intimate relationship joining the Lord to the community of believers.

"Biblical thought is expressed in parables and images taken up from generation to generation, in order to reveal the deepest spiritual truths to us."[1] The theme of bridegroom, or that of wedding, owes its origin to the desire to express familiarly the intimate union God wanted to realize with His people through the Covenant.

In the eighth century B.C. the Prophet Hosea proposed the image of the broken marriage to characterize Israel's behavior toward God. The period of unfaithfulness, however, will be followed by pardon and reconciliation. The unfaithful bride will once again be joined to her God: "So I will allure her; I will lead her into the desert and speak to her heart" (Hos. II: 16). More than a century later, Jeremiah will use again, for the benefit of the kingdom of Juda, the theme of the despised love of God, Bridegroom of a sinful people: "This word of the Lord came to me: I remember the devotion of your youth following me in the desert in a land unsown" (II: 2). Modifying the allegory, Ezekiel compares Jerusalem to an abandoned, foreign child whom God has saved, reared, and then wed (ch. XVI). Like

Jeremiah (XXXI: 31–34), he foresees the formation of a new eternal covenant founded on a free pardon (Ezek. XVI: 59–63). After the lamentations over the widowing of Jerusalem (cf. Lam. I: 1) there will come, near the end of the Exile, those poems of Joy in which the Prophet of Israel's Consolation, the author of Deutero-Isaiah, celebrates the reuniting of the bride with her divine Bridegroom:

> *Raise a glad cry, you barren one who*
>   *did not bear,*
> *break forth in jubilant song, you*
>   *who were not in labor,*
> *for more numerous are the children*
>   *of the deserted wife*
> *than the children of her who has a*
>   *husband, says the Lord. . . .*
> *For he who has become your husband*
>   *is your Maker,*
> *his name is the Lord of hosts.*
> *Your redeemer is the Holy One of*
>   *Israel,*
> *called God of all the earth.*
>   (Isa. LIV: 1, 5.)

The Song of Songs consists of a collection of poems that sing of the mutual love of a Lover and his Beloved. According to the allegorical interpretation, the work poetically renews a theme long popular, especially with the Prophets: the history of God's relationship with Israel symbolized in the joys and deceptions of conjugal love. The theme is more understandable if we recall that at one period in its history, the people of God was considered the spouse of the King-Messiah, David's heir (cf. Cant. II: 4). Psalm XLIV plays on that theme:

> *Fairer in beauty are you than the sons of*
>   *Men;*
> *grace is poured out upon your lips;*
> *thus God has blessed you forever. . . .*

*Therefore, God your God, has
  anointed you
with the oil of gladness above your
  fellow kings. . . .
Hear, O daughter, and see; turn
  your ear,
forget your people and your father's
  house,
So shall the king desire your beauty;
for he is your Lord, and you must
  worship him.* (vv. 3, 8, 11f.)

The Synoptic Gospels (cf. Mark II: 19f.) present Jesus as the Bridegroom in an allegory describing the effect of His departure on the subjects of the Kingdom—sorrow will follow upon joy. Already at the time, Mark notes, "the Pharisees . . . took counsel with the Herodians against him, how they might do away with him" (III: 6). The expression, "will be taken away" (Mark II: 20), corresponds to the Septuagint's Greek term used to signify the temporal end of the Suffering Servant (Isa. LIII: 8). Then the joy of the Messianic marriage will be interrupted by the brusque rejection of the invited bride, Jerusalem of the Jews.

Two *parables*, both proper to Matthew, take up the theme of the Wedding. In the parable of the wedding feast (XXII: 1–14),[2] the Bridegroom is no longer the Lord, as formerly among the prophets, but rather the Son of God, the Messiah, as in Psalm XLIV. Although members of the chosen people were invited by right to the wedding, they have become unworthy to attend because of their conduct. A general gathering, somewhat like a Church assembly, will have to fill the wedding room with guests. In the parable about the ten virgins (Matt. XXV: 1–13) the concern is over the final coming of the Lord as regards Christian souls: "They took their lamps and went forth to meet the bridegroom." While the eventual delay of the *parousia* can result in waiting, the duration of that waiting will be no excuse for those who would fail to be ready.

Writing to the Corinthians, St. Paul said: "For I am jealous for you with a divine jealousy. For I betrothed you to one *spouse*, that I might present you a chaste virgin to Christ" (II Cor. XI: 2). Like the entire Church, that particular community and its individual members *does* inherit "prerogatives that once belonged to the people of the former Covenant" (cf. Gal. IV: 21–31). In the Epistle to the Ephesians betrothal has given way to a true marriage: Christ is the spouse of the Church because He is its leader and loves it as His own Body. The baptismal allusions of Ephesians (V: 21–32) are based on a historical context. In ancient Eastern custom the bride-to-be was bathed, adorned, and brought to her husband-to-be by "the sons of the wedding." In the mystery of the Church, Christ Himself washed His fiancée free of every stain with baptism's water in order to present her to Himself (*BJ*).

Implicitly or explicitly, the nuptial theme appears in several pages of the Fourth Gospel's first chapters. The wedding feast of Cana (II: 1–11) mysteriously prefigures the Messianic banquet. The nuptial bath that the Son will give His Church, *when His hour will have come*, will not be a bath with water (cf. I: 33), but one with blood and the Spirit, symbolized by the wine at Cana. To this context also belongs the saying of John the Baptist: "He who has the bride is the bridegroom; but the friend of the bridegroom, who stands and hears him, rejoices exceedingly at the voice of the bridegroom. This my joy, therefore, is made full. He must increase, but I must decrease" (III: 29f.). The former Covenant joyfully gives way to the new one, the free woman, the Jerusalem from on high (Gal. IV: 24–26).

The episode of the encounter with the Samaritan woman can also be enlightening. Does not this woman represent in John's perspective that Northern kingdom whose "prostitutions" had been so often denounced by the Prophets? " 'I have no husband,' the woman answered. Jesus said to her, 'Thou hast said well, "I have no husband," for thou hast had five husbands, and he whom thou now hast is not thy husband. In this thou hast spoken truly.' The woman said to him, 'Sir, I see that thou art a prophet' " (IV: 17–19). Here as elsewhere John freely gives his historical characters a symbolic value.

Continuing the Johannine tradition, the Apocalypse mentions "the marriage of the Lamb" (XIX: 7) to symbolize the establishing of the heavenly kingdom. "The spouse of the Lamb" (XXI: 9) is the Messianic Jerusalem or the Church (XXII: 17). All these figures derived from marriage underline the intimate and indissoluble union of Christ with the community of the new Covenant that He won with the price of His precious Blood (cf. V: 9). In the course of Christian centuries the use of the image of betrothal and marriage to show the mystical union of individual souls with God has often hurt the diffusion of the properly Scriptural title of Bridegroom. "It is the union of Christ and the Church, His spouse, and not immediately the union of Christ and the soul, that marriage symbolizes. St. Paul also makes it clear to us that the grace of Christ comes down upon the baptized only by reason of his insertion into the Church."[3]

NOTES ON 13

[1] An observation found in *Évangile*, no. 18, entitled "L'Époux et l'épouse." On the same subject, cf. C. Wiener and J. Colson, *Un roi fit des noces à son fils* (Bruges, 1962). Père Paul-Marie de la Croix has treated the theme of the Bridegroom and the Bride in several sections of his work, *L'Ancien Testament source de vie spirituelle* (cf. pp. 475–548, 774–79). He reminds us of a patristic teaching: "The Fathers have always seen, in the gesture of God forming Eve from Adam's side, the image of the Church sprung from the open side of Christ (Gen. II: 22), and St. Augustine will write: the complete spouse is the head and the body; the body is His Church. Therefore Spouse and Bride: two in one flesh" (p. 516).

[2] See p. 75, n. 4.

[3] J. Huby, *Mystiques paulinienne et johannique* (Bruges, 1946), p. 31. F. X.

Durrwell links the notion of "Christian virginity" to the idea that the Church is the Bride of Christ (cf. Eph. V: 25ff.). "It does not appear," he adds, "that the Holy Spirit drew many people to virginity in the Old Testament. Since the bridegroom had not yet come, such virginity would merely have been renunciation" (*In the Redeeming Christ*, New York, 1963, p. 175).

14

THE HEAD OF THE BODY—THE LEADER OR THE AUTHOR

THERE seems to be nothing better to introduce these new titles than to cite at length a passage completely dedicated to the universal pre-eminence of Christ:

He is the image of the invisible God,
the firstborn of every creature.
For in him were created all things,
in the heavens and on the earth,
things visible and invisible,
whether Thrones or Dominations, or
        Principalities, or Powers;
all things have been created through and unto him.

And he is before all creatures, and in
        him all things hold together.
Again, he is the head of the body, *the Church.*

He is the beginning,
the firstborn from the dead,
that in all things he may have the first place.
For it has pleased God the Father that in
        him all his fullness should dwell,
and that through him he should reconcile
        to himself all things,
whether on the earth or in the heavens,
making peace through the blood of his cross.
                              (Col. I: 15-20.)

This text seems to consist of two strophes of a hymn to the glory of Christ, "firstborn of every creature" and "firstborn from the dead." The central section (vv. 17, 18a) would be directly Pauline and constitute an addition intended to supplement the eulogy in the sense of a Church theology dear to Paul. The hymn recalls various aspects of the absolute primacy of Christ: perfect image of God, He is the source of all creatures, their unifying principle and their purpose in the order of creation. In the redemptive plan He is also first in several areas: *principle of life*, firstborn from the dead, mediator of universal reconciliation.

In the affirmation, "Again, he is the *head of the body*, the Church" (Col. I: 18), one understands "pre-eminence" and "cohesion," but not exclusively, for Christ is also the *Principle*, the meaning of which is suggested in the reprimand to the false ascetic who "is not united to the head, from whom the whole body, *supplied* and built up by joints and ligaments, attains a growth that is of God" (Col. II: 19; cf. Eph. IV: 15f.). In the same sense, the Epistle to the Ephesians affirms that God made Christ "head over the Church, which indeed is his body, the completion of him who fills all with all" (I: 22f.).

St. Paul recommends as part of domestic morality: "Be subject to one another in the fear of Christ. Let wives be subject to their husbands as to the Lord; because a husband is head of the wife, just as Christ is *head of the Church*, being himself saviour of the body" (Eph. V: 21–23). Once again, the theme of authority comes to the foreground and the Pauline expression could echo the Old Testament metaphor of the "head" or "leader." For example, the word constantly reappears in the episode of Jephte, "leader of all the inhabitants of Galaad" (Judg. X: 18; XI: 8–11). So, too, David claims to be the "head of nations" set up by God (II Sam. XXII: 44). The same meaning can be derived from the contrast often mentioned between "the head" and "the tail," to distinguish the dominator from the dominated (cf. Deut. XXVIII: 43f.; Isa. IX: 13f.).

Four different epistles (Rom. I, Cor., Col., Eph.) show

Paul having recourse to the concept of "a single body" to express the nature of the union of Christians with Christ. To attribute the present-day sense of "body" (as in "social body," "corporation," "homogeneous group," "teaching body") to Paul's vigorous thought would be to weaken its meaning. Paul never says "the body of Christians" but always "the body of Christ," a conception that the Apostle presumes to be well known by Christians in his time even though ancient literature offered no instance of it. Paul envisages a single organism when he writes: "Now you are the body of Christ, member for member" (I Cor. XII: 27). Two other texts, "we are members of his body" (Eph. V: 30; cf. II Cor. XI: 2), and "do you not know that your bodies are members of Christ?" (I Cor. VI: 15), are found in passages devoted to the union described by Genesis: "The two become one flesh" (II: 24).

But St. Paul did not take the metaphor "body" from the Old Testament, which did not know it. On the contrary, the formulas of the Last Supper can be considered as having influenced the Pauline idea of a body of Christ, whose members are Christians. Paul himself gives us the principal datum when he writes: "Because the bread is one, we though many, are one body, all of us who partake of the one bread" (I Cor. X: 17). The intimate union of all members is not at all astonishing, if the flesh and blood of Christ become the food and drink of the Christian community.

Only in the Pauline writings is the "eucharistic body" worked into a theology of the communal body. At the basis of this new development must be placed Paul's unique experience on the road to Damascus and the saying: "Why dost thou persecute me?" (Acts XXVI: 14). From that it was easy to conclude: "Now you are the body of Christ, member for member" (I Cor. XII: 27), or again, "So we, the many, are one body in Christ, but severally members one of another" (Rom. XII: 5).

To introduce the Christological title "Head of the Body," a text from the Epistle to the Colossians (I: 15–20) was cited earlier. In the next chapter Paul once again uses some notions of that hymnal piece: "For in him dwells all the fullness of the Godhead bodily, and in him who is the *Head* of every Principality and Power you have received of that fullness" (II: 9f.). This passage attests a doctrinal progress as compared to Colossians (I: 18–24), where Christ is Head of the Body or the Church to the exclusion of the heavenly powers who form no part of it. A similar development is presented differently in the Epistle to the Ephesians "And all things he made subject under his feet, and him he gave as head over all the Church, which indeed is his body, the completion of him who fills all with all" (Eph. I: 22f.). Here Paul is apparently restricting to the Church the scope of the formulas "fullness" and "body," which can assume a cosmic significance. The idea that "Christ fills all things" is resumed by Ephesians (IV: 10). It lay in the background of the description of God's plan to *recapitulate* ("reduce under a single head") all things, heavenly and earthly, in Christ (I: 10). "Everything must be brought back under Christ as under a single Leader, a recognized leader and even a nourishing source for some, a leader imposed by force for others."[1] At one and the same time Christ can be Head of all creation and Head of the Church, for from the Church He radiates his invisible royalty over the world. A special presence, then, links Christ to the Church, which forms part of the total domain submitted to the Head of creation.

As Head of the Body, Christ holds the *authority* in the Church, whose cohesion and unity He guarantees, as the metaphor "cornerstone" clearly indicates. The title "Head," it has been said, implies that Christ is also the *life* of the Church. In the allegory of the vine, John will illustrate that aspect with greater insistence. For the Church, Christ is also the Bridegroom, a title that associates *love* and authority.

Another title, closely akin to that of Head, is one called ἀρχηγός in Greek, which can be translated "Author" or "Leader." The title appears twice in Acts and twice in Hebrews. In the Epistle it is read in the following context:

For it became him for whom are all things, who had brought many sons into glory, to perfect through sufferings the *author* of their salvation. (II: 10.)

Therefore let us also . . . put away every encumbrance and the sin entangling us, and run with patience to the fight set before us; looking towards the *author* and finisher of faith, Jesus, who for the joy set before him endured a cross despising shame, and sits at the right hand of the throne of God. (XII: 1f.)

The idea of an achievement or a *perfection* acquired by suffering is put forth in both these texts. The redemptive mission of the Saviour reached its achievement in the Passion to which His entire life had been destined as to its term and crown. "Leader of our faith," He was also its *Author* and beginner by His teaching and life, He brought our faith to perfection by His acceptance of the cross, for the Redemption "accomplishes" our faith and realizes the hope that it implies.

The book of Acts also applies the title ἀρχηγός to Christ by referring to Him as "the author [prince] of life" (III: 15), which is similar to the use in Hebrews (II: 10), "the author [leader] of their salvation": in Aramaic the same term, *hayye*, means "life" and "salvation". In another discourse (Acts V: 31) Peter calls Christ "*Prince* and Saviour" in a similar context. A parallel can also be seen there of the designation of Moses as ruler (ἄρχων) and redeemer of the Hebrews (Acts VII: 35). Christ is called "Prince and Saviour" by reason of the mission that He received at His resurrection to win salvation for "Israel." The Greek Bible calls the *heads* of family (Exod. VI: 14) or of tribes (Num. XIII: 3) by the term ἀρχηγός. A philosopher contemporary with Christ, Philo, calls Adam the "first leader" (*archegete*) of humanity, a title that equally suits Christ, the last Adam (cf. I Cor. XV: 45) and head of a new humanity.

Christ ἀρχηγός is Head, guide, initiator, pioneer in the economy of salvation whose *Author* He is totally. Leader of all the faithful, and their "precursor" (Heb. VI: 20),[2] He inaugurated for us "a new and living way," through His blood, to lead to the heavenly sanctuary (cf. Heb. X: 19f.). From many viewpoints, then, Christ is "head of his body, the Church" (Col. I: 18).

NOTES ON 14

[1] P. Benoit, "Corps, tête et plérôme dans les Épitres de la captivité," in *Revue Biblique* (1956), p. 31. On Christ, head and pleroma, cf. also *Rédemption Sacrificielle*, where we point out other interpretations of "recapitulation" (p. 390). Also see Pius XII's masterly encyclical *Mystici Corporis* (June, 1943).

[2] For Heb. II: 10; VI: 20, see C. Spicq, the *Épitre aux Hébreux*, vol. II.

15

THE VINE

THE allegory of the vine is familiar to Christians. Two sayings of Jesus concern our subject particularly: "I am the true vine, and my Father is the vine-dresser"; "I am the vine, you are the branches" (John XV: 1, 5).[1] A more expressive symbol for the vital union existing between Christ and Christians, between the Messiah and the community of the last days, would be difficult to find.

This title, *the Vine*, could be placed in another category. However, communal scope and other aspects justify its association with the Messianic titles. For example, it recalls the idea that the Christian community is a new Israel. "I am the *true* vine," Jesus insists, in contrast, it seems, to the degenerate vine described by Isaiah on the occasion of a grape harvest:

> *Let me now sing of my friend, my friend's*
> *song concerning his vineyard.*
> *My friend had a vineyard on a fertile*
> *hillside;*
> *He spaded it, cleared it of stones, and*
> *planted the choicest vines.*
> *Within it he built a watchtower, and*
> *hewed out a wine press.*
> *Then he looked for the crop of grapes*
> *but what it yielded was wild grapes . . .*
> *The vineyard of the Lord of hosts is*
> *the house of Israel,*

> *and the men of Juda are his cherished*
>   *plant;*
> *He looked for judgment, but see, bloodshed!*
> *for justice, but hark, the outcry.* (V: 1f., 7.)

For the same reason, because the chosen people did not
bear the fruit expected, Jeremiah will treat Israel as "a
spurious vine" (II: 21) and will transmit the divine order
to pull up its branches which "do not belong to the Lord"
(V: 10; cf. VI: 9). In the Johannine allegory the branches
are burned (John XV: 6); in the parable of the barren fig
tree, the entire tree is threatened (Luke XIII: 6–9) and
even condemned (Matt. XXI: 18–20).

On the other hand, in a late apocalyptic section of the
Book of Isaiah (chs. XXIV–XXVII) a distant disciple of the
prophet foresees Israel becoming the vine beloved of God
(XXVII: 2–5): "Israel shall sprout and blossom covering
all the world with fruit" (XXVII: 6). Ezekiel compares the
Messianic restoration of Israel to the marvelous development of a cedar branch:

> *On the mountain heights of Israel I will*
>   *plant it.*
> *It shall put forth branches and bear*
>   *fruit,*
> *and become a majestic cedar.*
> *Birds of every kind shall dwell beneath it,*
> *every winged thing in the shade of*
>   *its boughs.* (XVII: 22f.; cf. Matt. XIII: 32.)

Carried along by his plea, Ezekiel describes as worthless
the wood of the vine, as destined to be burned, a figure for
Jerusalem's lot (XV: 1–8; cf. XIX: 10–14).

The interest that biblical authors have in the vine corresponds partly to the information given us by profane
literature: the *ancients* esteemed the vine even to the point
of worship (cf. Deut. XXII: 9). In neo-Sumerian the terms
for "wine" and "life" are really etymologically alike. The
Babylonian texts more often give to wine "a vital force"

than to oil. In ancient pagan rites wine was poured over tombs to guarantee immortality to the deceased. According to the Bible itself, the life of man has its seat in the blood (cf. Lev. XVII: 11; Deut. XII: 23) and wine is called "blood of grapes" (Gen. XLIX: 11). A parabiblical tradition identifies the tree of knowledge (cf. Gen. II: 9, 17) with the vine (cf. Henoch XXXII: 4). When the *eschatological* aspect of the notion of creation is considered (cf. II Pet. III: 13), it is not surprising that the vine appears with the fig tree as a plant of Messianic times (cf. Mic. IV: 4; Zech. III: 10). The New Testament takes up this element by making "new wine" a symbol of Messianic times (cf. Matt. IX: 17; John II: 1–11).

Generally, *plantation*² is an image used to describe the Messianic community. And so in a post-exilic section of the Book of Isaiah we read about the "survivors" of Israel: "They will be called generations of justice and plantation (φύτευμα) of the Lord to show his glory" (LXI: 3 [Greek]). The apocryphal psalms of Solomon written in the first century B.C. added: "The paradise of the Lord, the tree of life—these are the saints; their plantation [φυτεία] is rooted for eternity; they will not be uprooted as long as heaven lasts" (XIV: 2f.). In the Qumrân writings the community of the just is also compared to an eternal plantation.

For St. Paul the Christian is in baptism associated with the crucified and resurrected Christ as a young branch is grafted to the trunk (cf. Rom. VI: 5: σύμφυτος). The term *"neophyte"* (νεόφυτος: I Tim. III: 6) belongs to the same family of images. A further development related to the Johannine theme of the vine is Paul's treatment of the factors that help the plant of the faithful community grow (I Cor. III: 5–9; cf. Matt. XV: 13). The first Psalm had described the steadfastness of the just man with a well-known metaphor: "He is like a tree planted near running water, that yields its fruit in due season, and whose leaves never fade" (cf. Jer. XVII: 8).

Messianic expectation counted on the establishing of a new Israel on the day of the Lord and so too of a new vine although the Messiah's identification with the vine was not even dreamed of. But such an allusion does appear in Psalm LXXIX, especially in the Greek version (v. 16), where the parallelism links the vine, Israel, with a Messianic "Son of Man." A first-century apocrypha is no doubt reflecting a pre-Christian tradition as it describes thus an eschatological turning point of history: "Then the principate of my Messiah will be revealed, which is like the fountain and the vine, and when it is revealed it will root out the multitude of its host"[3] (II Bar. XXXIX: 7). But the reality was to exceed all expectations.

In the Synoptics the vineyard represents the human community (especially Israel), worked by God's workers, the preachers of the kingdom (cf. I Cor. III: 6–9): parable of the vine-dressers (Mark XII: 1–12), parable of the laborers in the vineyard (Matt. XX: 1–16), parable of the two sons (Matt. XXI: 28–32). The Fourth Gospel (cf. XV: 1–17) uses certain data from the Synoptics but transforms them. The similarities are no longer concerned with the lot of any particular vine but generally with the cultivation of the vine. Furthermore, the eschatological coloration is softened, for John freely "actualizes" eschatology[4] and interiorizes it. The just man, for example, already somehow possesses the gifts of the future life (cf. V: 24–29). The atmosphere of polemic against the Pharisees has given way to peaceful meditations: the true Vine is Jesus Himself, the true life of the Church.

The interpretation of the Johannine allegory of the vine depends in part on the solution given to this problem: when was it delivered? In its present context it immediately follows the announcement of a departure: "Arise, let us go from here!" (John XIV: 31). Did Jesus, in John's perspective, develop His subject on the road to Gethsemani or rather on the porch of the Temple, whose façade offered an interesting symbolic ornament: a golden vine representing Israel? A less recondite explanation is perhaps preferable. A careful reading of chapters XV–XVI gives one the impression that they are John's paraphrase on the previous discourse, a new redaction, perhaps an alternate text destined as a liturgical reading. In fact, those two chapters take up the chief themes of Chapter XIV. According to this solution, the signal for departing (XIV: 31) is immediately followed by the "priestly prayer" (ch. XVII) and by the walk down to Gethsemani (XVIII: 1).

The suggested hypothesis puts the allegory in the immediate context of the Last Supper and suggests a Eucharistic meaning for the symbolism of the Vine. The Vine does appear in the accounts of the institution of the Eucharist: "Amen I say to you, that I will drink no more of the fruit of the vine, until that day when I shall drink it new in the kingdom of God" (Mark XIV: 25). John replaces that eschatological outlook with an ecclesial one where fraternal charity and love of Christ are mysteriously one (cf. John XV: 9–15).

"Greater love than this no one has, that one lay down his life for his friends" (John XV: 13). That saying recalls this one of the Last Supper: "This is my blood of the new covenant, which is being shed for many" (Mark XIV: 24). If hatred characterizes the world of unbelievers, love characterizes the group of disciples (cf. John XV: 18–27). By His death and resurrection[5] Jesus will reunite the Messianic community (cf. John XV: 32; XII: 32) and will become its life. Wine, which the ancients called "the blood of the grape" (cf. Deut. XXXII: 14), was fitting, by both its color and its origin, to symbolize the sacrificial blood of the Crucified, "crushed for our sins" (cf. Isa. LIII: 5). Along with the bread, the Eucharistic blood would make the divine life of the Saviour's Cross present in all places and in every generation. Through the whole vine, which is the whole Christ, courses only one life, symbolized by water springing up unto life everlasting (John IV: 14).[6] To the formal, external unity of the vine that Israel was (cf. Hos. X: 1) succeeds the vital union of all the branches to the Vine that nourishes them with its sap (John XV: 4; cf. Rom. XI: 16–24).

For John, Jesus is that *Wisdom* of God that biblical Revelation tended to personify. He is the Bread of Life (VI: 35) and nourishment for men, like Wisdom (cf. Sir. XXIV: 19–22). Quite appropriate too is this passage from the Discourse of Wisdom:

> *I spread out my branches like a terebinth,*
> *my branches so bright and so graceful.*
> *I bud forth delights like the* vine,
> *my blossoms become fruit fair and rich.*
> *Come to me, all you that yearn for me,*
> *and be filled with my fruits.* (Sir. XXIV: 16ff.)

NOTES ON 15

[1] The *Bible de Jérusalem* translated the Greek ἄμπελος as "stock" to distinguish it clearly from "branches," although the Evangelist did not seem pre-occupied with the distinction. In the parable of the Good Shepherd (John X: 1–18), for example, attention is turned from the flock and focused on the individual sheep and on the Shepherd. The allegory of the Vine is also careful to put aside any idea that the community enjoys an *autonomous* existence apart from Christ. St. Paul distinguishes more clearly Christ from Christians by the metaphor of the Body of which Christ is the Head and Christians are the members. This observation does not contradict A. Feuillet's opinion (*DBS*, vol. VI, c. 1409): "The perspective of the Church flowers throughout John's gospel . . . The woman at Cana (II: 4) and Calvary (XIX: 26) is Mary as the personification of the Church, which is to give Christians the Messianic wine (Cana) and to be their mother (Calvary)." Also see J.-L. D'Aragon, "Le caractère distinctif de l'Église johannique," in *L'Église dans la Bible* (collection "Studia," no. 13, Bruges, 1962), pp. 53–66.

[2] After studying the symbolic theme of "plantation," especially in Judaeo-Christianity, J. Daniélou writes: "We reach the conclusion that, of the catechetical images of the Church—the temple, the ship, the flock—one of the most primitive is the plantation. It is found in its pure state in the old documents, which took it over from Judaism. It sometimes developed under the form of God's vineyard. This image has to be distinguished from that of Christ as the tree of life or as the vine-stock on which shoots and branches grow; this last image represents the close connection between Christ and his members in the Church. But from the *Hodayoth* of Qumrân on, and from Ignatius of Antioch on, we find one metaphor passing into another. Finally

that of the φυτεία, the plantation, tends to give way to that of the mystical vine" (*Primitive Christian Symbols*, p. 40f.). He also notes that "the theme of the Church *planted* by the Apostles" is an old missionary theme renovated in modern missionary language. In the Synoptics Jesus had used the metaphor "vineyard" as the Old Testament did, but in St. John "the image is compressed for the revelation of unity in love which it is intended to convey" (L. Bouyer, *The Fourth Gospel*, Westminster, Md., 1964, p. 204). The unity of a vine and that of a vineyard belong obviously to a different level.

3 Translation of R. H. Charles, *op. cit.*, vol. II, p. 501.

4 "With the publication of C. H. Dodd's *Parables of the Kingdom* in 1935, the term 'realized eschatology' became an important part of the vocabulary of New Testament studies, and considerable discussion has centered around this topic in the twenty-five years which have followed . . . Dodd argued on the one hand, that Jesus viewed his total ministry (culminating in the cross and resurrection) as the crucial eschatological event; in short, the kingdom of God had *arrived* in the career of Jesus. On the other hand, he maintained that Jesus predicted no *future* eschatological crisis which would radically change or terminate history." Thus is a complex problem ably laid out by a recent writer: Robert F. Berkey in *Journal of Biblical Literature*, 1963, p. 177. Some authors consider "realized eschatology" as an overstatement and prefer to refer to "actualized eschatology", "inaugurated eschatology," or "eschatology in the process of being realized." Berkey would accept similar expressions "only if we do not allow words and phrases to negate an actual realization of the kingdom in the life and ministry of Jesus" (p. 186). See also, for John, pp. 109 and 114.

5 How Christians participate in the death and the resurrection of Christ is explained in Cerfaux's latest book, *Le chrétien dans la théologie paulinienne* (Paris, 1962), pp. 302–19.

6 In a recent study F. J. McCool suggests that in John (IV: 10–14) the two interpretations, living water = the Spirit and living water = the revelation of Jesus, are not necessarily exclusive of one another: the Holy Spirit's activity enables the revelation of Jesus to attain its end effectively (cf. "Living Water in John," in *The Bible in Current Catholic Thought* (New York, 1962), pp. 226–33.

16

THE BREAD OF LIFE

IN a discourse that follows the miraculous multiplication of the loaves, Jesus refers to Himself as "the bread of life" (John VI: 35) or "the living bread" (VI: 51). He expressed in that Eucharistic symbol one aspect of the mystery which was to be fully formulated later: "I am the way, the truth and the life" (John XIV: 6). The presentation of Jesus as *Life of the Community* also reflects the daily lived experience of the primitive Church whose interpreter John became.

ETERNAL LIFE, AN ESCHATOLOGICAL GIFT

The theme of *life* already has a deep theological sense in the Old Testament. Yahweh is the living God (Deut. V: 26; cf. Matt. XVI: 16), for He is active and powerful while the idols are inert and helpless (cf. Ps. CXIV: 4–7; Isa. XLIV: 9–20). He is also said to "live forever" (Tob. XIII: 1), a later expression (cf. Dan. VI: 27), sometimes included in an oath (Deut. XXXII: 40; Dan. XII: 7). Author of life (Gen. II: 7; Isa. XLII: 5), God remains its master (Ps. CIII: 29f; Wis. XVI: 13) and dispenser (Deut. XXXII: 39). The divine origin of life accounts for several expressions that refer to life: breath of life (Gen. II: 7), tree of life (Gen. II: 9), way of life (Ps. XV: 11; cf. Jer. XXI: 8), fountain of life (Ps. XXXV: 10), light of the living (Ps. LV: 14), book of life (Ps. LXVIII: 29). The just man often thanks God, who saves him from never-ending dangers that threaten to strike him from "the land of the living" (Ps. CXV: 9)

To stray from God, then, is to separate oneself from the source of life. Consequently, *death* has entered this world together with sin, revolt against God. It has revealed its work in manifold ways: the crime of Cain (Gen. IV), the decreasing longevity of the patriarchs (Gen. V: priestly tradition), the decree limiting age (Gen. VI: 3; Yahwist tradition), and finally the deluge, a divine punishment (Gen. VI: 5) that destroyed all life (Gen. VII: 22) except for a "Remnant," a token of God's mercy.

Throughout the entire Old Testament the privilege of a long life is linked to the observance of God's law (cf. Deut. XXX: 15–20; XXXII: 47). In Ezekiel (XIV: 12–23) personal responsibility conditions temporal survival (cf. XXXIII: 16). Wisdom, especially, and fear of the Lord are sources of life: "For he who finds me finds life, and wins favor from the Lord; but he who misses me harms himself; all who hate me love death" (Prov. VIII: 35f.). "The fear of the Lord is a fountain of life that a man may avoid the snares of death" (XIV: 27). However, sapiential thought (cf. Job XXI) on day-to-day existence and the premature death of the just would favor a more definite belief in future life. But we shall expose that process of gradual revelation under the title "Resurrection."

The New Testament notion of life easily goes beyond the temporal framework to express the interior state of the soul united to God or the existence of the just man after death. That deeper understanding of the *true* life appears in a saying of Jesus, reminiscent of Deuteronomy, which it renews: "Not by bread alone does man live but by every word that comes forth from the mouth of God" (Matt. IV: 4; Deut. VIII: 3). The basic truth repeated throughout the Bible is in no way laid aside: life belongs to God (cf. Luke XII: 20), and man cannot "add to his stature a single cubit" (Matt. VI: 27).

The Synoptic Gospels report this question asked by the young man: "Good Master, what shall I do to gain *eternal life?*" (Mark X: 17). The expression "eternal life" already appears in the last Old Testament books (cf. II Macc. VII: 9; Dan. XII: 3) and in the more recent apocrypha, the Parables of Henoch, for example. The identification of the true life with the eternal life of "time-to-come" (cf. Luke XVIII: 30) is so persistent that the adjective is often omitted: "How narrow the gate and close the way that leads to life! And few there are who find it" (Matt. VII: 14; cf. XIX: 17). This harmony is as constant in John's Gospel (cf. Ch. VI). Eternal life has such a price that one must be ready for any sacrifice to enter it (Mark IX: 43–48). Jesus taught that winning eternal life is linked to observing the commandments (cf. Matt. XIX: 17), particularly the one that enjoins love of God and neighbor (Luke X: 25–28). During the two centuries that precede the coming of Christ this conviction was well represented in Judaism. Other sayings of Jesus clearly distinguish present good from future life (cf. Mark X: 30).

In Paul's writings (cf. Rom. II: 7; Gal. VI: 8) and especially in the *pastoral epistles* (cf. I Tim. I: 15f.), eternal life (Tit. I: 2; cf. Acts XIII: 46), "the true life" (I Tim. VI: 19) is also thought of as *an eschatological good* possessed on earth only in hope (Tit. III: 7). By their immoral conduct the pagans are "estranged from the life of God" (Eph. IV: 18). On the other hand, it is declared to the baptized: "Thus do you consider yourselves also as dead to sin, but alive to God in Christ Jesus (Rom. VI: 11). The eternal life that will be ours already somehow exists in Him who is our life, "the firstborn from the dead" (Col. I: 18): "For you have died and your life is hidden with Christ in God. When Christ, your life, shall appear, then you too will appear with him in glory" (Col. III: 3f.; cf. Eph. II: 6).

Eternal life is also understood as a future eschatological gift in the majority of the texts of the Apocalypse, in these images, for instance, dear to Jewish apocalypses: "the tree

of life" (II: 7; XXII: 14); "river of life" (XXI: 1f.); "book
of life" (III: 5; cf. Phil. IV: 3); "crown of life "(Apoc. II: 10;
cf. Jac. I: 12). One passage from the Apocalypse seems, on
the other hand, to belong to a current of thought which
considers as "life" the interior state of the good Christian:
"And to the angel of the church at Sardis write: Thus says
he who has the seven spirits of God and the seven stars: I
know thy works; thou hast the name of being *alive*, and
thou art *dead*" (III: 1).

ETERNAL LIFE, A PRESENT REALITY

In the Synoptic Gospels, two expressions are equivalent:
"to enter Life" (Matt. XVIII: 9) and "to enter the kingdom
of God" (Mark IX: 47). Concretely, the kingdom is the
eschatological salvation. The future happiness of the elect
is also the subject of the conversation with Nicodemus who
learns what the conditions are that prepare the man who
wants "to see the *kingdom of God*" (John III: 3) and to what
"lifting up" the Son of Man must submit so that "those
who believe in him may have life everlasting" (III: 15).
A Lucan passage "the kingdom of God is within you"
(Luke XVII: 21) and the parables of Matt. XIII suggest that
the kingdom is a reality already present. This perspective
flows from the double phase recognized in the kingdom—
one present, the other future. The *Johannine* kingdom or
eternal life cannot be divided: the believer will partake of it
in the beyond, but he already possesses it, being as from now
a "child of God" (I John III: 1f.). "In St. John, the entire
eschatological event is shifted and with the person of Jesus
erupts into the present world."[1]

To believe in Jesus is effectively to make a decisive choice
that already assures eternal life:

Amen, amen, I say to you, he who hears my word, and believes
him who sent me, has life everlasting and does not come to
judgment, but has passed from death to life. (John V: 24.)

The believer escapes judgment because his lot is already fixed: he is "saved" if he persists in his faith (cf. John III: 16, 36). All believers—whether pagans who convert and turn to the knowledge of "the one true God" or Jews who recognize the one He has sent, Jesus Christ, already somehow possess eternal life (John XVII: 3). Only on "those who do not know God and who do not obey the gospel of our Lord Jesus Christ" (II Thess. I: 8) will the weight of his wrath fall. Such knowledge of salvation also entails conduct (cf. Rom. I: 21). The believer "does not commit sin . . . cannot sin" (I John III: 9) and has "passed from death to life" (John V: 24), for, by his firm hope, he escapes the power of real death, eternal death: "Whoever lives and believes in me, shall never die" (John XI: 26).[2]

JESUS, SOURCE OF LIFE

As we have seen, John actualizes eschatology. He also interiorizes it, for Johannine thought belongs to the post-paschal climate, that stage of revelation that identifies the Jesus of history with the Christ of faith who is the life of the Church. Christ is "the bread of life" (John VI: 35), "the living water" (IV: 10; cf. VI: 35), "the light of life" (VIII: 12). These expressions certainly mean that He who *is* life (XIV: 6) has as His mission obtaining eternal life for us with the power given Him by the Father: "For as the Father has life in himself, even so he has given to the Son also to have life in himself" (V: 26; cf. Luke XXII: 29).

Without thinking of the life of Jesus as "a divine fluid" transfused to believers, we can justifiably claim for the Johannine texts a greater depth of meaning than a certain exegesis is disposed to give it. The allegory of the vine (John XV), for example, obviously calls on the belief in a community of life that unites Christ and His disciples. The same conclusion is suggested by the interpretation that John gives the statements of Jesus, the source of living water: "He said this, however, of the Spirit whom they who believed in him were to receive" (John VII: 39). This can be linked to Paul's affirmation: "And hope does not disappoint, because the charity of God is poured forth in our hearts by the Holy Spirit who has been given to us" (Rom. V: 5). "Clarified by parallel passages, this text teaches the Christian's participation in the life of the Trinity through sanctifying grace" (*BJ*). According to the New Testament, the Holy Spirit is truly the principle of a new life, now interior and hidden, but one that will be *manifested* in the happiness of the afterlife (cf. I John III: 2).[3]

"You search the Scriptures, because in them you think that you have life everlasting. And it is they that bear witness to me, yet you are not willing to come to me that you may have life." (John V: 39f.). For the Jews, the Sacred Scriptures are a source of eternal life, because they point out the way to attain it. But for Jesus the *Messianic* Scriptures especially lead to life, because they announce the coming of one who was to be the life of the world (John I: 4). Even though John shows little interest in metaphysical speculations referring to "person" or "nature," he lets it be clearly understood that Jesus' Messianic activity and saving power spring from the riches of His being: "In the beginning was the Word, and the Word was with God; and the Word was God" (I: 1).

The notion of life is one of the major themes in the Johannine writings. The Prologue to his gospel presents Light and Life in a cosmic context that recalls the priestly account of creation (Gen. I: 1–II: 4) and the Psalmist's words to God: "For with you is the fountain of life and in your light we see light" (Ps. XXXV: 10). In the Prologue "the life was the light of men" (John I: 4), while in Gnostic thought Light (knowledge or gnosis) alone can gain Life or salvation.

For a long time John reflected on the meaning of the cures and temporal resurrections wrought by Jesus. It is

understandable, then, that his writings often call Christ
the life of the believers:

And as Moses lifted up the serpent in the desert, even so must
the Son of Man be lifted up, that those who believe in him may
not perish, but may have life *everlasting*. For God so loved the
world that He gave his only begotten Son, that those who believe
in him may not perish but may have life everlasting.

(John III: 14f.)

The water that I will give him shall become in him a fountain
of water, springing up into life *everlasting*.   (IV: 14.)

I am the *bread of life*. He who comes to me shall not hunger, and
he who believes in me shall never thirst.   (VI: 35.)

I came that they may have life and have it more abundantly.

(X: 10.)

But these signs are written that you may believe that Jesus is the
Christ, the Son of God, and that believing you may have *life* in
his name.   (XX: 31.)

THE BREAD OF LIFE

In the Incarnation of the Word John sees the descent to
earth of the true life that is God's (cf. John V: 26). Such an
abyss separates natural life from shared divine life that man
cannot accede to it without a rebirth (III: 3–8). The central
theme of the discourse on the bread of life belongs to this
conception: "For the bread of God is that which comes
down from heaven and gives life to the world" (VI: 33).
That miraculous bread in the desert, manna, was only an
earthly food although "come down from heaven" (VI: 31;
cf. Ps. LXXVII: 24). Jesus *is* "the bread *from* heaven, the
true bread" (VI: 32) or "the living bread that has come down
from Heaven" (VI: 51) with which the faithful are fed
through faith (VI: 35) and the Eucharist (VI: 51–63).

For several reasons, the *notion of bread* is an apt sign

for the Eucharist, both nourishment and sacrifice. Sacrifices in the Old Testament are called "bread of God" (cf. Lev. XXI: 6–22; Num. XXVIII: 2), an anthropomorphism inspired by extrabiblical conceptions. Furthermore, the term "bread" in Semitic language is known to be related etymologically to the words "flesh" and "to crush." This saying of Jesus' is also worth recalling: "Amen, amen, I say to you, unless the grain of wheat falls into the ground and dies, it remains alone. But if it dies, it brings forth much fruit" (John XII: 24).[4]

As for unleavened bread or azymes (cf. I Cor. V: 7), called "bread of misery" (Deut. XVI: 3), it is the nourishment for travelers and exiles (cf. II Cor. V: 6), prescribed for the Hebrews leaving Egypt (Exod. XII: 8; Heb. XI: 13), even though such use of azymes seems to reflect the later period of the Settlement. The "azymes" symbolize "purity and truth" (II Cor. V: 8), because for the ancients, leaven was considered as a corrupting element (cf. Matt. XVI: 6, 12). The sacrificial food offerings of the ancient law consisted of fine flour "in the form of *unleavened* cakes." (Lev. II: 4).

The discourse on the bread of life (John VI) has been prepared by the account of two impressive miracles in which Jesus revealed his creative and lordly power over the elements of this world: the multiplication of the loaves and the walking on the water. While the first of these prodigies contains a clearly Eucharistic orientation, the origin of Christian liturgical rites is less of a concern for John than the revelation of Jesus as the dispenser of Life. Unlike the Synoptics, John did not report the institution of the Eucharist,[5] but his discourse on the bread of life certainly reflects the Saviour's teachings which were to prepare the disciples for the mystery of the Last Supper. There Jesus is seen in His role as dispenser of Life. Understandably, too, Peter reproached the unbelieving Jews with having caused the death of "the prince of life" (Acts III: 15). According to Proverbs, Wisdom "has spread its table" and proclaimed on the heights, "Come, eat of my food, and drink of the wine I have mixed" (IX: 2–5). The tree of life in the earthly paradise symbolized mankind's early aspiration for an unquenchable life. The new Wisdom answered that expectation: "I am the living bread that has come down from heaven. If anyone eat of this bread he shall live forever; and the bread that I will give is my flesh for the life of the world" (John VI: 51).

NOTES ON 16

[1] J. Dupont, *Essais sur la christologie de saint Jean* (Bruges, 1951), p. 188. This work treats these four themes: Jesus as Word (λόγος), Light, Life, and manifestation of Glory. It is noteworthy that John (III: 5) is the only passage of the Fourth Gospel that uses the frequent Synoptic expression "*the kingdom of God*." Writing on the Fourth Gospel's "inaugurated" eschatology (cf. *Revue Thomiste*, 1960, pp. 345–53), F.-M. Braun believes that *John* can be described in the same terms used by Msgr. Cerfaux for *Paul*: "He considers successive periods less than the incomplete quality of Christian realities that are both in the future world and in this one" (p. 353). Braun also writes: "Since the eternal life expected in the future world is in Jesus and since through Him all men are called to enjoy it, John was right in sustaining that the ἔσχατον had become present at least virtually" (p. 360). Discussing "the Parousia" in the Johannine writings (*DBS*, VI, cc. 1394–1411), A. Feuillet offers several luminous explanations of Johannine eschatology. "The reader," he says, "who leaves the Synoptics or Paul to begin John's Gospel has the impression of going from the religion of hope directed to the future to one of possession in present time" (c. 1404). On so-called "realized eschatology" see p. 105, n. 4. The *now* to which the Christ of John so often refers (cf. IV: 23; V: 25; XII: 31; XIII: 31; XIV: 7; XVII: 1, 5) is not a timeless present, but the culminating point of a religion's history. Toward this *now* all life prior to Christ, and even the whole economy of the Old Testament, were directed. For example, if "the hour comes and is already there when true worshippers will adore the Father in spirit and in truth, then *that* is the high point of Old Testament worship" (c. 1407).

[2] The only true death, eternal death, cannot touch true believers (cf. John VIII: 51) who are graced with eternal life (cf. IV: 14; X: 28).

[3] On the biblical theme of *life*, cf. J. Guillet, *Themes of the Bible*, pp. 172–91. In particular, the author notes: "This certitude of having encountered life is one of the features which mark the physiognomy of St. Paul" (p. 188). "Paul does not separate the life of Christ from the life of the Church, from his own existence" (p. 190). The Apostle writes "Christ your life" (Col. III: 4), "for me to live is Christ" (Phil. I: 21), "I live, no longer I, but Christ lives in me" (Gal. II: 20). For John, however, "Jesus is not his, John's life. He is, without any other qualification, life" (p. 191). Having noticed that Jesus' words on "eternal life" most often consist in affirming its existence rather than in describing it, Guillet suggests this explanation for that

reserve: "Eternal life is a revelation of life after death" (p. 188). Jesus, he continues, apparently added nothing to the certitude of Daniel (cf. XII: 2f.) or of II Maccabees (cf. VII: 9, 14) on eternal life. But Jesus "speaks of it from the inside, and that is why He reveals it in the proper sense. In His words, and even more in His actions, in His spontaneous reactions, we find ourselves in immediate contact with the world of life" (*ibid.*).

4 The *Didache*, written in the first century A.D., says of the Eucharist: "As this broken bread was scattered over the hills and then when gathered became one mass, so may Thy Church be gathered from the ends of the earth into Thy kingdom. For Thine is the glory and power through Jesus Christ for evermore" (IX: 4.—translation from *Ancient Christian Writers* series, Newman Press, vol. VI, p. 20).

5 The silence of Jesus on the rites of the institution of the Eucharist is explained in several ways. Writing for readers well aware of these rites, the author of the Fourth Gospel did not deem it necessary to give the same detailed account as the Synoptics (cf. Mark XIV: 22–25) and Paul (I Cor. XI: 23–26). Again, the silence has been explained as care not to reveal "sacred formulas" to the hostile pagans (J. Jeremias). For a long time, the absence of any description of the Eucharistic rites has also been noted in the *Didache*, which, nonetheless, prescribes that only the baptized ought to be admitted to the preparatory meal. The writing founds its teaching on the saying of the Lord: "Do not give what is sacred to dogs" (Matt. VII: 6). Following the same hypothesis, the expression "breaking of the bread" would be a cryptogram connected with the discipline of the *arcana*. Let us add: if there was "a eucharistic secret," it was neither universal, nor absolute. According to Cullmann, the silence of the Evangelist is closely allied to his tendency to speak of the sacraments only *indirectly* by showing, for example, how the episodes of Jesus' life are related to them. With D. Mollat let us add that for John the mystery of the living bread is only an aspect of the very mystery of the Incarnation: "And the Word was made flesh" (σάρξ: I: 14). This is, undoubtedly, the source of the use of "flesh" (σάρξ: VI: 51) and not "body" (σῶμα: Mark XIV: 22) to designate the Eucharist. Besides, the term "flesh" is closer to the Aramaic word—bāsār—presumably used by Jesus. The term "body," a less Semitic rendering was more acceptable in Greek cultural communities (cf. *Lumière et Vie*, no. 31, p. 115). Since the Eucharist is for John the "memorial of the Incarnation," redemptive in all its amplitude, the Fourth Gospel does not directly associate the institution at the Last Supper with it. Yet it is clear that for John the Eucharist is also connected with the sacrifice on Calvary, as the symbolism of the blood flowing from the pierced side would seem to indicate, as well as this formula: "And the bread that I *shall give* is my flesh for the life of the world" (John VI: 51; cf. Isa. LIII: 10, 12 Gr.). "So then," writes A. Feuillet, "the Church or the glorious Christ will continue to accomplish the work of vivifying and saving souls by the sacraments and the fruit of the exaltation (Passion and Resurrection) of the Saviour. To put that truth into higher relief John recounts neither the baptism at Jordan nor the Last Supper" (*DBS*, vol. VI, cc. 1409f.; cf. *NRT*, 1960, p. 1059). On the theme "bread of life," cf. X. Léon-Dufour, "Le mystère du Pain de vie," in *Rech. Sc. Rel*, *1958*, pp. 481–523; A. Feuillet, "Les thèmes bibliques majeurs du discours sur le pain de vie (John VI)," in *NRT* (1960), pp. 803–22, 918–39, 1040–62.

17

THE STONE, THE ROCK

NUMEROUS Old Testament passages attest the use of the word "stone" as a metaphor. First of all, let us examine those texts that are somehow connected with the theme "Messianic stone."

In Canaanite religion *steles* or upright stones used to symbolize the masculine divinity. During a dream filled with revelations Jacob had localized the presence of God in Bethel: "Jacob arose in the morning, took the stone which he had placed under his head, set it up as a memorial pillar [Maççébâh] and poured oil over it" (Gen. XXVIII: 18). Such a cultural practice will later be prohibited (Exod. XXIII: 24), but the *notion of a sacred stone* had been introduced into biblical tradition. Jacob's oracle on the future of Joseph's tribe prophesies the annihilation of the enemy "by the *name* of the *Rock* of Israel" (Gen. XLIX: 24). If this conjectural interpretation of an obscure passage corresponds to the original text, then the designation of Yahweh as *the Stone* could refer back to the Bethel episode or could herald the use of the symbol "rock" to signify the stability and strength of God (cf. Deut. XXXII: 31; Ps. XVII: 3), the refuge of the just man (Ps. XXVI: 5).

In his first oracle about the *stone*, Isaiah reassures his own disciples and seeks to disassociate them from the conduct of "the two houses of Israel" which are tempted to join a confederation doomed to disaster. To resist the word of God is to go down in ruin; "Yahweh will become a sanctuary,

an obstacle and a *stumbling stone* to both houses of Israel, a
trap and a snare for those who dwell in Jerusalem" (VIII:
14). The second oracle delivered before the fall of Samaria
(721) again promises security to the small group that truly
believes in the power of Yahweh, and predicts that a remnant will survive the destructive judgment. "See, I am
laying a *stone* in Sion, a stone that has been tested a precious
cornerstone as a sure foundation; he who puts his faith in it
shall not be shaken" (XXVIII: 16). Here, this *stone* already
seems to recall the figure of the Messiah, clearly identified
in the New Testament (cf. Rom. IX: 32f., 1 Pet. II: 6).

Zechariah's oracles on the *stone* are more directly
Messianic and belong to a context that mentions "my
servant the Branch" (III: 8, VI: 12) or "shoot," one of
the Messianic names (cf. Isa. XI: 1; Jer. XXIII: 5). Here we
are plainly in a post-exilic climate where hopes for the
future center on "the two anointed" (Zech. IV: 14): Josue
the high priest and Zorobabel the Davidic candidate for
royal anointing (cf. Hag. II: 23). For the moment, the
Temple receives attention: "Look at the stone that I have
placed before Josue, one stone with seven facets, I will
engrave its inscription, says the Lord of hosts, and I will
take away the guilt of the land in one day" (III: 9). The
seven facets or eyes represent the watchful presence of
Yahweh (cf. IV: 10f) or even the seven spirits of the
Messiah-King (cf. Isa. XI: 2; Apoc. V: 6). The idea of an
opening in the side of the Temple (cf. Ezek. XLVII: 1) is
put into an eschatological context that foresees the presence
of a purifying fountain (cf. Ezek. XXXVI: 25) coming out of
the Temple: "On that day there shall be open to the house
of David and to the inhabitants of Jerusalem, a fountain
to purify from sin and uncleanness" (Zech. XIII: 1), a
symbol that the New Testament will use. In the other
oracle of Zechariah the subject is the material temple in
construction and not the eschatological, heavenly Temple:
"What are you, O great mountain? Before Zorobabel you

are but a plain. He shall bring out the capstone amid exclamations of 'Hail, Hail' to it" (IV: 7). The great mountain probably means the enormous mass of rubble from which the old capstone will be saved, for Zorobabel will be the one to finish the building (cf. IV: 9f.).

"The stone which the builders rejected has become the cornerstone. By the Lord has this been done; it is wonderful in our eyes" (Ps. CXVII: 22f.). This Psalm was sung in the post-exilic Temple in the course of a liturgical procession (probably the Feast of Tabernacles). The verses cited proclaim to humbled Israel its providential role: the rejected stone now crowns the saving work of God, the Messianic community which is this living temple.

Referring probably to a restored sanctuary or to the Messianic community, the last strophe of Dan. IX: 24 foresees that "a most holy will be anointed." Beyond the historical meaning of the term *"sanctuary"* we can see a Messianic meaning implied in that other enigmatic verse: "For 2,300 evenings and mornings: then the *sanctuary* shall be purified" (literally: "will be justified"—Dan. VIII: 14). In the stone that comes free by itself, causes earthly empires to crumble (cf. Luke XX: 18; Isa. VIII: 14) and becomes a great mountain filling all the earth (Dan. II, 34f., 45), we can detect a spiritual transposition of Mount Sion of which Isaiah said: "There shall be no harm or ruin on all my holy mountain; for the earth shall be filled with knowledge of the Lord, as water covers the sea (XI: 9). More directly the stone of Daniel recalls the memorial stone of Isaiah (XXVIII: 16). Toward that mountain and its temple the universal soteriology of Isaiah and Jeremiah had nations climb.

In the New Testament the notion of stone receives metaphorical application that follows the various aspects already mentioned: stumbling stone, stone of the temple, stone as water source. The Old Testament passages concerning the "Messianic" stone seem to have formed part of an oral or written collection of "Scriptural testimonies" (*testimonia*) for the use of Christian preachers. Certain literary peculiarities of these citations are more understandable in that light. For the two texts, I Pet. II: 6–8 and Rom. IX: 33, which are perhaps mutually dependent, a common source has been suggested: a primitive hymn. Independent instances of the notion *stone of the temple* are both rare and brief in the New Testament and will be treated in the various developments given the other two notions: stumbling stone, stone as water source.

THE STUMBLING STONE

The Synoptics cite Psalm CXVII: 22 to conclude the allegorical parable of the murderous vine-dressers: "And have you not read this Scripture: The stone which the builders rejected has become the cornerstone" (Mark XII: 10). The prophets' persecutors will have imitators in the murderers of the Son of God who came to work for the redemption of Israel, God's beloved vine. One teaching of the text cited runs as follows: God often realizes His plan with what is humble and scorned. The ambition of the evil vine-dressers will bring about only one result: their punishment and the exaltation of their victim.

For Matthew (XXI: 43) the rehabilitation of the rejected stone seems relevant to the religious preferment of the Gentile world. Once again we recognize Matthew's tendency to adapt the parables to the circumstances of his time and to the needs of the pastorate. In an addition inspired by Isa. VIII: 14–16 and Dan. II: 32, 44, Luke has the theme of the destructive stone intervene, to describe the lot of the Messiah's enemies: "Everyone who falls upon that stone will be broken to pieces; but upon whomever it falls, it will grind him to powder" (XX: 18). From that parable one allegorical detail serves to illustrate a certain literary characteristic of the Synoptics: Mark reproduces

Jesus' words more literally; Matthew and Luke accentuate their allegorical significance through slight changes and so give them a meaning more in conformity with foreseen events. And so, in Mark the son is killed and then thrown outside the vineyard (XII: 8), in Matthew (XXI: 39) and Luke (XX: 15) he is thrown outside the vineyard and then killed, as Jesus was crucified outside the Holy City (cf. Heb. XIII: 12).[1]

In a discourse to the Sanhedrin, Peter applies the testimony of the Psalm to the Resurrection of Christ and His saving power: "This is the *stone* that was rejected by you, the builders, which has become *the corner stone*. For there is no other name under heaven given to men by which we must be saved" (Acts IV: 11f.). To the theme of the stone, Peter's First Epistle consecrates a many-sided development:

Draw near to him, a *living stone*, rejected indeed by men but chosen and honored by God. Be you yourselves as living stones, built thereon into a spiritual house, a holy priesthood, to offer spiritual sacrifices acceptable to God through Jesus Christ. Hence Scripture says, Behold, I lay in Sion a chief *cornerstone*, chosen, precious, and he who believes in it shall not be put to shame. For you, therefore, who believe, is this honor, but to those who do not believe, A stone which the builders rejected, the same has become the *head of the corner*, and A *stumbling-stone*, and a rock of scandal, to those who stumble at the word, and who do not believe. For this also they are destined. (II: 4–8.)

The complex symbolism of this passage groups several applications that the first Christian interpreters had drawn from the Old Testament with regard to "the Messianic stone": Isa. VIII: 14f.; XXVIII: 16; Ps. CXVII: 22. Jesus is the *living* stone, for He *lives* now in heaven and makes the other stones live. Living bread (John VI: 51), living water (John IV: 14), life (John XIV: 6), He inaugurated through His blood "a new and living way" (Heb. X: 20) which leads to the heavenly sanctuary. As *cornerstone*

(I Pet. II: 6; cf. Eph. II: 20) of the spiritual edifice, the
Church, Jesus guarantees unity for Christians; as "foundation" (I Cor. III: 11), He sustains everything by His ever-
active power, on which also depend "the apostles and
prophets" in their role of "foundation" (Eph. II; 20) for
the "holy temple," "God's dwelling place" (II: 21f.; cf. I
Cor. III: 16).

The image of the *stumbling-stone* is then introduced
(I Pet. II: 7f.) to illustrate a well-established truth already
affirmed in the New Testament prophecy over the child
Jesus: "And Simeon blessed them, and said to Mary his
mother, Behold, this child is destined for the fall and for
the rise of many in Israel, and for a sign that shall be contradicted. And thy own soul a sword shall pierce, that the
thoughts of many hearts may be revealed" (Luke II: 34f.).[2]
The saying of Jesus, "He who is not with me is against me"
(Matt. XII: 30), expresses somewhat differently the same
idea, which is also present in the Johannine "judgment,"
dividing men into two categories, believers and unbelievers
(cf. I Pet. II: 7; Isa. VIII: 14). The author of I Peter quotes
in the same context Isa. XXVIII: 16, which gives a symbolic
and prophetic name to the precious stone that is the new
Jerusalem, "he-who-believes-shall-not-be-shaken" (cf. Isa.
I: 26). These two Isaian texts are quoted together in a
Pauline text on *faith*: depending on their own works the
Israelites "stumbled at the *stumbling-stone*," as it is
written, "Behold I lay in Sion a *stumbling-stone* and rock of
scandal: and *whoever believes in him shall not be disap-
pointed*" (Rom. IX: 32f.).

THE ROCK AND THE WATER

To the Samaritan woman Jesus suggests the desire for
living water which *He* can give (John IV: 10f.). On the last
day of the Feast of Tabernacles He addressed this invitation
to every believer: "If anyone thirst, let him come to me and

drink, he who believes in me!" Then, referring to *Himself*,
according to the earliest interpretation,[3] He added: "As
the Scripture says, From within him there shall flow rivers
of living water" (John VII: 37f.). It seems that this
"citation" derived its present formulation from an Aramaic
text of Ps. LXXVII: 16:

> *He made streams flow from the rock*
> *and rivers of flowing water run downhill.*

The end of the verse (John VII: 38) would have had the
following form in Aramaic: "From *him* (literally: "from his
belly") will flow rivers of living water."

Père Boismard holds that the *typology of the Rock* is
actually called upon in the exclamation on Living Water.
The author of the Fourth Gospel, we know, liked to describe
Christ's activity in reference to the events of the Exodus:
the gift of the Law through Moses (I: 17); the episode of the
brazen serpent (III: 14), the manna fallen from heaven
(VI: 30f.). Connections have even been proposed between
the miraculous crossing on the Sea of Galilee (John VI: 1ff.)
and the passing of the Red Sea. Reference to Moses had
been made earlier (V: 45f.) and John is careful to note that
"the Pasch, the feast of the Jews, was near" (VI: 4).

"Let us point out the following fact whose importance
would be difficult to determine. The typological interpretation of John VII: 38 supposes . . . a close link between John
VII: 38 and John XIX: 34; when Christ was struck by the
Roman soldier's lance, from His side flowed blood and water.
Then did Christ make real in His own person the figure of
the rock struck by Moses. On the other hand, in Num. XX:
11 (parallel to Exod. XVII: 7), it is added that Moses had to
strike the rock *twice* before the water flowed freely. In the
Targum of the Pseudo Jonathan (Jerusalem I) this is the
explanation offered: 'Moses struck the rock twice; the first
time, *blood* flowed and the second, *water*.' Although the
resemblance with John XIX: 34 could be purely coincidental,

it is probable that there is an interdependence between both texts".[4] An explanation is also suggested for the modifier "immediately" in the passage: "One of the soldiers opened his side with a lance, and *immediately* there came out blood and water" (John XIX: 34): "John would like to underscore a certain opposition: Moses had to strike the rock twice for the water to flow; on the contrary, *as soon as* Christ was struck by the Roman soldier, there flowed water and blood."

In the strict sense, *living water* is distinguished from stagnant water. In the figurative sense, the image appears in a reproachful word of Yahweh to his people: "They have forsaken me, the source of *living waters*" (Jer. II: 13). In the Fourth Gospel, living water recalls now baptismal water (cf. John III: 5; IV: 14) and now the Holy Spirit (VII: 39). The symbolism is only apparently distinct, since baptism, the new birth (III: 5, 8), gives the Holy Spirit (John I: 33; Mark I: 8): "John indeed baptized with water, but you shall be baptized with the Holy Spirit not many days hence" (Acts I: 5; cf. XI: 16). In the *Didache*, perhaps contemporary with the Gospels, we read this: "On the subject of baptism, baptize thus in the name of the Father and of the Son and of the Holy Spirit, in *living water* (VII: 1). For Ezekiel, the eschatological effusion of divine life is already designated by water symbolizing the Spirit (cf. XXXVI: 25ff.). The theme is clarified and unified in John, perhaps through the intermediary of this Qumrân text that describes the final judgment of God, who "will purify with His truth all the works of man . . . will pour on him a spirit of truth *as lustral waters*, [washing] all the abominations of deceit" (*Manual of Discipline*, IV: 20f.).[5]

The other examples of the theme of water, the source of life, in the New Testament, are in the Apocalypse. A first text joins two citations from Isaiah (XXV: 8; XLIX: 10) to describe the blessedness of those "who have come out of the great tribulation," the persecution of Nero: "For the

Lamb who is in the midst of the throne will shepherd them, and will guide them to the fountains of the waters of life." (Apoc. VII: 17). Further on, these fountains are identified with greater precision: "He who sits on the throne," God Himself, declares: "I am the Alpha and the Omega, the beginning and the end. To him who thirsts I will give of the fountain of the water of life freely" (Apoc. XXI: 6; cf. XXII: 17). A final text states that there is really only *one fountain* or *source* whose location amid the *trees of life* is an evocation of the earthly paradise:

And he showed me a river of the water of life, clear as crystal, coming forth from the throne of God and of the Lamb. In the midst of the city street, on both sides of the river, was the tree of life, bearing twelve fruits, yielding its fruit according to each month, and the leaves for the healing of the nations.

(Apoc. XXII: 1f.)

Centuries earlier, the prophetic glance of Ezekiel had contemplated a similar scene: a source, springing from under the Temple's threshold, became a brook, then a stream and headed for the Red Sea whose waters it was to purify (XLVII: 1–12). The paradisal theme (cf. Gen. II: 8–17) is clearly recalled:

Along both banks of the river, fruit trees of every kind shall grow; their leaves shall not fade, nor their fruit fail. Every month they shall bear fresh fruit, for they shall be watered by the flow from the sanctuary. Their fruit shall serve for food, and their leaves for medicine. (Ezek. XLVII: 12.)

This marvelous water, the source of life, will also stock the "dead" water of the salt sea (Ezek. XLVII: 9f.) with fish, as did the primordial water, fecundated by the Word (Gen. I: 20). Here the symbol of the *fish* (see the title "Saviour") finds one of its Scriptural foundations.

For the Old Testament *living water* is a *Messianic* theme in this respect: as a symbol of life, water is often mentioned among the benefits that are to accompany the days of national restoration, a type for another yet more marvelous restoration. In a post-exilic context of Isaiah, a word of consolation is addressed to the exiles for the day of return. "With joy you will draw water from the wells of salvation" (Isa. XII: 3). This comforting promise will be repeated by Deutero-Isaiah: "Ho, every one who thirsts, come to the waters; and he who has no money, come, buy and eat!" (Isa. LV: 1, *RSV*; cf. Apoc. XXI: 6).

We noted in the beginning of the chapter "Light of the World" one aspect of the connection of the theme of *living water* with the *Jewish feast of Tabernacles or tents* (cf. John VII: 37ff.). There are many more. In his study *Primitive Christian Symbols* Père Daniélou showed that, from the prophetic times until the fourth century A.D., Jewish tradition gave the Feast of Tabernacles (i.e., Huts or Booths) a Messianic and eschatological interpretation.

Psalm CXVII, a *Messianic* one, belongs to the post-exilic liturgy of the Feast of Tabernacles, one of whose rites it recalls, the procession with psalms:

> *Blessed is* he who comes *in the name of the Lord;*
> *we bless you from the house of the Lord.*
> *The Lord is God, and he has given us* light.
> *Join in the procession with leafy boughs*
> *up to the horns of the altar*
>
> (Ps. CXVII: 26f.)

We have already suggested that the title "He-Who-Comes," together with the theme of *light,* is also associated in John's perspective (VIII: 12) with living water in the context of the Feast of Tabernacles.[6] The psalm's Messianic character is made indubitable by the presence of one of its verses in a scriptural collection of the first Christian preachers: "The stone which the builders rejected has become the cornerstone" (Ps. CXVII: 22).

Now, in the last chapter of the Deutero-Zechariah (IX: 14), a fourth-century compilation manifestly Messianic in character, it is said that *"living waters* shall flow from Jerusalem" (XIV: 8) and "all who are left of all the nations that come against Jerusalem, shall come up year after year to worship the King, the Lord of hosts, and *to celebrate the feast of Tabernacles"* (XIV: 16). This feast, then, appears as a figure for the *Messianic kingdom*. It is no surprise that Jesus calls Himself a source of living water on the occasion of this solemnity. We can now also grasp more fully the significance of Peter's action on the mount of the Transfiguration: at the appearance of the Transfigured Christ, he thinks that the Messianic kingdom has begun and talks of erecting three *tents* (σκηνή—Mark IX: 5), perhaps remembering a Messianic text from Isaiah: "My people will live in peaceful country, in secure *dwellings* [miškenôt] and quiet resting places" (XXXII: 18). The eschatological meaning of these tents or huts also appears in Jesus' recommendation, pronounced at the end of the parable of the unjust steward (proper to Luke): "And I say to you, make friends for yourselves with the mammon of wickedness, so that when you fail they may receive you into the everlasting *dwellings* [σκηνή]" (XVI: 9; cf. II Cor. V: 1, 4).[7] The same conclusion is true of numerous texts in the Apocalypse (cf. VII: 15; XII: 12), which describe the heavenly dwellers as living under God's tent (cf. XIII: 6).

*
*   *

In Chapter X of the First Epistle to the Corinthians, St. Paul brings out the *typological* meaning (cf. I Cor. X: 6; I Pet. III: 21) of Exodus: persons, events, institutions associated with leaving Egypt and the sojourn in the desert prefigure in the divine pattern New Testament realities. Paul says of the Israelites: "And all ate the same spiritual food, and all drank the same spiritual drink (for they drank from the spiritual rock which followed them, and the rock

was Christ)" (I Cor. X: 3f.). The image of the wandering
rock is legendary and rabbinic in origin, but the miraculous
sources of Raphidim (Exod. XVII: 1–7) or Cades (Num. XX:
1–13) found the symbolism of the rock as a source of water.

For the prophets, God the Rock (cf. Ps. XVII: 3) is also
a source of living water (cf. Jer. II: 13), a prerogative
adopted by the Johannine Christ in His conversation with
the Samaritan woman by the well of Jacob (John IV: 10–15).
According to John the Evangelist, the living water dis-
pensed by Christ symbolizes "the Spirit whom they who
believed in him were to receive; for the Spirit had not yet
been given, since Jesus had not yet been glorified" (VII:
39).

Still another tradition has a purifying water spring from a
side of the Messianic temple (cf. Ezek. XLVII: 1). Having
presented Christ as the New Temple (John II: 19; cf. Mark
XIV: 58f.), John has us assist at a final symbolical drama:
from the open side of the Victim springs purifying water
and blood of expiation, certain figures of Baptism and
the Eucharist. John's insistence on his eyewitness testimony
at this historic deed (XIX: 31–37; cf. Zech. XII: 10)[8] shows
what importance he attaches to its religious value. Although
we have already associated the episode of the lance piercing
the Crucified with those of the miraculous Rock, this
association does not exclude allusion to the Temple, itself
also a springing source. The themes of "stone" and "temple"
are, in fact, related, and even tend to fuse: in the former
economy the Temple rises on the Rock; in the new, Christ
is the Rock and the Temple. It is no coincidence that He is
in the Temple (John VII: 14; VIII: 2) when He calls
Himself a source of living water (VII: 37f.).[9] For the
author of the Epistle to the Hebrews the immolated body of
Christ is the *altar* (XIII: 10), the center of the new worship.

These texts, especially that of Paul (I Cor. X: 3f.), on
Jesus "the Rock," also affirm the pre-existence of one who
could say: "Before Abraham came to be, I am" (John VIII:

58; cf. I: 1).[10] The Stone is invisible now, but it *always* remains the support of that temple that is the Messianic community:[11] it is represented on earth by the successor of him to whom it was said:

"Thou art Peter, and upon this rock I will build my Church, and the gates of hell shall not prevail against it" (Matt. XVI: 18).

NOTES ON 17

[1] A different interpretation is offered by X. Leon-Dufour, "La parabole des vignerons homicides" in *Sc. Eccl.*, 1965, pp. 365–96.

[2] Afraid that the *faith* of the Apostles (John XIV: 1) would be shaken by the trials that await them, Christ reveals a glimpse of the future to them (John XIII: 19), adding: "These things I have spoken to you that you may not be *scandalized*" (XVI: 1). The term σκάνδαλον, however, means "snare set on a road, stumbling block." Cf. σκανδάληθρον, "the springing of a trap," and the Sanskrit *skándati*, "to leap, to jump, to burst forth."

[3] Chief witnesses: St. Justin, Hippolytus, St. Cyprian, Aphraatus, St. Ephraim. The anonymous little work *De montibus Sina et Sion*, written between 210 and 240, would be the first dated work to link John VII: 38 and John XIX: 34 explicitly (cf. M. E. Boismard, "De son ventre couleront des fleuves d'eau (John VII: 38)," in *Revue Biblique*, 1958, p. 527). It is not easy to determine precisely to which *Scripture* Christ alludes. All those passages "where there is question of the rock (a type of Christ) struck by Moses and from which water flows freely to quaff the thirst of the Israelites: Exod. XVII: 1ff.; Isa. XLVIII: 21; Ps. LXXVII: 15f.; CIV: 41" (M. E. Boismard, *art. cit.*, p. 524) could be invoked as well as three texts which were read in Jewish assemblies during the feast of the Tabernacles: Isa. XII: 3; Ezek. XLVII: 1ff.; Zech. XIV: 8; cf. Jer. II: 13. The interpretation suggested does not deny that the water received from Christ can become in the believer "a source springing up into eternal life" (John IV: 14). Another reading of John VII: 37f. is possible: "If anyone thirst let him come to me and drink. For the man who believes in me, as Scripture says, living waters will flow from within him." The Bodmer II Papyrus (a manuscript from about the year 200) attests this reading. Furthermore, a good number of the Fathers, *following Origen*, have read the text in this manner and understood that the rivers of living water will flow *from the believer's bosom*. By his perfect knowledge of the Scriptures, Origen affirmed, the believer becomes for all other believers a source of light and sanctification: "You in turn will become teachers and from you there will flow rivers of living waters" (*Homilies on Genesis* XIII: 4). Cf. Isa. LVIII: 11; Prov. V: 15.

[4] M. E. Boismard, *art. cit.*, p. 539. According to Boismard, the text of the *Targum* on blood and water probably depends on John XIX: 34. The relationship between the two texts still retains its interest. Other articles on John VII: 38 have appeared in *Revue Biblique* in 1959; pp. 369–74 (Grelot); 374–78 (Boismard); 379–86 (Audet).

[5] Here, as in John VII: 37f., living water symbolizes the Holy Spirit, while

in Ezek. XXXVI: 25ff. and in Matt. III: 11 purification by water precedes the gift of the Spirit. On this subject, cf. J. Daniélou, "Le symbolisme de l'eau vive," in *Rev. Sc. Rel.* (1958), pp. 335–46.

[6] Cf. p. 76.

[7] Recall the assonance that relates the root *skn* of the Greek σκήνη, "tent," ἐσκήνωσεν "to dwell" (John I: 14), with the Hebrew *šekīnāh*, "glorious presence of God," and *šakan*, "to dwell" (cf. Exod. XXIV: 16; XL: 35). Cf. p. 86, n. 4.

[8] Apoc. I: 7 also cites Zech. XII: 10 to describe the *parousia* of the Pierced One, which the allusion "to the coming on the clouds" identifies with the Son of Man (cf. Matt. XXIV: 30; Apoc. I: 13).

[9] See pp. 76, 85. In a fresh study (cf. p. 128, n. 4), Père Grelot arrives at the following conclusion on the subject of John VII: 38: "In the same manner [i.e., rabbinic procedure] the evangelist, I believe, in John VII: 38 has related a text on water in the desert to another one on the eschatological source of the Temple (exactly, Zech. XIV: 8) by looking for the key to both texts in Christ's words at the Feast of Tabernacles, pronounced in connection with the libation rite performed at the water gate. John borrowed the matter for that complex citation from rabbinic tradition on the Feast of Tabernacles, more precisely, a Targum nourished on that tradition furnished him with it" ("John VII: 38: Eau du rocher ou source du Temple?" in *Revue Biblique*, 1963, p. 50). Cf. A. Feuillet, "Les fleuves d'eau vive de Jo, VII: 38," in *Parole de Dieu et sacerdoce* (Tournai, 1962), pp. 107–20, where the Johannine text's relation to the Septuagint is studied.

[10] In Deutero-Isaiah we read: "Listen to me, you who pursue justice, who seek the Lord; look to the *rock* from which you were hewn, to the pit from which you were quarried; look to Abraham, your father, and to Sara, who gave you birth" (Isa. LI: 1f.). This passage seems to be related to Matt. III: 8f.: "Bring forth therefore fruit befitting repentance, and do not think to say within yourselves, 'We have Abraham for our father'; for I say to you that God is able out of these *stones* to raise up children to Abraham." "At first sight," L. Ligier writes, "the metaphor surprises. Does it not rather suit the context? For it tends, according to the Semitic word play already pointed out (cf. Gen. II: 22) to compare children, *banim*, to a building that is erected, *banah*, with stones, *abanim*. To give birth to children is then, also to *erect* these stones, according to the two meanings of the Greek ἐγείρειν; it is to build the *true Temple of God* that the genuine descendants of Abraham must be" (*Péché d'Adam et péché du monde*, vol. II, pp. 44f.).

[11] The *temple* theme has been treated by A. Leboisset in "God in our Midst," in *The God of Israel* . . . , pp. 76–88; also by Y. Congar, *Le Mystère du Temple* (Paris, 1958).

SOTERIOLOGICAL TITLES

18

THE SAVIOUR—THE "REDEEMER"

AT the head of Part IV it is fitting to place the title "Saviour," a translation of a Greek term (Σωτήρ) which is the root of the expression "soteriology." The soteriological titles, then, describe Christ in His functions as author of salvation.

The angel of the Lord announced a great joy to the shepherds of Bethlehem: "A *Saviour* has been born to you, who is Christ the Lord" (Luke II: 11). Toward the end of the first century John wrote to the communities of Asia: "And we have seen, and do testify, that the Father has sent his Son to be *Saviour* of the world." (I John IV: 14). The irregular application of the title "Saviour" to Jesus in the New Testament raises many problems that we must face. Yet the constant use of this title by the Christian Church, from Ignatius of Antioch down to the present, requires special inquiry despite the reserve shown it by an important part of the New Testament.

THE NOTION OF SALVATION

Any adequate treatment of the title Σωτήρ, "Saviour," also entails treatment of the notion of σωτηρία, "salvation," for they are correlative. Their use in the New Testament reveals deep biblical roots and so the Old Testament must be examined first.

Leaving aside that notion of salvation that refers to mere deliverance from temporal evils (cf. I Sam. X: 19), let us go immediately to a higher, spiritualward meaning: the salvation of the chosen people worked, for example, on the occasion of their passage through the Red Sea (Exod. XIV: 13) or their return from Babylon: "Israel, you are saved by the Lord, saved forever" (Isa. XLV: 17). In biblical thought the places of servitude or exile represented lands of sin, for idolatry and vice flourished there. If "liberations" from such lands did prefigure Messianic salvation, then the more perfect notion of salvation as "deliverance from sin" is not far off. We read in the Septuagint: "God shall save us . . . for their sin will be pardoned" (Isa. XXXIII: 22, 24); "You shall be my people, and I will be your God. I will save you from all your iniquities" (Ezek. XXXVI: 28f.; cf. XXXVII: 23).

Successive deceptions, however, have carried the perspectives of salvation forward to the end of time. According to the *prophetic* notion, such an eschatological salvation will entail the establishment of the chosen people in Palestine and the inauguration of the Messianic kingdom (cf. Isa. XI: 1–10). In the *apocalyptic* perspective of *eschatological* salvation the Messianic era shall have for theater "new heavens and a new earth" (Isa. LXV: 17), after the old universe has been crushed under the devastating judgments of Yahweh (cf. Isa. XXIV: 4, 19f., 23). This apocalyptic notion of salvation dominates paracanonic Judaic literature.

New Testament usage of the title "Saviour," it will be seen, refers back constantly to an Old Testament context. The same is true of the notion of salvation, as for example in these words of Zachary:

Blessed be the Lord, the God of Israel, because he has visited and wrought redemption for his people, and has raised up a horn of salvation for us, in the house of David his servant . . . to give to his people knowledge of salvation through forgiveness of their sins . . . (Luke I: 68f., 77.)

Luke again will complete the Evangelists' citation of

Isaiah (XL: 3–5) in the preaching of John the Baptist: "And all mankind shall see the *salvation of God*" (Luke III: 6). The formula "those who are saved" used by Luke (XIII: 23, Acts II: 47) and St. Paul (I Cor. I: 18) recalls the idea of the *Remnant of Israel* (cf. Ezra. IX: 15)[1] and forms the counterpart of "those who perished" (I Cor. I: 18; II Cor. II: 15).

The notion of salvation in the New Testament prolongs that of the Old Testament. One category of texts sees salvation as a deliverance from whatever threatens *temporal life*: sickness (cf. Mark III: 4), unbridled elements (cf. Matt. VIII: 25), death (cf. Mark XV: 31). If Luke uses the same term, "to save," for bodily healing and the spiritual cure of the Magdalene (Luke VII: 50), is it not for the purpose of suggesting that temporal salvation heralds and somehow inaugurates spiritual, Messianic salvation (cf. Luke VIII: 12)? The same perspective is in Peter's discourse to the Sanhedrin: the cure of a lame man showed that "there is no other name [Jesus = "God saves"] under heaven given to men by which we must be saved" (Acts IV: 12). Bodily infirmities, too: nervous maladies (cf. Mark IX: 17ff.), deafness and blindness (Matt. XII: 22), paralysis (Luke XIII: 11), are attributed to evil spirits, and their cure is a prelude to the decline of Satan's power. In Cornelius' home, Peter described the anointing of One who "went about doing good and healing all who were in the power of the devil; for God was with him" (Acts X: 38). Deutero-Isaiah had described, in the fourth song, the *saving* action of the Servant:

> *Yet it was our infirmities that he bore,*
> *our sufferings that he endured,*
> *While we thought of him as stricken*
> *as one smitten by God and afflicted.*
> *But he was pierced for our offenses,*
> *crushed for our sins; upon him was*
> *the chastisement that makes us whole,*
> *by his stripes we were healed*
> (Isa. LIII: 4f.)

By his sacrifice the Servant expiated and took away sin. So Matthew quite correctly applied this passage of the prophet to the miraculous cures of Jesus: "He himself took up our infirmities, and bore the burden of our ills" (VIII: 17; cf. Isa. LIII: 4). Interestingly enough, only Matthew adds the note "unto the forgiveness of sins" to the central saying of the institution of the Eucharist: "for this is my blood of the new covenant, which is being shed for many *unto the forgiveness of sins*" (XXVI: 28; cf. Mark XIV: 24).

Nonetheless the majority of the uses of the verb σώʒειν, "to save," and all the instances of the noun σωτηρία in the New Testament are associated to some degree with *Messianic salvation*.[2] The liberation from Egypt's bondage had already heralded it (cf. Acts VII: 25). The first hint of that notion of salvation that was to become part of the biblical tradition of the *Remnant* is the rescue of Noe:

Noe, found just and perfect, renewed the race in the time of devastation. Because of his worth there were *survivors*, and with a sign to him the deluge ended; a lasting agreement was made with him, that never should all flesh be destroyed.

(Sir. XLIV: 17f.)

The First Epistle of Peter sees Noe's salvation as a figure of the salvific action of baptism (III: 20f.), while other writings (cf. Luke XVII: 26f.; Matt. XXIV: 37f.) see the destructive character of the waters of the deluge as a concrete incarnation of God's judgment (cf. Heb. XI: 7).

*

*   *

Messianic salvation is *directly* called to mind in a great number of texts. Upon informing Joseph about Mary, the angel of the Lord concludes: "And she shall bring forth a son, and thou shalt call his name Jesus; for he shall save his people from their sins" (Matt. I: 21). This salvation is associated with different contexts: perseverance (Matt. X: 22), the danger of riches (Mark X: 26), the power of the Gospel (Rom. I: 16), the conversion of the pagans (Rom. XI: 11), the exigencies of the Christian life (Rom. XIII: 11), the uncertainty of final grace (Phil. II: 12). *Saving* is from one's sins (Matt. I: 21; Luke VII: 50), from condemnation (John III: 17; XII: 47), from perdition (I Cor. I: 18), from the wrath of God (Rom. V: 9), from eternal death (Mark VIII: 35). Yet these aspects of the notion of salvation are only apparently negative, for in the New Testament Messianic salvation wins every blessing such as those mentioned in the section on the themes of *life* and *light*. Through the symbol of the banquet, both Old (cf. Isa. XXV: 6) and New Testaments (Matt. VIII: 11; Apoc. III: 20) teach of the unspeakable joy that awaits the prodigal son's returning to the Father's house (Luke XV: 24).

For St. Paul, salvation, strictly defined, is a future *eschatological gift* (cf. Phil. III: 20f.), which is distinct from justification,[3] or reconciliation, already brought about by the sacrificial death of Jesus:

But God commends his charity toward us, because when as yet we were sinners, Christ died for us. Much more now that we are justified by his blood, shall we be saved through him from the wrath. For if when we were enemies we were reconciled to God by the death of his Son, much more, having been reconciled, shall we be saved by his life. And not this only, but we exult also in God through our Lord Jesus Christ, through whom we have now received reconciliation. (Rom. V: 8–11.)

In a wider sense, salvation is a reality both present and future. Certainly, the just man must await the last judgment to be saved definitively and completely. Christians are on the path of salvation, not at its end. The *tension* that characterizes the waiting for what is already in progress is the basis of all Christian moral life. *Total salvation* implies the body's resurrection promised by the abiding Spirit but still expected along with "liberation" from the material world:

For we know that all creation groans and travails in pain until now. And not only it, but we ourselves also who have the first fruits of the Spirit—we ourselves groan within ourselves, waiting for the adoption as sons, the redemption of our body. For in hope were we saved. But hope that is seen is not hope. For how can a man hope for what he sees? (Rom. VIII: 22ff.)

Other epistles place greater emphasis on salvation as already achieved: we are risen with Christ in baptism (Col. II: 12); with Him, by grace, we are saved (Eph. II: 8) and brought to His sides in heaven (II: 6). Only in hope are Christians saved, the Apostle adds, however, and this recommendation applies to them: "work out your salvation with fear and trembling" (Phil. II: 12).

THE SAVIOUR

The explanation of those titles of Jesus that underline His divinity often lead to a procedure dear to readers of the New Testament: applying the attributes of God to Christ or citing Old Testament texts about Yahweh and referring them to Christ. This theological reflection is particularly apparent in the Scriptural use of the title "Saviour."

Those liberators of the people of God whom we call "Judges" are called "Saviours" in three texts from the Septuagint (Judg. III: 9, 15; Neh. IX: 27). Although Scripture does not call Moses "saviour," the role assigned to him by God is certainly that of a saviour. In a remarkable, universal vision, Isaiah predicts the conversion of the oppressed Egyptians: "When they cry out to the Lord against their oppressors, he will send them a *saviour* to defend and deliver them" (XIX: 20). If the function of Saviour is rarely attributed to the Messiah (cf. Zech. IX: 9, Gr.), it is doubtless due to the Old Testament custom of reserving the title and role of Saviour to *God Himself*, a custom followed by the majority of books, especially Isaiah (cf. XII: 2; XLV, 21f.) and the Psalms:

Shall my soul not give itself to the Lord? For with him is my salvation. He is my God and my Saviour [Σωτήρ], my refuge; I shall not falter. (Ps. LX: 1f. Gr.)

The biblical authors often affirm that *God alone* truly saves. The Book of Judith proclaimed it fervently in a poetic passage that ends this way: "Make it known to every people and tribe that you are the Lord, God of all power and strength, and that the people of Israel have no other protector but you" (IX: 14). Isolated or in groups, human forces could not save the king (Ps. XXXII: 16) or the people (Isa. XXXI: 1; Hos. V: 13).

In the religious literature of Hellenism gods or supermen receive the title Σωτήρ when they deliver mankind from temporal evils such as sickness or public catastrophes. Mystery religions also grant this title to the divinity that wins immortality. But outside of biblical use, the deified sovereign is most often called Saviour and also frequently Κύριος, Lord. Extrabiblical usage of the title Σωτήρ may have exerted an influence on its *diffusion* as a Christological title. However, the Christian use of the title Saviour owes its origin to three chief factors: Old Testament usage, the name of Jesus, the advent of Messianic salvation.

The fact that Christ is called Saviour *especially* in the *more recent* New Testament works has been explained in different ways. Would it indicate opposition to Jewish hopes for the coming of a political "Saviour"? (Cf. John VI: 15.) In the spiritual domain, Qumrân testifies, Jesus' contemporaries awaited the advent of a *master of doctrine* and persisted in considering God the only possible Saviour. Perhaps, too, pagan religious use of the title has delayed its Christian usage. One matter is certain: because the name *Jesus* meant Saviour in Hebrew and Aramaic, this *title* was to know only a limited diffusion in Palestine. It is equally clear that the title Σωτήρ was applied to Jesus only in a post-paschal climate when belief in His divinity was openly expressed. And so we should not be surprised that the two titles, Σωτήρ and Κύριος, are often associated, as in the Nativity account (Luke II: 11) and especially in the Second Epistle of Peter (I: 11; II: 20; III: 2). This literary juxta-position also appears in the single Pauline text which applies the title "Saviour" to Christ, before the Pastoral Epistles:

But our citizenship is in heaven from which also we eagerly await a *Saviour*, our Lord Jesus Christ, who will refashion the body of our lowliness, conforming it to the body of his glory by exerting the power by which he is able also to subject all things to himself. (Phil. III: 20f.)

At first the Risen Christ was called *Lord*, a title attributed to God in the Old Testament, and only later was He called *Saviour*.

The Pastoral Epistles freely associate the title of Saviour with the name of *God*. Paul attributes the origin of his apostolate to an "order of God our *Saviour*" (Tim. II: 10; Tit. I: 3). "For we work and are reviled for this reason," he adds, "that we hope in the living God, who is the *Saviour* of all men, especially of believers" (I Tim. IV: 10; cf. II: 3f.). He advises the slaves to honor "the teaching of God our *Saviour*" (Tit. II: 10) by their conduct. In a text that stresses the mystery of God and the gratuitousness of salvation through baptism, the title Saviour is applied now to God, now to Christ:

But when the goodness and kindness of God our *Saviour* appeared, then not by reason of good works that we did ourselves, but according to his mercy, *he saved us* through the bath of re-generation and renewal by the Holy Spirit; whom he has abundantly poured out upon us through Jesus Christ our *Saviour*, in order that, justified by his grace, we may be heirs in the hope of everlasting life. (Tit. III: 4–7.)

The doxology of the Epistle of Jude, according to one interpretation (*BJ*), would be stated thus: "To the one God, our Saviour through Jesus Christ, glory." That would seem to be a splendid theological affirmation, but parallels (cf. Rom. XVI: 27) invite a different reading: "To the one God, our Saviour, glory, majesty, strength and power, through Jesus Christ our Lord, before all time, now and forever. Amen" (v. 25).

Using a saying from Habakkuk (III: 18), the Virgin Mary in her Magnificat had exclaimed: "My soul magnifies the Lord, and my spirit rejoices in God my *Saviour* (Luke I: 46f.). To this aspiration corresponds the happy announcement of the heavenly heralds: "Today in the town of David a *Saviour* has been born to you, who is Christ the Lord" (Luke II: 11). The explanation furnished by Matthew for Jesus' name "for he shall save his people from their sins" (I: 21), defines the salvific role of the Messiah in terms used by the Old Testament to describe the work of God *Saviour:*

> *The Lord our judge, the Lord our lawgiver,*
> *The Lord our king, he it is who will save us.*
> *No one who dwells there will say, I am sick;*
> *the people who live there will be forgiven*
>   *their guilt.*
>
>   (Isa. XXXIII: 22, 24.)

EPIPHANY

In the religious language of the ancient Greeks the term ἐπιφάνεια meant the brusque but beneficent apparition of a liberating divinity. Later on, the occasional visits of deified sovereigns considered as "saviours" (cf. "Antiochus Epiphane") will be called "epiphanies" (or "Parousias"). By describing the coming of Jesus as *epiphany*, the Pastoral Epistles recall who the true Saviour is. II Maccabees depicted God as multiplying His miraculous epiphanies to save His people (cf. XII: 22; XIV: 15). In the Septuagint (cf. Zeph.

II: 11; Joel III: 4.) the "day of the Lord" is announced as an epiphany, a thought resumed by the Benedictus (Luke I: 79): the rising sun is to show itself (ἐπιγᾶναι) to those sitting in darkness and the shadow of death (cf. Isa. IX: 1; XLII: 7).

According to the Pastoral Epistles, "the grace of God our Saviour has *appeared* to all men" already with the first coming of Jesus:

This grace is now made known by the *manifestation* of our Saviour Jesus Christ. He has destroyed death and brought to light life and incorruption by the gospel, of which I have been appointed a preacher and an apostle and a teacher of the Gentiles.
(II Tim. I: 9–11.)

This *epiphany* of Jesus coincides with the day "when the goodness and kindness of our *Saviour appeared*" (Tit. III: 4). Other texts from the same books announce the *eschatological* epiphany (cf. II Tim. IV: 1, 8) of the Saviour. In this present world we must live in watchfulness, justice and piety,

looking for the blessed hope and glorious *coming* of our great God and Saviour Jesus Christ, who gave himself for us that he might redeem us from all iniquity and cleanse for himself an acceptable people, pursuing good works.
(Tit. II: 13ff.; cf. I Tim. VI: 14.)

CHRIST THE SAVIOUR

Although the oldest texts did not attribute the title Σωτήρ to Christ, the primitive Church understood very soon that *Jesus* was truly what the name signifies: the Saviour. Paul could write to the Philippians: "We eagerly await a Saviour, our Lord Jesus Christ, who will refashion the body of our lowliness, conforming it to the body of his glory" (III: 20f). This eschatological perspective is absent from Eph. V: 23, which adds: differing from the husband in regard to his wife, Christ is not only Head but also "the *Saviour* of the Body" which is the Church.

The Samaritans said to the woman of Sichar, who had told them about Jesus: "We no longer believe because of what thou hast said, for we have heard for ourselves and we know that this is in truth the *Saviour of the world*" (John IV: 42). This popular persuasion indeed answers John's theological conviction: God sent His Son into the world "that the world might be saved through him" (John III: 17); Jesus is "the lamb of God, who takes away the sin of the world" (John I: 29); He came "to *save* the world" (John XII: 47); "The Father has sent his Son to be Saviour of the world" (I John I: 14). This universalist conception discovers in Jesus' saving work the fulfillment of the prophecy: "Everyone shall be rescued who calls upon the name of the Lord" (Joel III: 5). The Book of Wisdom had also called God "the Saviour of all" (XVI: 7).

Stephen's discourse to the Sanhedrin (Acts VII) presents Moses as a *figure* of Jesus and describes the similar attitude of the Jews toward both. Twice (vv. 7, 35) there appears the saying of the Egyptian to Moses: "Who has appointed you ruler and judge over us?" (Exod. II: 14). This *Moses* whom they had disowned, Stephen adds, "him God sent to be *ruler and redeemer* with the help of the angel who appeared to him in the bush" (Acts VII: 35). This context clarifies the passage in Acts that calls Jesus "Prince and Saviour" (ἀρχηγὸς καὶ Σωτήρ):

The God of our fathers raised Jesus, whom you put to death, hanging him on a tree. Him God exalted with his right hand to be *Prince and Saviour*, to grant repentance to Israel and forgiveness of sins. (V: 30f.)

Speaking to the Jews, Paul applies the title of Saviour to the Risen Christ too (cf. Acts XIII: 32f.) after a reminder of David's divine vocation: "From his offspring, God according to promise brought to Israel a *Saviour*, Jesus" (Acts XIII: 23).

To the Romans he will write: "For if when we were enemies we were reconciled to God by the death of his Son, much more, having been reconciled shall we be *saved* by his life" (V: 10). In fact, union with the Risen Christ, the normal condition for Christians, saves us from the judgment of condemnation.

Ἰχθύς

The growing popularity that the title Saviour enjoyed in the first Christian centuries depends partly on its inclusion in the acrostic Ἰχθύς: Jesus Christ, Son of God, Saviour. The symbol of the *fish* (Ἰχθύς), as representative of Christ, is even older than the acrostic (beginning of the third century) and could have determined the order of its letters. The gospel text to which the fish symbol owes its origin is not easy to pinpoint. Naturally, we immediately think of the fish associated with the miraculous multiplication of the loaves (Mark VI: 41; cf. John XXI: 13). Seeing the Christian's redeeming symbolized by the payment of the tax (Matt. XVII: 27), Origen commented: "In this fish was represented Him whom we call the Fish." For St. Augustine, "Ἰχθύς," the Fish, mystically designates Christ who survived from the deep waters, that is the gulf of our *mortality*."

More likely the emblem of the fish *designated Christians at first*, as in Jesus' saying to the apostles: "Come, follow me, and I will make you fishers of men" (Matt. I: 17). Christian art made an early association between baptism and fishing scenes. A blessing before baptism asked the Christ Spirit to come down upon the water to engender new Christians there: this rite explains the transfer of the symbol to Christ Himself, the Fish *par excellence*. Now the famous text of Tertullian is understandable: "We little fish are born in the water by virtue of our Ἰχθύς, Jesus Christ, and to be saved we must remain in the water."[4]

It is possible to clarify further the biblical origins of the anagram Ἰχθύς, in the symbolic context explained above in relation with *living water* (pp. 127ff.). Sprung from the side of the *Temple*, the living water will make trees of life along its course grow and will produce a marvelous transformation in the Dead Sea:

This water flows into the eastern district down upon the Araba, and empties into the sea, the salt waters, which it makes fresh. Wherever the river flows every sort of living creature that can multiply shall live and there shall be abundant *fish*, for wherever this water comes the sea shall be made fresh. *Fishermen* shall be standing along it from En-gaddi to En-eglaim spreading their *nets* there. Its kinds of *fish* shall be like those of the Great Sea, *very numerous.* (Ezek. XLVII: 8ff.)

Jesus Himself compared His immolated and risen body to a new *Temple* (John II: 19, 21). Extending that idea, John will recognize in the episode of the lance thrust the actuation of the prophetic symbolism of Ezekiel: the side of the new Temple is a source of water whose life-giving fecundity reaches believers through baptism. And so the first Christian writers, Tertullian and St. Ambrose for example, saw Christians being born in the water of baptism as little fish engendered by the water that the Spirit fecundates (cf. Gen. I: 2, 20).

Certain symbols of Jewish art already used to represent the fish as a symbol of resurrection, perhaps under the influence of the prophetic parable of Jonas (cf. Matt. XII: 40). For Daniélou "the fish denotes the Christian quickened by the outpouring of eschatological water which has its source in Jerusalem."[5] The text already cited from Tertullian clearly illustrates how easily the symbol first applied to Christians passed on to Christ.

The *miraculous hauls of fish*, reported by Luke (V: 1–11) and John (XXI: 1–4), doubtlessly appeared in the Evangelists' perspective as signs of the power of Jesus over nature. Perhaps they may have also been seen as a symbolical illustration of the presence of the Living Water generative of fish. Did the Septuagint not add a significant note to the text from Ezekiel cited above: "This water flows *into Galilee*, down the eastern district" (XLVII: 8)?

The fish figured among the symbols of several primitive religions. The strange circumstances of its aquatic life lent it a mysterious character. Magical techniques borrowed elements from it, and certain priestly castes even fed themselves with sacred fish. For the first Christians the formula Ἰχθύς, the mysterious acrostic perhaps used as a password, compactly expressed the essentials about the true Saviour of humanity.

THE "REDEEMER"

Although Jesus is not called "Redeemer" in the New Testament, the function corresponding to this title is constantly recalled there.[6] In the Johannine writings Christ is sometimes designated by a central *function* of His saving mission, "Expiation" for example (I John II: 2; IV: 10), or "Resurrection" (John XI: 25). Earlier, Paul had also had recourse to a literary abridgement to underscore the intimate union between Christ and His work: "Christ Jesus . . . has become for us God-given wisdom, and justice, and sanctification, and *redemption*" (I Cor. I: 30). The redemption wins us the justice of God and also marks the end and crown of our sanctification, for we shall be fully redeemed only at the glorious resurrection: "We ourselves who have the first fruits of the Spirit—we ourselves groan within ourselves, waiting for the redemption of our body" (Rom. VIII: 23).

The *eschatological* aspect of redemption is expressed elsewhere in a formula that presents Christian salvation as the true deliverance prefigured by deliverance from Egypt (cf. Exod. XIX: 5f.): the Holy Spirit is "the pledge of our inheritance sealed for a *redemption* of possession, for the praise of his glory" (Eph. I: 14; cf. I Pet. II: 9). The same idea is repeated: "And do not grieve the Holy Spirit of God, in whom you were sealed for the day of *redemption*" (Eph. IV: 30). When the signs of the end will begin to appear, Jesus said, "look up, and lift up your heads, because your *redemption* is at hand" (Luke XXI: 28).

The word "redeemer" (λυτρωτής) appears only once in the New Testament, in that passage already cited on Moses "ruler and redeemer" (Acts VII: 35). The notion of redemption is, in fact, related to those of "liberation" or "deliverance" which, in turn, are connected with the idea of ransom (λύτρον) or redeeming: "For the Son of Man also has not come to be served but to serve and to give his life as a ransom for many" (Mark X: 45; cf. I Tim. II: 6). Containing a direct allusion to the Servant's sacrifice (cf. Isa. LIII: 10–12), this saying of Jesus' expresses the core of His mission to fill the longing that Zachary's Benedictus recalls: "Blessed be the Lord, the God of Israel, because he has visited and wrought *redemption* for his people" (Luke I: 68). At the Presentation Anna the prophetess spoke openly of the Child "to all who were awaiting the *redemption* of Jerusalem" (Luke II: 38). The deception of the disciples of Emmaus was happily unfounded: "But we were hoping that it was he who should *redeem* Israel" (Luke XXIV: 21). The Psalmist had written: "He it is that will *ransom* Israel from all its iniquities" (CXXIX: 8).

This universal (cf. Rom. III: 24) and eternal (cf. Heb. IX: 12) redemption is connected with Jesus' blood, shed as the precious price of our freedom (I Pet. I: 18f.). In Christ, in fact, "we have *redemption through his blood*, the remission of sins" (Eph. I: 7; cf. Col. I: 14). On the night before His death Jesus pronounced a statement that is connected with that teaching: "This is my blood of the new covenant, which is being shed for many unto the forgiveness of sins" (Matt. XXVI: 28).

For a long time now Christian thinkers have asked the question: "To whom was the price of blood paid?" Some falsely believed that it was paid to the devil; óthers, allegedly better informed, taught that it was paid to God and shed, to appease Him. With St. Augustine we must keep the metaphor within limits: our very burdensome redemption frees us from our sins, by which the devil held us enslaved. Dying to His flesh by spilling His blood, Christ killed the old humanity (cf. Rom. VIII: 3) and substituted for it a new creature—the new man, the paschal traveler: "Our old self has been crucified with him, in order that we may no longer be slaves to sin" (Rom. VI: 6); "If then any man is in Christ, he is a new creature" (II Cor. V: 17); "For Christ, our passover, has been sacrificed" (I Cor. V: 7).

By freeing man from Evil, Christ gave him back to God. In St. Paul's Greek-inspired image of freedom from slavery, the biblical theme of "redemption" is illustrated in this way:

For when you were the slaves of sin, you were free as regards justice. But what fruit had you then from those things of which you are now ashamed? For the end of these things is death. But now set free from sin and become slaves to God, you have your fruit unto sanctification and as your end, life everlasting. For the wages of sin is death, but the gift of God is life everlasting in Christ Jesus our Lord.   (Rom. VI: 20–23.)

NOTES ON 18

[1] The theme of the "Remnant" is abundantly present in Scripture: cf. Gen. XII: 2; XVIII: 26; XLV: 7; Exod. XIX: 6; XXXII: 10; Lev. XXVI: 36, 39; Num. XIV: 12; I Kings XIX: 17f.; II Kings XIX: 31; XXV: 12; Amos III: 12; IV: 11; V: 14; IX: 8f.; Mic. II: 12; IV: 6f.; V: 2, 6f.; Isa. I: 9; IV: 2f.; VI: 13; VII: 3; X: 20–23; XI: 11f.; XIV: 30; XV: 9; XVII: 5f.; XXVIII: 5; XXX: 17; XXXVII: 31f.; Zeph. II: 7, 9; III: 12f.; Jer. V: 18f.; XXIV: 5ff.; XXXI: 2; XL: 11, 15; XLII: 2, 15, 19; XLIII: 5; XLIV: 12ff., 28; L: 20; LI: 50; Ezek. VI: 8; IX: 8; XI: 13, 17; XIV: 22; XXXVII: 12; Zech. VIII: 11–15; XIII: 8f.; XIV: 2; Obad. XVII; Joel III: 5; Esd. IX: 15; Sir. XLIV: 17; Rom. IX: 27; XI: 5. The notion of the "Remnant," in the words of G. Pidoux, answered a

theological necessity that aimed at assuring the transition between the inevitable misfortune and the final re-establishment (cf. *Le Dieu qui vient*, p. 41).

2 On the notion of "salvation" and the title "Saviour," cf. *Lumière et Vie*, no. 15; the periodical *Évangile*, no. 26; the article "Salut" in the *Vocabulaire biblique* of J.-J. von Allmen and in the *Vocabulaire de théologie biblique* (Édit. du Cerf); O. Cullmann, *The Christology of the New Testament*, pp. 238–45; also the article in the *DBS*, vol. IV, cc. 1337–43 (R. Pautrel); W. C. van Unnik in *La formation des Évangiles* (Bruges, 1957), pp. 178–94; S. Lyonnet, "Le Sauveur" in *Introduction à la Bible*, vol. II, pp. 86off. where the reference by the Pastoral Epistles to the pagan use of the title "Saviour" is declared to have involved a polemical intention. On the notion of "salvation," consult also Père Lyonnet's work *De Peccato et Redemptione*, vol. II (Rome, 1960), pp. 7–23.

3 Cf. S. Lyonnet in *Littérature et théologie pauliniennes* (Bruges, 1960), pp. 168f.

4 *De Baptismo*, I: 3. The collection *Sources Chrétiennes*, vol. XXXV, proposes a different translation: "But we little fish, who have our name from our Ἰχθύς Jesus Christ, we are born in the water and only by remaining in it are we saved" (p. 65).

5 J. Daniélou, *Primitive Christian Symbols*, p. 51.

6 The periodical *Lumière et Vie* dedicated the entire no. 36 (1958) to the title "Le Rédempteur"; cf. especially pp. 39–44. We have translated ἱλασμός by "expiation" and not "propitiation" as in the Confraternity Bible (I John II: 2; IV: 10). The problem will be discussed pp. 169ff.

19

THE SERVANT

ONE of the most remarkable features of the personality of
Jesus presents Him to us as conscious of His own destiny.
The course of His public life unfolds in an atmosphere
totally devoid of the adventurous or fatalistic. His tragic end
followed by triumph is set in a providential plan familiar
to Him long in advance; His Passion and Resurrection form
an integral part of His Messianic vocation. In a spirit of
obedience and love Jesus conformed Himself to the destiny
that the heavenly Father sealed for Him.[1] Jesus Himself,
the Apostles and Evangelists after Him, showed that the
salvific plan of God had been expressed long since in the
Messianic heraldings. In particular, we shall see that
numerous texts on the redemptive mission of Jesus are
inspired in their formulation by a group of prophetic
writings known as the *Servant Songs* or *Poems.*

In Deutero-Isaiah these songs appear as "four lyric
enclaves depicting a perfect disciple of Yahweh sent to
preach the true faith to nations and destined to be handed
over as an expiating sacrifice with the hope of a mysterious
rehabilitation." The poems do not follow a very definite
plan and the same themes are taken up repeatedly. In the
first song (XLII: 1–9) Yahweh Himself speaks: He intro-
duces His Servant, His chosen one, to whom He grants His
spirit to accomplish the mission entrusted—teaching the
true religion to all nations and acting as mediator of a
universal alliance. The *second* song (XLIX: 1–6) returns to

the same ideas and completes them, now with the Servant speaking, now with Yahweh. In the *third* song (L: 4–11) the Servant describes the mistreatment that the fulfillment of his mission draws down on him. Yet he renews his trust in Yahweh, in the one who exhorts believers to listen to the voice of his messengers. The *fourth* song[2] describes the Servant's sacrifice in its various aspects: expiatory suffering, intercession, personal rehabilitation, and justification of the many.

The salvific mediation of the Servant represents an astonishing theological progress for the age. Certainly it is a prayer of intercession (Isa. LIII: 12), as in the Prophets; it is also a sacrifice of expiation (cf. Isa. LIII: 10), as in the priestly idea. This remarkable synthesis was suggested perhaps by the tormented life of Jeremiah, who was set aside from his birth (cf. Isa. XLIX: 1; Jer. I: 5), was persecuted for his intransigeance and led to the slaughterhouse like a lamb (cf. Isa. LIII: 7; Jer. XI: 19). Jeremiah, however, had not reached the Servant's deep insight and did not perceive the secret of victory hidden in defeat and death. The suffering of the prophets was not redemptive as it was for the Servant; in fact, they could hardly grasp its meaning.

More than individual piety, the *national* role is what constitutes the fundamental fitness of the title "Servant," bestowed like a grace and by virtue of a free choice: "From Jacob I will save an offspring, from Juda those who are to inherit my mountains; my *chosen ones* shall inherit the land, my *servants* shall dwell there" (Isa. LXV: 9). Underlying the biblical notion of "servant" is the ever-present idea of a service rendered to accomplish a mission, to realize the saving plan of God.

Many Old Testament figures were honored with the title "servants": the ancestors of the chosen people (cf. Exod. XXXII: 13; Deut. IX: 27), the prophets (Isa. XX: 3; Jer. VII: 25), Moses (Num. XII: 7f.), Joshua (XXIV: 29), David (II Sam. VII: 5), Zorobabel (Hag. II: 23), the Messiah (cf.

Ezek. XXXIV: 23f.; Zech. III: 8), and even Cyrus (Isa. XLIII: 10) and Nabuchodonosor (Jer. XXV: 9) as performers of God's will. In Deutero-Isaiah, Israel is called "servant" on several occasions (cf. XLI: 8; XLIV: 1). For that reason, the Servant of the Lord in the Songs has been seen by some to be Israel at its best, the elite, the "Remnant" that is finally reduced to one individual in the person of the Servant.

The identification of the enigmatic Servant figure could not effectively abstract from the well-known Israelite tendency to incarnate an entire people's destiny in an individual representative (cf. p. 206, n. 6). Attempts made to identify *the man of sorrows* of Isaiah LIII with some individual from the past are doomed to failure. Why is the Servant of Deutero-Isaiah not called the Messiah?[3] The scandalous behavior of the majority of Israelite kings, the final failure of the royalty, and perhaps too the fear of offending the Persian monarch motivated such discretion. But the Servant, who did, in fact, receive an investiture with the Spirit (Isa. XLII: 1), like the expected Davidic king (Isa. XI: 2), transcends the picture then drawn of the Messiah, although he draws on some similar features. Finally, the figure of the Servant, who personifies and even surpasses the most beautiful of Israel's features, cannot be a mere conception of the human mind. Born of a prophetic vision, it traces, centuries in advance, the general pattern of the Saviour's redemptive career. The prophet's inspired vision discerns in the future a figure, some features of whom he thought he had seen in the past. That Christ Himself and His disciples had such frequent recourse to these Songs to formulate an explanation of the first events of the Christian era should not surprise us.

New Testament texts that present Jesus' death as accomplished in the *manner* willed by God and at a *moment* fixed by Him abound. This explains why frequent recourse to Scripture is made in relation to the sacrifice of Jesus. To guard against the scandal of the cross (cf. Gal. V: 11; I Cor.

I: 23), it was fitting to show that the crucifixion did not result from a judicial error, but from God's salvific plan. St. Paul reflects both the thought of Christ and the conviction of the primitive Church when he writes to the Corinthians: "For I delivered to you first of all, what I also received, that Christ died for our sins *according to the Scriptures*" (I Cor. XV: 3). One of Peter's discourses is inspired by the same tradition: "But in this way God fulfilled what he had announced beforehand by the mouth of *all* the prophets, namely that his Christ should suffer" (Acts III: 18; cf. XIII: 29). The First Epistle of Peter attributes the inspiration of the prophets to the pre-existing Christ: "They searched what time or circumstances the Spirit of Christ in them was signifying, when he foretold the sufferings of Christ, and the glories that would follow" (I Pet. I: 11).

THE "SERVANT" IN THE GOSPELS

A series of sayings transmitted by the Evangelists attests that Jesus enjoyed a foreknowledge of His imminent death (cf. Mark VIII: 31; Luke XVII: 25). Others affirm that this event was announced by the Scriptures: "The Son of Man indeed goes his way, as *it is written* of him" (Mark XIV: 21; cf. Luke XXII: 22). The arrest at Gethsemani marks the first step toward the end: "I was daily with you in the temple teaching, and you did not lay hands on me. But it is so that the Scriptures may be fulfilled" (Mark XIV: 49; cf. Luke XXII: 53). The Risen Christ gives "the pilgrims to Emmaus" a Scripture lesson: "But he said to them, 'O foolish ones and slow of heart to believe in all that the prophets have spoken! Did not Christ have to suffer these things before entering into his glory?' And beginning then with Moses and with all the Prophets, he interpreted to them in all the Scriptures the things referring to himself" (Luke XXIV: 25–27). The principal passage explained was, doubtlessly, the fourth song of the Deutero-Isaiah, describing the expiatory and redemptive mission of the Suffering Servant.

The Messianic investiture of Jesus at His *baptism* often recalls the divine proclamation establishing the Servant's mission:

> *Here is my servant whom I uphold,*
> *my chosen one with whom I am pleased;*
> *Upon whom I have put my spirit,*
> *he shall bring forth justice to the nations.*
> (Isa. XLII: 1.)

As the Servant, Jesus receives the Spirit and is the object of divine pleasure (cf. Mark I: 10f.). He is not called "Servant," but Luke (cf. IX: 35; XXIII: 35) and John (I: 34) see in Him *the chosen one*. Perhaps even one of John the Baptist's well-known sayings may originally have read: "Behold the *Servant* of God, who takes away the sin of the world!" (John I: 29). According to Matthew (XII: 17f.), Jesus' apostolic method fulfills Isaiah's oracle on the Servant. Significant, too, is the Evangelist's substitution of the word "beloved" (ἀγαπητός), the title bestowed on the Son by the Father at the baptism (Matt. III: 17) and the Transfiguration (Matt. XVII: 5), for the word "chosen" (ἐκλεκτός). Luke (IV: 18f.) characterizes Jesus' ministry with the aid of a citation (Isa. LXI: 1f.) which implicitly evokes the figure of the Servant through the functions mentioned.

Several Greek *expressions* used by the Evangelists in relation to the Passion of Jesus had been used before to describe the sufferings of the Servant: (Isa. L: 6; LIII: 3–12). Certain *actions* performed by Jesus in the last days of His life even recall the same Isaian context. The *silence* He observes before the Sanhedrin (Mark XIV: 61), before Pilate (Mark XV: 5), before Herod (Luke XXIII: 9) corresponds to the Suffering Servant's attitude—"a sheep before the shearers he was silent and opened not his mouth"

(Isa. LIII: 7). Like the Servant too, Jesus *intercedes* for sinners (Luke XXIII: 34) although He has been ranked with scoundrels (Luke XXII: 37; Isa. LIII: 12). Furthermore, the anointing at Bethany suggests (cf. Mark XIV: 8) that in normal circumstances the Crucified would have received only a dishonorable burial as did the Servant who "was assigned a grave among the wicked and a burial place with evildoers" (Isa. LIII: 9).

THE MEDIATION OF THE SERVANT

Two sayings of Jesus' will hold our attention a little longer: "For the Son of Man also has not come to be served but to serve, and to give his life as a ransom for many" (Mark X: 45); "And he said to them, This is my blood of the new covenant, which is being shed for many" (Mark XIV: 24). The two main ideas of the *first* saying recall the figure of the Servant: *service and ransom for many*. The need for service or the generosity of "the servant" can attain that extreme that is the gift of life; Jesus wanted to express that generosity in this text and in another that clarifies it: "Greater love than this no one has, that one lay down his life for his friends" (John XV: 13). To designate the beneficiaries of the redemptive sacrifice by the expression "many" (πολλοί) was to refer to an equivalent term (*rabbim*) used five times in the fourth song (Isa. LII: 14f.; LIII: 11f.). "To give one's life as a ransom" is exactly what the Greek text of Isaiah LIII: 10 affirmed of the Servant. The redemption excludes no one: Christ Jesus "gave himself a ransom for *all*" (I Tim. II: 6). The same universalism is expressed in the *second* saying: "This is my blood of the new covenant, which is being shed for many" (Mark XIV: 24), for if Pauline tradition speaks of the body "given for *you*," of "blood shed for *you*" (Luke XX: 19f.; I Cor. XI: 24), it is due to the influence of the liturgical rite for the distribution of the sacred species.

Several reasons invite us to recognize under the formulas of the Eucharistic institution the intentional suggestion of a certain *parallelism* with the covenant sealed at Sinai: "As intermediary between Yahweh and the people, Moses unites them symbolically by pouring on the altar, that represents Yahweh, and upon the people the blood of one and the same victim. Thus, the pact is ratified with blood, as the New Covenant will also be with the blood of Christ" (*BJ:* Exod. XXIV: 8). There also seems to be attention given to Eucharistic rites in the manner that the Epistle to the Hebrews cites (in Greek) the words of Moses: "This is the blood of the covenant which God has commanded for you" (Heb. IX: 20: the Greek τοῦτο, "this," replaces ἰδού, "behold," of Exod. XXIV: 8). Let us note one difference: on Sinai, aspersion constitutes the rite of the covenant; on the Cross immolation plays an essential role. In the humanity of Jesus, immolated and then transformed by the Spirit, sinful man is, in principle, delivered from his sins and reunited to God, because His flesh, as mortal, represented sinful mankind (cf. Rom. VIII: 3).

Nevertheless, it seems to us that the context of the covenant recalls the *mediation of the servant* even more directly. The establishing of a covenant represents an element in the restoration announced by the Deutero-Isaiah. To the Servant, Yahweh declares: "I set you as a *covenant* of the people and a light for the nations" (Isa. XLII: 6). With a ritual sprinkling of blood the Servant fulfills his role as mediator of that covenant, in accord with a passage from the Deutero-Isaiah whose Hebrew text can be interpreted thus:[4]

> *Behold, my servant shall prosper,*
> *he shall be high and lifted up and very exalted.*
> While the many looked on amazed,
> I, by my unction, bestowed on him a bearing
> superhuman, a splendour outshining the mortals.
> So shall he sprinkle many nations

and the kings in awe will remain speechless
because they have seen what had never
been told them, and become attentive to something
of which they had never heard the like.

(Isa. LII: 14f.)

Two disconcerting events explain the general awe: the
supernatural anointing of the servant and the ritual
sprinkling of the nations with blood of this mediator of a
universal covenant. The anointing of the servant (by the
Spirit? cf. Isa. XLII: 1; Acts IV: 27) consecrated him for his
priestly role (representative), as mediator by the blood.
His purifying works the reunion (*at-one-ment*)[5] of humanity
with God. Let us note that this description of the Servant
(Isa. LII: 13–15) as a person of a "divine" power (ritual
or priestly?) is not opposed to the later description of his
pitiable state (LIII: 2ff.), but rather serves to underline
the sense of the expiatory mission that he must accomplish in his mediating sacrifice. The question that opens
Chapter LIII could evoke an abrupt reversal in the situation: the transfigured Servant becomes the defigured
Servant.

We are authorized, then, to conclude: by virtue of the
mission received and of his expiatory sacrifice for sin, the
Servant-Pontiff reconciles men with God; by his purifying
blood, he is mediator (as a type?) of the new covenant and
thereby also intercessor (cf. Isa. LIII: 12). There is thus
reason to take the affirmation of Isa. XLII: 6 literally:
"I set you as a covenant of the people." On the eve of
accomplishing His sacrifice, Jesus presents Himself as the
true and only Mediator-Pontiff: "This cup is the new covenant in my blood, which shall be shed for you" (Luke
XXII: 20). Doubtlessly, the Messianic and prophetic figure
of the Servant was present in the mind of the Saviour in
that solemn moment of His life.

The figure of the Servant is also called on at the Last
Supper, if instead of covenant, we think of the related

concept *testament*. About to leave this world, Jesus the Servant reveals His "last dispositions" to his intimates:

For which is greater, he who reclines at table, or *he who serves?* Is it not he who reclines? But I am in your midst as *he who serves*. But you are they who have continued with me *in my trials*. And I appoint to you a kingdom, even as my Father has appointed to me, that you may eat and drink at my table in my kingdom; and you shall sit upon thrones, *judging* the twelve tribes of Israel. (Luke XXII: 26–30.)

This passage marvelously expresses the conception Jesus had of His mission. He is the *Son of Man*, who in His first coming will play the role of the *Suffering Servant* and who in His second coming or *parousia* will fill that of the *glorious* Son of Man, judge of the world. His followers will share both His trials and His glory, for somehow they are one with Him.

THE "SERVANT" IN THE WRITINGS OF PAUL AND PETER

In the *Pauline writings* the theology of the Servant reveals its presence by a series of allusions, especially apparent in those passages that Paul draws directly from kerygmatic tradition. "For I delivered to you first of all, what I also received, that *Christ died for our sins according to the Scriptures*, and that he was buried, and that he rose again the third day, according to the Scriptures . . ." (I Cor. XV: 3; cf. Matt. XXVI: 28). It is not always possible or necessary to find the exact text to which the expression "according to the Scriptures" refers, for this formula often constitutes but a reminder of this truth: the facts of Jesus' life testify to the fulfillment of the prophecies that announced the saving intervention of God through His intermediary, the Messiah. Certain privileged passages, however, are more directly concerned.

Thus the addition *"for our sins"* recalls the often expressed finality of the *Servant's* sacrifice: "He was pierced for our *offenses*, crushed for our *sins* . . . the Lord laid upon him the *guilt* of us all . . . he was stricken for the transgression of my people . . . through his suffering, my servant shall *justify* many and their *guilt* he shall bear . . . he surrendered himself to death and was counted among the wicked; and he shall take away the *sins of many*, and win pardon for their *offenses*" (Isa. LIII: 5–12).

To this context the formula *"delivered up for our sins and rose again for our justification"* (Rom. IV: 25) also belongs. In its Greek version the first part of this statement is almost a citation of Isaiah LIII: 12. Incidentally, it would be as false to disassociate death and resurrection as to separate remission of sins and infusion of grace in justification. Jesus has died *and* risen from the dead for our justification. So, too, expiatory suffering and the Servant's rehabilitation appear intimately associated with the lot of the redeemed (Isa. LIII: 10–12).

The assertion "He surrendered himself to death" in the Hebrew literally affirms: "He emptied himself by generously pouring out his soul" or his blood which symbolizes his life (cf. Lev. XVII: 11). St. Paul attributes the same sacrificial generosity to the Servant Jesus, who "annihilated himself" (Phil. II: 7) or "emptied himself." Such an interpretation manifests one of the many literary affinities that link the Christological hymn (Phil. II: 6–11) to the fourth Servant Song.

Other New Testament writings consider Jesus as the "Suffering Servant" of Deutero-Isaiah. The majority of texts concerned are related to traditions dependent on the Apostle Peter. Jesus' reprimand (Mark VIII: 33) bore fruit: he who was opposed to his Master's sacrifice seems to have been the first and ultimately the most ardent in recognizing Jesus as the Suffering Servant. The discourses in Acts prove this: You have *delivered up* Jesus, he said to the Jews (III:

13; cf. Isa. LIII: 12). In a prayer recited with Peter, the community calls Jesus "the holy servant" of God (IV: 27–30). It is not surprising that a passage in the First Epistle of Peter (II: 21–25) is formed by a grouping of citations drawn in great measure from Isaiah LIII.

The influence of the Servant Songs extends to many other New Testament texts. Several will be mentioned in relation with the soteriological titles "expiation" and "lamb." The relationships pointed out have stressed the importance of the role that the "theology of the Servant" played in the primitive community. The conversion of the high official of Candace, Queen of Ethiopia, furnishes a concrete example of it. Starting with the fourth Servant Song, Philip "preached Jesus to him" (Acts VIII: 35). One of Jesus' sayings has never failed to inspire generosity in Christians: "The Son of Man also has not come to be served but to serve, and to give his life as a ransom for many" (Mark X: 45).

NOTES ON 19

[1] See a detailed exposé of these ideas in *Rédemption Sacrificielle*, pp. 193–203. In this same work the theme of the Servant is studied in a deeper and more extensive manner (pp. 192–255). A useful bibliography and a comprehensive discussion of the problems will also be found in W. Zimmerli and J. Jeremias, "The Servant of God" (*Studies in Bibilical Theology*, no. 20, London, 1957). There is no consensus yet on the exact extent of the Servant Songs.

[2] G. von Rad in *Theologie des Alten Testaments*, vol. II (Munich, 1960), p. 268, characterizes the fourth song as "a prophetic liturgy," a sort of "elegy" (*Leichenlied*), in which can be distinguished God's oracles (Isa. LII: 13–15; LIII: 11f.) and the choir's responses (cf. LIII: 2–10).

[3] Granted that our interpretation of Isa. LII: 14f. (cf. p. 156) is correct, the Servant is equivalently named the Messiah, that is, "the anointed."

[4] In this translation the roman indicates what is ours; the italic lines are borrowed from C. R. North, *The Second Isaiah* (Oxford, 1964), p. 64. Our interpretation takes into account a number of recent scientific works mentioned in *Rédemption Sacrificielle*, pp. 352ff. It is favored by the newly discovered Qumrân manuscripts. St. Jerome had already translated by "So shall he sprinkle many nations" (also Douay version) the most difficult and important passage. The explicit mention of "unction" is conjectural.

[5] Etymologically "atonement" would mean "reconciliation" rather than "expiation" or "propitiation."

20

THE LAMB

THIS soteriological and sacrificial title appears prominently in the writings of John. Jesus is called "the lamb of God" twice in the Fourth Gospel (I: 29, 36) and thirty times or more "the Lamb" in the Apocalypse. The only two other explicit uses appear in the First Epistle of Peter (I: 19) and in a citation from Isaiah in Acts (VIII: 32). The figure of the lamb can call up various contexts which we will now try to determine.

In the account of Jesus' baptism, John the Evangelist only retains the descent of the Holy Spirit (cf. John I: 32f.) upon Him whom he calls "the *chosen* of God" (I: 34).[1] An even more obvious allusion to the *Servant* perhaps figured in the original formula of Jesus' introduction by His precursor: "Behold the lamb of God, who takes away the sin of the world" (John I: 29). The Aramaic term *talya*, in fact, can mean either "lamb" or "servant." In applying the title "lamb of God" to Jesus, the author of the Greek Gospel would have opted for the first sense. This explanation is possible, though not certain or necessary.

This apparently premature identification of Jesus with the redemptive lamb is surprising to many scholars. Has not the Saviour delayed and only gradually disclosed the revelation of His tragic destiny in the other Gospels? In fact, the Baptist's proclamation seems more appropriate if it was addressed to Christians: it reflects the way in which the primitive Church understood the work of Redemption and illustrates once again how John occasionally integrates his theology into the Gospel pattern. Besides, the Johannine character of the sayings contained in John III: 31–36 and attributed to the Baptist is quite obvious.

Another question arises: *What lamb* is considered in the phrase "behold the lamb of God" (John I: 29, 36)? Any allusion to the daily holocausts of lambs must likely be put aside (cf. Exod. XXIX: 38–42), for such rites were not properly expiatory. Doubtless, the Evangelist is thinking of the *paschal lamb*, as when he sees the fulfillment of Scripture in this episode of the death on the cross: "Not a bone of him shall you break" (John XIX: 36). This ritual custom (Exod. XII: 46) reflects an old belief in a certain revivification (in the fecundity of the flock?) of the victim offered to the divinity; its Johannine symbolism means that Jesus was destined for resurrection. Earlier, the use of a hyssop stalk to bring the vinegar to Jesus' mouth (John XIX: 29) also referred to the paschal ritual (cf. Exod. XII: 22). Insistently John notes that Jesus died on "the Preparation Day for the Passover" (XIX: 14, 31). Incidentally, reminiscences of the Exodus abound in the Fourth Gospel. Furthermore, the Eucharistic sacrifice was instituted during a paschal meal. The rites of the Institution need not mention the lamb, for *Jesus is the true paschal lamb* who sealed the new covenant with His blood. In the silence of the Evangelists we can also see an influence of the primitive Church's Eucharistic formulas.

Jesus, the Lamb of God, John tells us (I: 29), *takes away the sin of the world*. In fact, the immolation of the paschal lamb can be viewed as a *deliverance rite*.[2] In prophetic thought, Egypt was the land of sin (cf. Ezek. XX: 7f.). Actually, the vision of the Evangelist overflows the Exodus framework: it fuses into one reality the two figures—that of the paschal lamb and that of the Suffering Servant, "like a lamb led to slaughter" (Isa. LIII: 7; cf. Jer. XI: 19). The conclusion suggested by a literary hypothesis is thus reached differently. According to the Isaian texts the Servant bears the sins (LIII: 4, 11), a still inexact term meaning that *he takes them away*. The association of the paschal lamb and of the suffering just man had already been prepared in this passage from the Psalm: "He watches over all his bones; not one of them shall be broken" (XXXIII: 21; cf. John XIX: 36).

By His expiatory sacrifice, then, Jesus, like the Servant (Isa. LIII: 10) takes away the sin of the world. The Baptist's saying (John I: 29) is set in a baptismal context that is both literary (cf. John I: 28–34) and *theological*. For the baptism of Jesus was the prelude to the drama of His *death* and resurrection (cf. Luke XII: 50; Rom. VI: 4). Like *Isaac* (Gen. XXII: 2, 12, 16), Jesus is called "beloved son" at His baptism (Mark I: 11), but unlike in Genesis (XXII: 8), Mark does not say that God "will provide the sheep for the holocaust." Nonetheless, God did provide and like Abraham toward Isaac (Gen. XXII: 16), He did not spare His Son (Rom. VIII: 32) but gave Him to the world for a Saviour (John III: 16f.).

A baptismal homily prior to the year 60 seems to have inspired, in the First Epistle of Peter, an important statement about Christ the lamb:

You know that you were redeemed from the vain manner of life handed down from your father not with perishable things, with silver or gold, but with the precious blood of Christ, as of a *lamb* without blemish and without spot. Foreknown, indeed, before the foundation of the world, he has been manifested in the last times for your sakes. (I: 18–20.)

Evident allusions to the Exodus guide the interpretation: Christ is the new paschal lamb who redeemed mankind from a slavery prefigured by the oppression of the Hebrews in Egypt. At the time of the Exodus the blood of the lamb was a sign; on the Cross the blood of Jesus is the price of our redemption: He reconciles man with God (Col. I: 20), wins forgiveness for sin, seals the new covenant (Matt. XXVI: 28). Earlier, around Easter of the year 57, St. Paul had written to the Corinthians: "Christ, our passover, has been sacrificed" (I Cor. V: 7; cf. Deut. XVI: 5).[3]

The term that designates the victorious and redeeming Lamb in the Apocalypse is no longer ἀμνός (John I: 29) but ἀρνίον. Yet the *Exodus context* is always present, as for example in the song that the four elders sing to the Lamb:

> *Worthy are thou to take the scroll*
> *and to open its seal;*
> *For thou wast slain, and hast redeemed*
> *us for God with thy blood,*
> *Out of every tribe and tongue and*
> *people and nation,*
> *And hast made them for our God a*
> *kingdom and priests,*
> *And they shall reign over the earth.*
>
> (V: 9f.)

As the Hebrews were redeemed or delivered from the land of sin and slavery (Exod. XX: 2; Deut. V: 6) that Egypt was, so Christ's disciples, marked with the blood of the Lamb (Apoc. XIV: 1), are redeemed, purchased from the *earth* (Apoc. XIV: 3) or the Johannine "world" of rebellion against God, and won for God (cf. Eph. I: 14; I Pet. II: 9).

Other Apocalypse texts betray a different feature of the Lamb, that of the *victorious Leader*. In His train, for example, walk the 144,000 virgins (cf. XIV: 4), those, that is, who are not defiled with that prostitute, idolatry (cf. Hos. I: 2), by worshipping the Beast (XIV: 9; XX: 4). They shall be invited to the marriage supper of the Lamb (XIX: 9). The Lamb of the Apocalypse is both the triumphant Messiah, who leads His people to victory, and the suffering Messiah who gave His life for His followers. In the Servant figure the sacrificial interpretation of the Saviour's death was already announced and prepared. By way of conclusion, let us listen to the majestic refrain of the heavenly hymnody:[4]

Worthy is the Lamb who was slain to receive power and divinity and wisdom and strength and honor and glory and blessing.

(Apoc. V: 12.)

About the domineering Beast the Apocalypse reveals: "And all the inhabitants of the earth will worship it whose names have not been written in the book of life of the *Lamb* who has been slain from the foundation of the world" (XIII: 8). "The Lamb can effectively be called 'slain from the foundation of the world' because the Redemption is eternally present in divine thought and it has borne fruit before Christianity" (A. Gelin). To these two reasons Bossuet adds a third drawn from typology:

In Abel the just man was massacred; when Abraham wanted to sacrifice his son, he began in figure what was to be realized in Jesus Christ. In Him, too, we see fulfilled what Joseph's brothers began. Jesus was hated, persecuted, pursued to death by his brothers: in the person of Joseph He was sold, thrown into a cistern (or delivered over to death): with Jeremiah He was in the deep lake, with the children in the furnace, with Daniel in the Lion's den. In every sacrifice it was He whom they immolated in spirit. He was in the sacrifice that Noe offered upon leaving the ark and seeing the sacrament of peace in the rainbow; in those, too, that the patriarchs offered on the mountains, in those that Moses and all the Law offered in the tent and later in the temple: and having been always immolated in figure, He comes now to be so in reality.[5]

NOTES ON 20

[1] Another, more common, reading is: "the Son of God."

[2] Enriching the primitive theme, M. E. Boismard writes "Jewish tradition subsequently gave a redemptive value to the blood of the lamb: 'Because of the blood of the Covenant of the circumcision, and because of the blood of the Pasch, I have delivered you from Egypt,' *Pirqe R. Eliezer*, 29; cf. *Mekhilta* on Exod. XII" (*Vocabulaire de théologie biblique*, c. 18). Cf. Ezek. XLV: 18–21. On the Paschal Lamb in Judaism see also: L. Sabourin, "Mysterium paschale et vox messianica," in *Verbum Domini*, 1966, pp. 65–73.

[3] The "paschal" interpretation of the death of Christ seems suggested in the sense of "dying" attributed to "suffering" (cf. Acts I: 3; III: 18; XVII: 3; XXVI: 23). About I Pet. III: 18 (where we read in one Lesson: ἔπαθεν . . . θανατωθείς), Père Boismard writes: "But, probably under the influence of the word 'Pasch,' which an ancient exegesis would derive from the verb *paschein*, to suffer, and to underline that by dying Christ had fulfilled the figure of the Paschal Lamb (cf. Luke XXII: 15), primitive Christianity gave this verb the meaning 'dying' as in the kerygmatic formulas of Luke XXIV: 26, 46, where the 'passion' and 'the resurrection' of Christ are contrasted" (*Quatre hymnes baptismales dans la Première Épître de Pierre*, p. 59).

[4] On Apoc. I: 5–7, A. Gelin writes: "The Apocalypse contains a certain number of heavenly *carmina* which could easily be specimens and transpositions of earthly acclamations" (*La Sainte Bible*, vol. XII, p. 597). Perhaps my treatment of the title "Lamb" will seem somewhat succinct. For fuller treatment on this subject and on the idea of expiation, cf. *Rédemption Sacrificielle*, pp. 328–58.

[5] *Élévations sur les mystères*, XXIVe sem., élév. XI (édit. Outhenin-Chalandre, vol. III, p. 699). The phrase "from the foundation of the world" is perhaps more often linked with "were written" (Apoc. XIII: 8; cf. XVII: 8; Matt. XXV: 34). But compare I Pet. I: 18–20 quoted on p. 163. An often recurring verse in Advent runs thus in the Latin Breviary: "Emitte agnum, Domine, dominatorem terrae" (Isa. XVI: 1). St. Jerome understood it as a prayer to God: "Send, Lord, the lamb, the master of the world," the Messiah, that is. The meaning of the original text is doubtful but the general idea seems to be: "Send lambs to the ruler of the country," that is, to the king of Juda. Moabite refugees wished to acknowledge his sovereignty.

21

THE EXPIATION

ON two occasions the First Epistle of John calls Jesus, ἱλασμός, a Greek term translated here by "expiation," and not by the more current version "propitiation":

My dear children, these things I write to you in order that you may not sin. But if anyone sins, we have an advocate with the Father, Jesus Christ the just; and he is an *expiation* for our sins, not for ours only but also for those of the whole world.

(1 John II: 1f.)

In this is the love, not that we have loved God, but that he has first loved us, and sent his Son an *expiation* for our sins.

(1 John IV: 10.)

The idea of *propitiation*[1] is not, of course, absent from this context but merciful initiative plays a predominant role, whereas human effort to appease a god's wrath is quite common in pagan or very primitive religions. The Old Testament prophets gradually freed the Jewish religion from a merely pagan conception of propitiation. No New Testament text states that the sacrifice of Jesus was ordained to appease God's wrath or that Jesus Himself was the object of that wrath in the place of sinners. But through the mediation of His Son, ἱλασμός, God forgave our sins and freed us from our iniquities (cf. Rom. V: 8. f.).

The authorized commentators admit that the author of the Epistle is looking for a way to express a Hebrew thought in Greek. Now in biblical thought "expiation *wipes away* the sin precisely by giving back God's *presence* in the midst of His people Israel and by reuniting man once more to God."[2] "God does not reconcile Himself with the world," Dom Dupont writes, "He reconciles the world with Himself." This interpretation of Scripture (cf. II Cor. V: 18–20) corresponds to the mainstream of Catholic tradition which St. Thomas Aquinas expressed in his own fashion in the *Summa Theologica:*[3]

By sinning a man offends God. Now an offense is remitted to anyone, only when the soul of the offender is at peace with the offended. Hence sin is remitted to us when God is at peace with us, and this peace consists in the love whereby God loves us. Now God's love, considered on the part of the divine act, is eternal and unchangeable; whereas, as regards the effect that it imprints on us, it is sometimes interrupted, inasmuch as we sometimes fall short of it and once more regain it. (1–2, q. 113. a. 2.)

It is impious and cruel to hand an innocent man over to suffering and death against his will. That is not how God the Father handed Christ over, but rather He inspired in His Son the will to suffer for us. Thereby we can find first "the severity of God" who did not want to remit sin without a penalty (the Apostle underlines this when he says: "He did not spare His own Son"), and then too, the goodness of God, for when man could not offer a sufficient satisfaction for the penalty that he would himself undergo, God gave him someone who would satisfy for him (the Apostle means this when he says: "He delivered Himself up for all of us" and again of Christ "God set Him as a propitiation through faith in His blood." (III[a], q. 9. 47, a. 3, ad 1.)

The Council of Trent again ratified the tradition by declaring that our Lord Jesus Christ "merited our justification by His holy Passion on the wood of the cross and satisfied for us to God, His Father" (sess. VI, ch. 7). Here too we must recall a warning from the encyclical *Humani Generis* (1950): "Not content with that [suggesting that it would be impossible for God to create rational beings without equipping them for the beatific vision and calling them to it], they throw over the definitions of the Council of Trent by misrepresenting the whole nature of original sin, and indeed of sin in general, considered as an offense against God; the whole nature, too, of satisfaction which Christ offered on our behalf."

By translating ἱλασμός (I John II: 2; IV: 10) by a single word, "expiation," we wanted to retain the term's proper character of title, as in Greek. The meaning of ἱλασμός is diversely expressed. In his commentary on the Johannine Epistle, Père Bonsirven writes: "He Himself *serves as expiation* for our sins and not only for our sins but for the entire world." Other translations could be: "victim of expiation," "sacrifice of expiation,"[4] "victim of propitiation" (*BJ*), "agent of propitiation" (*Crampon*), "propitiation" (*Vulgate, Confraternity*). There is agreement, however, on the translation of ἱλασμός in II Macc. III: 33 as "sacrifice of expiation," "expiatory sacrifice," or "the expiation." What Scriptural reason motivates the substitution of the idea of propitiation for that of expiation? Since the Reformation there certainly exists a tendency to underline the aspect of penal substitution in the Redemption worked by Christ.

The designation of Jesus as the *Expiation* identifies Him once more with the Suffering Servant of God of whom the prophet had written: "The Lord was pleased to crush him in infirmity. He gives his life as *'āshām* (or as offering for sin, as *sacrifice of expiation*). . . . Through his sufferings,[5] my servant shall justify many" (Isa LIII: 10f.). Two Hebrew terms, *'āshām* and *ḥaṭṭa't*, mean both "sin" and "sacrifice for sin." Now we can understand why St. Paul could write: "For our sakes he [God] made him to be *sin* who knew nothing of sin, so that in him we might become the justice of God" (II Cor. V: 21). Of the Servant too (Isa. LIII: 9–11) it had been said that an innocent man became a victim for sin to justify sinners. The Hebrew *ḥaṭṭa't* is translated at least once by ἱλασμός in the Old Testament (Ezek. XLIV: 27), a precious indication of the similarity of the concepts. In a statement very similar in meaning to that of II Cor. V: 21, St. Paul affirms that "By sending his Son in the likeness of sinful flesh, *as a sin-offering*, he has condemned sin in the flesh" (Rom. VIII: 3). An attentive examination of the Greek terminology confirms that this translation is the exact one. Jesus offered himself in sacrifice for sin as God's true Suffering Servant. With the immolation of His flesh, sin was destroyed; with His Resurrection, a new humanity began to exist.

Still another passage from the Epistle to the Romans belongs to the same context:

All have sinned and have need of the glory of God. They are justified freely by his grace through the redemption which is in Christ Jesus whom God has set forth as a propitiation (ἱλαστήριον) by his blood through faith, to manifest his justice at the present time, so that he himself is just and makes just him who has faith in Jesus. (III: 23–26.)

In this ἱλαστήριον[6] there is a definite allusion to the propitiatory or *kapporet* of the ark of the covenant, that plaque of heavy gold set above the coffer containing the tables of the Law and sprinkled on various occasions with the blood of the victims. As will be true of the "socle" (*ăzārâh*) in the temple of Ezekiel (XLIII: 14, 17), the propitiatory (cf. Exod. XXV: 17–21), in the old Temple, served as "mercy-seat" (Ps. LXXIX: 2) from which Yahweh spoke to Moses (Num. VII: 89) and forgave his sins. Related to this was the sevenfold sprinkling with blood performed either toward the veil in the course of a year or on the propitiatory itself on the great Day of Atonement (Lev. XVI).

At the death of Jesus the veil of the Temple was torn from top to bottom (Mark XV: 38), for henceforth the throne of mercy is no longer hidden from sight, but accessible to all (Rom. III: 25). The event also shows that by His death Jesus becomes the living way to the eternal sanctuary (Heb. X: 19f.). The First Epistle of John, therefore, sees in "Jesus Christ the just," an "advocate with the Father" and "the Expiation" (II: 1f.). This dual role corresponds to the propitiatory's dual function and even more to the Suffering Servant's dual mission—expiatory victim and intercessor (Isa. LIII: 10, 12). By setting the prayer of the Suffering Christ into sharp, high relief, did the author of the Epistle to the Hebrews not want to represent the entire Passion "as one solemn prayer of intercession,"[7] answered from above (Heb. V: 7) by the sacrificial passing of the Son to the Father and by the victory of the first Risen One over death?

The idea of expiation is expressed in Hebrew and in Greek by words derived respectively from *kipper* and from ἱλάσκεσθαι. In agreement with doctrines of a "forensic justice," which does not really change man but covers his guilt with Christ's holiness, Protestants frequently lend these terms the meaning "to cover."[8] Another incorrect interpretation sees in the concept of expiation only the suffering of a pain incurred in an attempt to appease an angered divinity. Although the idea of satisfaction is implied in the term *kipper*, expiation or *at-one-ment*[9] tends basically to re-establish men in the society of God's friendship. For that reason, in his commentary on the Fourth Book of the Sentences, St. Thomas follows the doctrine of a predecessor (the Pseudo-Augustine): "St. Augustine defined satisfaction as being made to God, from whom, in fact, nothing can be taken away, although the sinner tries as much as he can to take something away from Him. For that reason, in a satisfaction made to God, the sinner's amendment for the future is more important than his compensation for the past. That is why St. Augustine defined satisfaction in terms of the future" (D. 15, q. 1, a. 1, sol. 3, ad 4).[10]

By the medium of blood or life, whose origin is in God,

man is reconciled with God, because his sin, "expiated" and pardoned, is no longer an obstacle to friendship with God. The text from Romans (III: 25) cited previously reveals that the saving justice of God is now exercised more intensely because of the Cross of Jesus: "God commends his charity towards us, because when as yet we were sinners, Christ died for us" (Rom. V: 8). By stating that Jesus is the Expiation, John makes a name of that redemptive function. Of Himself the Johannine Christ said: "I am the resurrection" (John XI: 25). This was a way to formulate the identification of the redemptive mystery with the person of the Saviour.

NOTES ON 21

[1] "Propitiation" is here used in its more common meaning of "appeasement" (of the wrath of God); cf. *Denzinger, Enchir. Symb.*, No. 940. According to its frequent use in biblical Latin (cf. Dan. IX: 9), we know that the term "propitiation" also often means the "benevolence" of God, who shows Himself "propitious" and who pardons (cf. the "collects" of the Roman missal: 14th Sunday after Pentecost; Wednesday of the third week in Lent; All Saints). The Bible's vocabulary for "expiation" (and related themes) is explained by Lyonnet in *De Peccato et Redemptione*, vol. II (Rome, 1960), pp. 67–117. On the "appeasement of the wrath of God" in the Bible, cf. P. van Imschoot, *Théologie de l'Ancien Testament*, vol. II, pp. 318–21.

[2] S. Lyonnet in *Lumière et Vie*, No. 36 (1958), p. 45; J. Dupont, *La réconciliation dans la théologie de saint Paul*, p. 15.

[3] Quoted here from the Anton Pegis edition.

[4] In *Mystiques paulinienne et johannique* (Bruges, 1946), J. Huby translates ἱλασμός in at least three different ways: "expiation" (p. 207), "victim for expiation" (p. 183) and "victim of propitiation" (pp. 151, 158). L. Moraldi translates ἱλασμός by "expiatory sacrifice" and ἱλαστήριον of Rom. III: 25 by "instrument of expiation" (in art. "Expiation," *Dictionnaire de Spiritualité*, c. 2039f.). In this same article Moraldi recalls that in the Old Testament "sin" and "suffering" are closely related: "afflicted with suffering the people turn or at least should turn toward God, understanding that suffering is from God because of sin" (cf. c. 2033). According to Moraldi the Servant Songs "identify sacrificial and moral expiation" (cf. 2036).

[5] See p. 191, n. 2.

[6] The term ἱλαστήριον is preferably translated "expiation" (*RSV*) or "instrument of expiation" (Lyonnet in *Introduction à la Bible*, II, p. 868, and Ligier in *Péché d'Adam et péché du monde*, II, p. 247). Other translators follow the Vulgate's *propitiatio*. The meaning "expiation" is also attributed to ἱλαστήριον by J. Dupont in *Le discours de Milet* (Paris, 1962), p. 184 n.

[7] Cf. S. Lyonnet, "Expiation et intercession" in *Biblica* (1959), p. 899. This article (pp. 885–901) is concerned with contexts in which St. Jerome

translates the Hebrew verb *kipper*, "to expiate" (Greek: ἐξιλάσκεσθαι) by a word meaning "to pray" (cf. Lev. IV: 20, 26, 31, 35). Therein lies a theological intent to relate "expiation" and "intercession," an intent which also appears in the Epistle to the Hebrews, when it defines the essential function of Christ's priesthood in the heavenly liturgy (cf. Wis. XVIII: 21), as "an intercession" (VII: 25; IX: 24). Cf. R. Le Déaut, *La nuit pascale* (Rome, 1963), p. 109, n. 114. Prayer, in the Old Testament, is considered one way of expiating (cf. L. Moraldi, *art. cit.*, c. 2033). The *Bible de la Pléiade*, vol. I (Paris, 1956) translates *yôm hakkippurim* by "day of forgiveness" (*jour des Pardons*). It would seem that such an interpretation is too far removed from the idea of ritual purification.

8 The typology of the imposition of sins on the *scapegoat* (Lev. XVI) has been used, mainly *since the Reformation*, in connection with the covering of our sins by Christ's justice. This can be shown from the history of the interpretation of II Cor. V: 21: "For our sakes he made him to be *sin* who knew nothing of sin, so that in him we might become the justice of God" (cf. "Le bouc émissaire, figure du Christ?" *Sciences Ecclésiastiques* (1959), pp. 45–79; S. Lyonnet, *De Peccato et Redemptione*, vol. II, pp. 135–38). To my mind "sin" in II Cor. V: 21 means "sacrifice for sin" (cf. Rom. VIII: 3), as I have shown in the first part of *Rédemption Sacrificielle* and, more briefly, in *Sc. Eccl.* (1959), pp. 419–24 and *Verbum Domini* (1963), pp. 159–62. Is it not significant that W. Barclay should list among his Titles of Jesus that of *Scapegoat* (*Jesus as They Saw Him*, pp. 312–15), although such typology is entirely absent from the New Testament perspective in regard to Jesus?

9 Cf. p. 161, n. 5. Blood, a "divine" element, constitutes a sort of "sacrament" of union and, therefore, of expiation. In Lev. XVII: 11 it is said: "It is blood which expiates, by the life which is in it." Cf. L. Moraldi, *art. cit.* (c. 2030), and L. Sabourin, "Redemptio nostra et Sacrificium Christi," *Verbum Domini* (1963), pp. 162–64. In connection with "blood," the word "expiation" has a meaning which is close to that of "purification."

10 On "sin" as "offense of God" and its reparation see F. X. Durrwell, *In the Redeeming Christ* (New York, 1963), pp. 30ff.

22

THE HIGH PRIEST
THE ADVOCATE
THE MEDIATOR

I<small>T</small> is to the Epistle to the Hebrews[1] that we owe the application of the title "High Priest" to Jesus: "Wherefore, it was
right that he should in all things be made like unto his
brethren, that he might become a merciful and faithful
high priest before God to expiate the sins of the people"
(II: 17). On several occasions the Epistle calls Jesus "Priest"
(V: 6; VII: 11) or "High Priest" (V: 10; VI: 20) for eternity,
according to the order of Melchisedec (Ps. CIX: 4; Heb.
VII: 17). Only three writings in the Bible (Gen., Ps. CIX,
Heb.) mention Melchisedec. According to Gen. XIV: 17–24,
this person was king of Salem and *priest* of the Most High.
Upon Abraham's return he brings bread and wine and
blesses the patriarch who gives him a tenth of everything.

"In the sacred account this Melchisedec makes a brief,
mysterious appearance as king of Jerusalem, where Yahweh
will choose to live. Priest of the Most High before the
institution of the Levites and the one who is paid a tithe by
the Father of the chosen people, he is presented by Psalm
CIX: 4 as a figure of the Messiah, king and priest. Finally,
Hebrews VII applies to Christ the typology of His priesthood.
Patristic tradition developed and enriched this allegorical
exegesis: the bread and wine brought to Abraham were a
figure of the Eucharist and even a true sacrifice that prefigured the Eucharistic sacrifice; this interpretation is now
found in the Canon of the Mass. Several Fathers had even

admitted that in Melchisedec the Son of God had appeared in person" (*BJ*).

The *Messianic* character of Psalm CIX also appears in the many applications made to Christ from the very first verse: "Sit at my right hand till I make your enemies your footstool." For example, let us mention the enigma proposed to the Pharisees (Matt. XXII: 44), Peter's discourse to the crowd (Acts II: 34f.), the Scriptural proof that places Jesus above the angels (Heb. I: 13), the repeated affirmation of the sitting at the right of the Father (cf. Mark XVI: 19; Col. III: 1). In the Psalm this divine protection assured to the King-Messiah is associated with the priestly character: "The Lord has sworn, and he will not repent. You are a priest forever according to the order of Melchisedec" (v. 4).

At a certain period in the Old Testament (cf. Lev. VI: 15; XVI: 32) *anointing* set the High Priest apart from the other priests. The splendor of the ceremony (cf. Exod. XXIX; Lev. VIII) stressed the importance accorded the High Priest as leader of the community. Nonetheless the sovereign function of the High Priest seems to have been fully recognized only after the Exile, when royal anointing was transferred to him (cf. Zech. IV: 14; VI: 11). The figure of a Messiah, King and Priest, is sharply drawn in the Qumrân texts which speak of a Messiah of Juda and a Messiah of Levi, of a Messiah of Israel and a Messiah of Aaron. In these writings the priestly Messiah is declared superior to the royal Messiah.[2]

The Gospel texts furnish us with little explicit information on the consciousness *Jesus* had of being the High Priest of the New Covenant.[3] The dialogue with the Pharisees, recorded by the Synoptics (cf. Matt. XXII: 41–46), shows that Jesus admits the Messianic character of Psalm CIX. To the temporal High Priest's question, "Art thou the Christ, the Son of the Blessed One?" Jesus gives an answer (Mark XIV: 62) that reveals His awareness of being the eternal High Priest: "I am. And you shall see the Son of Man sitting *at the right hand of the Power* and coming with the clouds of heaven" (cf. Ps. CIX: 1; Dan. VII: 13).

Jesus also considered Himself the Suffering Servant of Yahweh, and the primitive community often elaborated this conviction. Now on many counts *the notion of the Suffering Servant* touches on that of the High Priest, whose central function also consists in doing expiation for sin and in taking it away by sacrifice (cf. Heb. IX: 28; Isa. LIII: 12). In both notions the voluntary and personal character of the sacrifice offered is stressed, along with the idea of intercession (Heb. VII: 25). Let us add this passage from the Epistle to the Hebrews which announces the eschatological return of Jesus the High Priest: "So also was Christ offered once *to take away the sins of many*; the second time with no part in sin he will appear unto the salvation of those who await him" (IX: 28). The underlined words are borrowed from the fourth Servant Song (Isa. LIII: 12). The expression "without sin" seems to us to signify "without [being] sacrifice for sin,"[4] in contrast with the first coming (cf. II Cor. V: 21; Isa. LIII: 10). As a matter of fact, we read several verses later on: "Now where sins are remitted, there is no longer oblation for sin" (vv. 10, 18).

Numerous literary affinities connect the Epistle to the Hebrews with the Johannine writings. Here especially we must recall that the Epistle to the Hebrews and the fourth Gospel *have the theme of the priesthood of Christ in common.* According to Hebrews, Jesus is essentially a king-priest officiating in heaven. Compassionate and helpful to His brothers in humanity, He helps them with His intercession before God and with the merits won by His sacrifice (cf. Heb. II: 17f., IV: 14ff.). Now St. John, a disciple known to the High Priest (John XVIII: 15) and especially interested in the Temple and the rites of the cult, is the only other New Testament writer to present the Saviour as supreme

Pontiff, exercising a properly priestly ministry."[5] The Epistle and Gospel agree in stressing the reality of both the humanity of Jesus and His divinity. Both also insist on the glorification that followed the abasement and both underscore the cultual aspect of the New Covenant.

Let us recall what sign Jesus had given the Jews of His authority over the temple: "Destroy this temple, and in three days I will raise it up" (John II: 19). John explains that He was speaking of the temple of His body (II: 21). "When He purifies the sanctuary of heaven (Heb. IX: 23), Christ renews the action performed in Jerusalem at the start of His earthly ministry and gives to it its fuller sense, its true efficacy, for henceforth the High Priest has at His disposal the blood that He shed on the cross. Just as John (II: 19) related the purification of the temple to the death of Jesus and insinuated that the humanity of the Risen Saviour would be the center of the cult in which the Father would be worshipped neither on Moriah nor on Garizim (John IV: 21–24), so too, by purifying the temple, the Christ of Hebrews gives men access to God and fulfills perfectly His priestly office, having at His disposal the holiest victim imaginable, His own flesh and blood! This conception of the heavenly Christian cult in Hebrews is in absolute conformity with that of the Apostle of religion in spirit and in truth; it certainly derives from him."[6]

Several ideas of the Epistle to the Hebrews concerning the High Priest are found also in "the priestly prayer of Jesus" (John XVII). For example, it is the Sovereign Sacrificer who pronounces these words: "And for them I sanctify myself, that they also may be sanctified" (John XVII: 19; cf. Heb. X: 10). He who is going to prepare places for His disciples (John XIV: 1f.) is the author (Heb. II: 10), pioneer and forerunner (Heb. VI: 20), who has entered the heavenly sanctuary before His followers to "prepare" the eternal city for them (Heb. XI: 16). A final priestly feature of the Johannine Christ, the seamless tunic worn by Christ at the

hour of His sacrifice (John XIX: 23), would recall the priestly
garment of the high priest as the Jewish historian Josephus
describes him. The Son of Man in John's Apocalypse "clothed
with a garment reaching to the ankles, and girt about the
breasts with a golden girdle" (I: 13), also describes the
glorified Christ as a priestly figure.

The Epistle to the Hebrews stresses the doctrine that
Jesus was truly man. "For in that he himself has suffered
and has been tempted, he is able to help those who are
tempted" (II: 18); "for we have not a high priest who
cannot have compassion on our infirmities, but one tried
as we are in all things except sin" (IV: 15). Tempted
particularly at the moment of the agony (V: 7; cf. Luke
XXII: 28), Jesus prayed (cf. Mark XIV: 39) and God heard
His prayer (Heb. V: 7), since He accepted the chalice of
suffering offered Him. "On the last day in His flesh He was
accomplished (cf. John XIX: 30) in His priestly office,
thanks to obedience (Heb. V: 8f.) or the total acceptance of
the conditions God had set for His mediation, and the fullest
experience of pain."[7]

Several Christological titles mentioned in the Prologue of
the Fourth Gospel are involved in the Prologue of the
Epistle to the Hebrews:

God, who at sundry times and in divers manners spoke in times
past to the fathers by the prophets, last of all in these days has
spoken to us by his Son, whom he appointed heir of all things,
by whom also he made the world; who being the brightness of
his glory and the image of his substance, and upholding all
things by the word of his power has effected man's purgation
from sin and taken his seat at the right hand of the Majesty on
high, having become so much superior to the angels as he has
inherited a more excellent name than they. (I: 1–4.)

These divine attributes suit one who is next called God
(I: 8) and Lord (I: 10) and also the God-Man, become High
Priest at the Incarnation through the anointing of the
Divinity. His redemptive work began with his entrance

into this world and his full acceptance of the sacrifice entailed
(Heb. X: 5–10). This desire to suffer was expressed in the
sacrificial act itself, accomplished "once for all" (Heb. X:
10) because it was by its very nature decisive and definitive
(cf. Heb. IX: 12, 26). The sacrifice of the Mass makes this
unique sacrifice, that cannot be repeated, because of its
infinite worth, present to all generations and in all places
(cf. Mal. I: 11). It can therefore be stated with Father
Mersch: "Jesus is not a Priest among priests, greater than
the others or holier; He is the only Priest . . . He exhausts
in Himself, so to speak, the entire priesthood."[8]

THE ADVOCATE

The priestly work of Jesus continues in heaven. Christ is
called "minister of the Holies and of the true tabernacle,
which the Lord has erected and not man" (Heb. VIII: 2).
Obviously the insistence on this eternal and heavenly liturgy
is explained by the desire to contrast it with the declining,
temporal and earthly Jewish liturgy, especially that of the
great Day of Atonement (Lev. XVI). It is not easy to
determine the precise nature of this heavenly liturgy. As we
have seen, such a liturgy cannot be a renewal of the Sacrifice of the Cross. Yet Christ with his glorious wounds (cf.
John XX: 24–29; Apoc. V: 6) continually reminds the
Father of the work fulfilled on earth and prolongs its effects
into eternity: "But he, because he continues forever, has an
everlasting priesthood. Therefore he is able at all times
to save those who come to God through him, since he lives
always to *make intercession* for them" (Heb. VII: 24f.). On
Calvary, sinful humanity represented by the mortal flesh
of Jesus (Rom. VIII: 3), has been virtually put to death, and
in the glorified humanity of the Risen One, a new world
has begun to exist. In heaven Christ also *intercedes* for His
own as He who entered "into heaven itself, to appear now
before the face of God on our behalf" (Heb. IX: 24).

According to the Epistle to the Romans, the presence of Christ the Intercessor keeps believers from every condemnation (VIII: 34). A similar subject for confidence is proposed to us in the First Epistle of John: "But if anyone sins, we have an *advocate* (παράκλητος) with the Father, Jesus Christ the just" (II: 1). The etymology (passive form) of the term παράκλητος suggests the meaning *advocate*, "he who is called" (Latin: *ad-vocatus*). According to legal language, then, he fulfills the roles of defender, mediator, or intercessor.[9] The Johannine Christ had promised to send *another* "paraclete" (John XIV: 16), the Holy Spirit, considering Himself in His role as intercessor. An allusion to that effect also appears in this word of Jesus': "And I say to you, everyone who acknowledges me before men, him will the Son of Man also acknowledge before the angels of God" (Luke XII: 8). Applied to the Holy Spirit by the Fourth Gospel, the term παράκλητος designates rather the witness of Christ (XV: 26) and His interpreter (XIV: 26), who will convince unbelievers of error (XIV: 8) and will console the true disciples (XIV: 16; XVI: 7).

THE MEDIATOR

Another title is intimately connected with that of High Priest. Both by their respective Latin etymology and meaning, the titles "Pontiff" and "Mediator" are related and eminently suit one who unites humanity and divinity in his person. In the Epistle to the Hebrews Christ is called Mediator of a new (IX: 15; XII: 24) and better covenant (VIII: 6; cf. Gal. IV: 25). Drawing on the double meaning of the Greek term διαθήκη, the epistle speaks now of *covenant*, now of *testament* (IX: 15, 17), and does so rightly. As the covenant was the heritage promised the Patriarchs (cf. Gal. III: 15–18), so the new covenant in the New Testament is the heritage won by the Saviour's redemptive death (cf. Gal. IV: 1–7; Rom. VIII: 17). The new covenant in His blood is also the testament of Christ, His last will. Therein He gives Himself to men and potentially makes them heirs of all the Father's goods. By the Saviour's death, all the old debts are wiped away, and "the representative return" of the Son to the Father's bosom is a pledge of our eventual possession of future goods.

The role of blood in concluding the Sinai covenant is also recalled by a formula that evokes the Last Supper: "This is the blood of the covenant which God has commanded for you (Heb. IX: 20; cf. Matt. XXVI: 28). At the Sinai covenant the sprinkling of blood constituted the essential rite (according to the elohist tradition), but Christ's sacrifice does not require sprinkling because of the theandric character of the person immolated. Secondary in the first covenant, immolation itself is here a constituent of the covenant-testament: by the representative death of Jesus and His passage to God, sinful humanity dies to sin and potentially recovers its life in God, who is now totally disposed to grant it back. In the other New Testament writings, *the title of Mediator*[10] is applied only once to Christ, in relation to His redemptive death: "For there is one God, and one *Mediator* between God and men, himself man, Christ Jesus, who gave himself a ransom for all" (I Tim. II: 5f.; cf. Mark X: 45). Such reserve toward so expressive a title seems due to the less appropriate current meaning given to the term at the time.[11] The term μεσίτης, besides, appears only once in the Septuagint, in Job. In writings prior to the Pastoral Epistles, Paul also uses it once only, in relation to the promulgation of the Law (Gal. III: 19f.).

High Priest, Sovereign Sacrificer, Stainless Victim, Intercessor, Advocate, Jesus Mediator[12] is the Supreme Pontiff, the Intermediary between God and man, the one who renders vain the sorrow of Job, struck powerless before the majesty and holiness of God: "No arbiter (μεσίτης) between us to lay his hand on us both" (Job IX: 33). The attitude of the believer is completely opposite:

For we have not a high priest who cannot have compassion on our infirmities, but one tried as we are in all things except sin. Let us therefore draw near with confidence to the throne of grace that we may obtain mercy and find grace to help in time of need. (Heb. IV: 15f.)

NOTES ON 22

[1] The Epistle to the Hebrews is special in "the Pauline collection"; for, if it reflects the Apostle's doctrine on many points, it was not redacted by him but by one of his disciples, "a biblist and a prophet," perhaps Apollos (cf. Acts XVIII: 24–28). The latter's sojourn at Ephesus could explain his knowledge of the Johannine catechesis, which also inspired the Epistle to the Hebrews. As for the literary genus of the Epistle, it is considered by some to be a carefully composed homily, with a farewell message added (XIII: 22ff.). Cf. A. Vanhoye, *La structure littéraire de l'Épître aux Hébreux* (Paris, Bruges, 1963), p. 215, n. 1.

[2] On "priestly Messianism," cf. A. Gelin, in *DBS*, vol. V, cc. 1196–1199. Concerning the Qumrân texts, the Zadokite Document and the Testaments of the Twelve Patriarchs, Cullmann writes: "The important thing is that the identification of the High Priest with the Messiah is accomplished in these texts" (*The Christology of the New Testament*, p. 86.)

[3] According to A. George, if "Jesus does not even once attribute the title of Priest to Himself," it is because "that title designates in his *milieu* a definite function reserved to members of the tribe of Levi. Now Jesus sees His task as very different from theirs, much more ample and creative. He prefers to call Himself the Son and the Son of Man. However, He uses priestly terms to define His mission. As usual, these expressions are implicit and figurative" (*Vocabulaire de théologie biblique*, c. 964).

[4] This interpretation was common among the medieval commentators: Sedulius Scotus, Rabanus Maurus, Lanfranc, St. Bruno, Hervé de Bourg-Dieu, Peter Lombard, St. Thomas Aquinas, and first of them all perhaps: Alcuin (†804). See also p. 173, n. 8.

[5] C. Spicq, *L'Épître aux Hébreux*, vol. I, p. 121. After this passage the author illustrates his thought with many examples,

[6] C. Spicq, *op. cit.*, vol. I, p. 107.

[7] C. Spicq, *op. cit.*, vol. II, p. 118; also J. Bonsirven, *Épître aux Hébreux*, in the *Verbum Salutis* collection.

[8] *Morale et Corps Mystique* (Bruges, 1937), p. 144.

[9] More precisely: in I John II: 1, παράκλητος means "advocate, defender" (cf. John XVI: 26), while in Rom. VIII: 34 (cf. VIII: 27) the idea of intercession is accentuated. All the problems relating to the "Paraclete" have been discussed recently by O. Betz in his book *Der Paraklet. Fürsprecher im häretischen Spätjudentum, im Johannesevangelium und in neu gefundenen gnostischen Schriften* (Leiden, Köln, 1963); cf. H.-M. Dion, "L'origine du titre de Paraclet: à propos d'un livre récent" in *Sc. Eccl.* (1965), pp. 143–49.

10 The majority of the titles of Jesus describe one or another aspect of his work of mediation. If the term "Mediator" is rarely used by the New Testament, the notion that corresponds to this title is nonetheless present throughout (cf. M. Schmaus, *Katholische Dogmatik*, vol. II, 2, Munich, 1955, p. 279). The notion of mediation has been amply covered by C. Spicq in *DBS*, vol. V, cc. 938–1083.

11 In the popular speech of the day, writes V. Taylor, μεσίτης meant "arbitrator," "umpire," "guarantor," "surety"; it was a legal and commercial expression (*The Names of Jesus*, p. 111). The term "surety" can be considered a title of Jesus since it is written in the Epistle to the Hebrews: "All the more has Jesus become *surety* (ἔγγυος) of a superior covenant" (VII: 22). It is described as a separate title by W. Barclay in *Jesus as They Saw Him*, pp. 329–33. The Vulgate translates ἔγγυος by "sponsor."

12 On Christ, Mediator of the New Covenant, see also pp. 155ff. ("The Mediation of the Servant").

23

THE RESURRECTION

To Jesus' promise "thy brother shall rise," Martha answers: "I know that he will rise at the resurrection, on the last day." Then Jesus said to her: "I am the resurrection and the life; he who believes in me, even if he die, shall live; and whoever lives and believes in me, shall never die" (John XI: 23ff.). It is characteristic of John, as we have already seen, to make a title of a function (cf. "the Expiation") and to insist on those sayings of Jesus' that begin with the revelation formula, "I am." The resurrection of Lazarus, an undeniable historical fact, takes on a symbolical value: the return of this dead man to temporal life prefigures and "signifies" the general resurrection at the end of time and attests the reality of what Jesus claims when He declares: "I am the resurrection."[1]

The Bible is witness of the *progressive revelation* of the mystery of the resurrection of bodies to an extraterrestrial life. The origins of the doctrine are connected with a firm and constant belief in Israel from the beginning: *living God* is stronger than death (cf. Deut. XXXII: 39; Luke XX: 37f.) He proved it by the taking up of Henoch (Gen. V: 24; Wis. IV: 10f.) and of Elias (II Kings II: 11; I Macc. II: 58), and especially by the resurrections to temporal life as answers to the prayers of Elias (I Kings XVII: 17ff.) and of Eliseus (II Kings IV: 29; cf. XIII: 21).

Many centuries had to pass before religious thought in Israel would go beyond the primitive concept of a vague, gloomy afterlife in *sheol*, that dark place in the center of the earth, where the dead descend to lead a silent, diminished life:

> *Will you work wonders for the dead?*
> *Will the shades arise to give you thanks?*
> *Do they declare your kindness in the grave?*
> *your faithfulness among those who have perished?*
> *Are your wonders made known in the darkness,*
> *or your justice in the land of oblivion?*
> (Ps. LXXXVII: 11–13.)

> *For it is not the nether world that*
> *gives you thanks,*
> *nor death that praises you;*
> *Neither do those who go down into the pit*
> *await your kindness.*
> (Isa. XXXVIII: 18.)

The exigencies of a just retribution initiated the idea of a *different lot* for the just and the unjust. The latter, like their fathers, "shall never more see light" (Ps. XLVIII: 20), but the just man thus expresses his hope: "God will redeem me from the power of the nether world by receiving me" (XLVIII: 16). Another psalmist declares that he had worried in vain about the happiness of the wicked "till I entered the sanctuary of God and considered their final destiny" one of irreparable catastrophe. "Yet with you I shall always be. You have hold of my right hand; with your counsel you guide me and in the end you will receive me in glory" (Ps. LXXII: 23f.). The Servant of Deutero-Isaiah personifies the suffering just man who has been doubly restored: by the splendor of his saving work and by a privileged, personal afterlife:

> *If he gives his life as an offering for sin,*
> *he shall see his descendants in a long life,*
> *and the will of the Lord shall be*
> *accomplished through him.*

Because of his affliction he shall see the
light in fullness of days;
Through his suffering, my servant shall
justify many,[2]
and their guilt he shall bear.
Therefore, I will give him his portion
among the great,
and he shall divide the spoils
with the mighty
Because he surrendered himself to death
and was counted among the wicked.
(Isa. LIII: 10ff.; cf. Ps. XXI: 23–32.)

To describe *the national restoration* the prophets often use
the image of resurrection. Contemplating a valley filled with
bones, Ezekiel hears God say: "Son of man, can these bones
come to life?" (XXXVII: 3). The word of God covered them
with flesh and the spirit of God put life into them. This
eloquent symbol would suggest the possibility of an
individual resurrection of the flesh, already less distant
in that post-exilic oracle of Isaiah:

But your dead shall live; their
corpses shall rise;
awake and sing, you who lie in the dust.
For your dew is a dew of light,
and the land of shades gives birth.
(XXVI: 19.)

Redacted toward the year 165 B.C., the Book of Daniel
offers us the first clear affirmation of individual resurrection
to a life beyond the tomb.[3] It is not yet stated that *all* men
will rise, but the wicked do not seem to be excluded. A
shining corporal glory (cf. Matt. XIII: 43) is foreseen for one
category of the risen:

Many of those who sleep in the dust of the earth *shall awake;*
some shall live forever, others shall be an everlasting horror and
disgrace. But the wise shall shine brightly like the splendor of

the firmament, and those who lead the many to justice shall be like the stars forever. (XII: 2f.)

A clear teaching on the resurrection also emerges from several texts of the Second Book of the Maccabees, an inspired work written for the Alexandrian Jews near the end of the second century B.C. Before dying the second of the seven martyred brothers warned the persecuting king: "Thou indeed, O most wicked man, destroys out of this present life: but the King of the world *will raise us up*, who die for his laws" (VII: 9). The fourth brother tells the king: "It is better, being put to death by men, to look for hope from God, *to be raised up again* by him; for as to thee thou shalt have no resurrection unto life" (VII: 14). Composed in Greek about the year 50 B.C. by a Hellenized Jew, the book of Wisdom replaces the Hebrew notion of the soul (*nephes̆*) with the Greek notion (ψυχή). This change modified the perspective: although he does not exclude resurrection, the Wisdom author insists on incorruptibility (VI: 18) and immortality (cf. III: 4, VIII: 17). Paracanonical apocrypha of the last two centuries before Christ reveal a rather general hope in an eternally happy life for the just. In the Book of Henoch, for example, we read: "The just shall be in the light of the sun and the chosen in the light of an eternal life; and the days of their life shall be without end, the days of the saints shall be without number" (LVIII: 3).

*
*   *

The New Testament clearly testifies to the faith in the general resurrection. Besides Lazarus (John XI), Jesus raised from the dead the daughter of Jairus (Mark V: 21ff.) and the son of the widow of Naim (Luke VII: 11–17), all astonishing deeds that herald the even greater miracle of resurrection to eternal life. To one of his hosts Jesus will recall that it would be better to invite to table "the poor, the crippled, the lame, the blind": "blessed shalt thou be, because they have nothing to repay thee with; for thou shalt be repaid at the *resurrection of the just*" (Luke XIV: 14). To the gross error of the Sadducees who denied the resurrection, Jesus opposed a clear doctrine that conformed to Scripture:

And Jesus said to them, The children of this world marry and are given in marriage. But those who shall be accounted worthy of that world and of the *resurrection* from the dead, neither marry nor take wives. For neither shall they be able to die any more, for they are equal to the angels, and are sons of God, being *sons of the resurrection*. But that the dead rise, even Moses showed in the passage about the Bush, when he calls the Lord the God of Abraham, and the God of Isaac, and the God of Jacob. Now he is not the God of the dead, but of the living, for all live to him.
(Luke XX: 34–38.)

That Jesus' death was already a victory achieved over death appears in this episode told by Matthew:

And behold, the curtain of the temple was torn in two from top to bottom; and the earth quaked, and the rocks were rent, and the tombs were opened, and many bodies of the saints who had fallen asleep arose; and coming forth out of the tombs after his resurrection, they came into the holy city, and appeared to many. (XXVII: 51ff.)[4]

St. Paul bases belief in the resurrection of the flesh on the fact of Jesus' resurrection (cf. I Cor. XV: 12–19). "For as in Adam all die, so in Christ all will be made to live" (I Cor. XV: 22). As for the living, they shall be transformed at the *parousia* (I Cor. XV: 51). The resurrected bodies will be "spiritual" (I Cor. XV: 44). This will be possible, for St. Paul sees the spirit as synonymous not with immateriality, but with strength, light, holiness, and whatever is heavenly or divine in origin. For him, the resurrection—especially Christ's—is an irruption of the Spirit of God into the world:

"But if the Spirit of him who raised Jesus from the dead dwells in you, then he who raised Jesus Christ from the dead will also bring to life your mortal bodies because of his Spirit who dwells in you" (Rom. VIII: 11; cf. I: 4). Paul always attributes the resurrection to the Father (cf. I Cor. VI: 14), except in this passage: the Lord Jesus Christ "will refashion the body of our lowliness, conforming it to the body of his glory by exerting the power by which he is able also to subject all things to himself" (Phil. III: 21).

For John, the resurrection is the work of the Son, and reaches *all* men, the just and sinners:

> Do not wonder at this, for the hour is coming in which all who are in the tombs shall hear the voice of the Son of God. And they who have done good shall come forth unto resurrection of life; but they who have done evil unto resurrection of judgment.
>
> (John V: 28f.)

For Paul, too, the resurrection is somehow also *present*: "With him [Christ] He has raised us up together and seated us together in heaven in Christ Jesus" (Eph. II: 6; Col. III: 1). A tendency of the Captivity Epistles to anticipate eschatology appears still more sharply in Johannine theology:[5]

> Amen, amen, I say to you, he who hears my word, and believes him who sent me, has life everlasting, and does not come to judgment, but has passed from death to life. Amen, amen, I say to you, the hour is coming, and now is here, when the dead shall hear the voice of the Son of God, and those who hear shall live. (John V: 24f.)

The statement "he who believes has life everlasting" (John VI: 47) is easily connected with this other one by Jesus about him whom the Father draws: "I will raise him up on the last day" (VI: 44; cf. VI: 54). In fact, the resurrection is already *present* for all, in Christ who can state: "I am the *resurrection* and the life" (XI: 25). The supernatural life that Jesus brings already contains the seeds of the final resurrection. Lazarus, Jesus' friend, has risen from the dead, but he shall be raised once again to eternal life. He who eats the bread of the Eucharist "shall live forever" (John VI: 51–58), for eternal death, the only death deserving that name, cannot affect the believer. The Epistles to the Thessalonians reflect the feverish climate of expectation that stirred in certain primitive communities (cf. I Thess. IV: 15; II Thess. II: 2). John's pacifying theology played a great role in leading the Church to the calm possession of the undefined presence of its Lord through the firm hope in the resurrection.

This title "the Resurrection" does not appear here among the *soteriological* titles of Jesus by mere chance. We wanted to present the resurrection for what it is: a mystery of salvation.[6] Following Jesus Himself who openly foretold His death and resurrection as a single mystery, the New Testament considers Jesus' glorification (Resurrection and Ascension) as an essential element in the Redemption. In St. John this theology appears every time that he sets Jesus' death in *a paschal context*. John considers Jesus' death as a Passover (XIX: 14, 31), a passing from this world over to the Father (XIII: 1; XX: 17), a return to the God (XIII: 3) who sent Him. Jesus fulfilled this ascent to the Father (VI: 62) as head of mankind: "Father, I will that where I am, they also whom thou hast given me may be with me" (XVII: 24). The sacrificial transformation (I: 29) of Jesus' body into the new Temple (II: 21), the center of the new worship, will be effected by the passing from the carnal to the spiritual through death and resurrection.

Saint Paul will insist further: "If Christ has not risen, vain is your faith, for you are still in your sins" (I Cor. XV: 17); "He was delivered up for our sins, and rose again for our justification" (Rom. IV: 25). As we have said before (p. 159), this sentence means: Jesus died and rose for our sins and our justification. With one and the same movement there is destruction of sin through death and rebirth to life through resurrection. A *sacrificial* interpretation of redemption, then, makes the most of the soteriological aspect of the resurrection. The sacrifice is a double phase movement that leads to rest in God. On the other hand any explanation too exclusively juridical and penal does not bring out correctly the fullness of the "return," and leaves the prodigal son a prey to his misery. By sin man strayed from God; by sacrifice consummated in the resurrection, he returns to the Father offering full satisfaction for his offense. Without Christ this return would have been impossible for man.

Through Baptism the Christian experiences what Christ lived in His flesh: "The death that he died, he died to sin once for all, but the life that he lives, he lives unto God. Thus do you consider yourselves also as dead to sin, but alive to God in Christ Jesus" (Rom. VI: 10f.).[7] Jesus' declaration, "I am the resurrection," terminated and recapitulated the long history of biblical revelation about the resurrection. In the full sense, it justified the ancient adage of Israel's religious thought: "Seek good and not evil, that you may live" (cf. Amos V: 14; Lev. XVIII: 5), more so the word which the Master of truth and life addressed to everyone: "Do this and thou shalt live" (Luke X: 28).

NOTES ON 23

[1] Some manuscripts add: "and the life."

[2] The translation "through his suffering" represents a change from the Massoretic Hebrew text. *Bible de la Pléiade* renders it thus: "Because of the affliction experienced by his soul he shall see the light, he shall be satisfied. *Through his knowledge* my servant shall justify many and their guilt he shall bear" (Isa. LIII: 11). For Father M. Dahood, the Hebrew term translated "knowledge" could here mean "sweat," as its Ugaritic equivalent does: "By his sweat (Ugar.: d't) the just one shall justify . . ." (*Gregorianum*, 1962, p. 63). Compare p. 169.

[3] A text from Job, "in my flesh I shall stand up . . ." (XIX: 25) is often interpreted as an affirmation of hope in the resurrection. However, the author seems to have in mind rather the possibility of a fleeting return to life, in view of a rehabilitation.

[4] In this somewhat difficult passage the rending of the Temple veil is mentioned by the three Synoptics. Whether or not a "material veil" is meant, the *velum scissum*, writes V. Taylor, "symbolizes the opening of the way to

God effected by the death of Christ, or alternatively, and perhaps at the same time, the end of the Temple system . . . G. Lindeskog suggests that the theological idea of the opening of the way to heaven has been dressed in a cultic pattern which is interpreted symbolically in Hebrews (cf. X: 19f.) and realistically in Mark" (*The Gospel according to St. Mark*, London, 1955, p. 596). Each Synoptist may have understood the event differently (cf. A. Pelletier, "La tradition synoptique du voile déchiré," *Rech. Sc. Rel.*, 1958, pp. 161–80). "Matthew adds some miraculous touches not found in the other sources. The raising of many bodies of the saints is more than a portent. It suggests that Jesus' resurrection is the first fruits of the general resurrection (I Cor. XV: 20) and that at his second coming, when all the dead are raised, he will be accompanied by the departed saints (I Thess. IV: 16)" (*The Interpreter's Bible*). It is hardly conceivable that the "bodies of the saints" would have risen from the dead on Good Friday and come forth from the tomb only on Easter Sunday. The sequence of events is perhaps more theological than chronological. Other explanations are possible (cf. *Scripture*, 1948, pp. 86f.). The resurrection of the bodies accompanies quite naturally the earthquake which caused the opening of the tombs. Amos had also mentioned "earthquakes" among the portents that would accompany the "Day of the Lord" (VIII: 8).

5 See also p. 102.

6 This aspect of the Resurrection is well presented in two recent works: F. X. Durrwell, *The Resurrection* (New York, 1960); D. M. Stanley, *Christ's Resurrection in Pauline Soteriology* (Rome, 1961); more briefly by F. Höltz, "Soteriological value of the Resurrection of Christ," *Theology Digest* (1955), pp. 101–06, and S. Lyonnet, "Redemptive Value of the Resurrection," *Theology Digest* (1960), pp. 89–93.

7 St. Paul also writes: "For we *were buried* with him by means of baptism into death, in order that, just as Christ has arisen from the dead through the glory of the Father, so we also may walk in newness of life" (Rom. VI: 4). Christ's stay in the tomb, *awaiting the resurrection*, somehow symbolized Christian life. For the ancients, burial was the ultimate imprint of death. By baptism the Christian dies totally to sin, but he remains marked by its consequences. Yet he lives a new life, graced by the Spirit who is the gage of his future resurrection. On the relationship of Rom. VI: 4–5 with the ancient baptismal rites, see two articles by E. Stommel in *Römische Quartalschrift* (1954, pp. 1–20, and 1955, pp. 1–21). The notion of baptism as "bath" (cf. I Cor. VI: 11; Tit. III: 5) is older than the one insisting on complete immersion and emersion (fourth century). Cf. also P.-E. Langevin, "Le Baptême dans la Mort-Résurrection," *Sc. Eccl.* (1965), pp. 29–66.

V

*PROPERLY CHRISTOLOGICAL TITLES**

* The titles of Part V more directly answer the question: "Who is Christ?" (cf. V. Taylor, *The Names of Jesus*, p. 124).

24

THE SON OF MAN

ACCORDING to the Gospels Jesus almost always used the expression "Son of Man" in the third person to designate Himself: "The foxes have dens and the birds of the air have nests, but the Son of Man has nowhere to lay his head" (Matt. VIII: 20). That such a description is practically restricted to the *Gospels* which always attribute it to Jesus Christ Himself (except once, when the expression is taken up by the crowd that has just heard Him: John XII: 34),[1] is remarkable and reaffirms the Evangelists' faithfulness to a firm, historical tradition. In the rest of the New Testament only once is Jesus called "Son of Man"—by the dying Stephen: "He said, Behold I see the heavens opened and the Son of Man standing at the right hand of God" (Acts VII: 56). Two visions from the Apocalypse also describe the Messiah as a "Son of Man," exercising his function as an eschatological judge.

Jesus did not attach the title of the Son of Man to any particular aspect of the mystery of His person, for the uses of the word vary with the context: thirty instances concern the *parousia*, twenty-five evoke the Passion and Resurrection, twenty or so describe the different circumstances of Jesus' life on earth. Some Gospel texts associate "Son of Man" and pre-existence: "No one has ascended into heaven except him who has descended from heaven: the Son of Man who is in heaven" (John III: 13). Doubtless, Jesus preferred calling Himself Son of Man because this title was suitable to describe the threefold aspects of His being and His work: pre-existence, earthly life, future life. Furthermore, the indefinite character of the notion with its imprecise association served the gradual revelation of the Messianic mystery. Although Jesus gave the expression "Son of Man" a new meaning, He did not invent it. Now we are invited to search into the preparation and progress of this title preferred by Jesus.

THE "SON OF MAN" IN THE OLD TESTAMENT

First, let us read the famous oracle of Daniel: "As the visions during the night continued, I saw one like a son of man coming, on the *clouds* of heaven" (VII: 13). Two of Jesus' sayings recall the content of that oracle: "And then they will see the Son of Man coming *upon clouds* with great power and majesty" (Mark XIII: 26; cf. Matt. XXIV: 30); "And Jesus said to him, 'I am. And you shall see the Son of Man sitting at the right hand of the Power and coming with the *clouds* of heaven' " (Mark XIV: 62). The answer of the man accused before Caiphas associates Dan. VII: 13 and the beginning of a Messianic Psalm, "The Lord said to my Lord: Sit at my right hand till I make your enemies your footstool" (Ps. CIX: 1). The *first* saying of Jesus recorded by Mark is also revelatory: "The *time* is fulfilled, and the kingdom of God is at hand" (I: 15). Daniel had predicted the eschatological advent thus: "The *time* came when the holy ones received the *kingdom*" (VII: 22).

Every time that the description of Jesus' return contains the theophanic element of the *cloud* (cf. Acts I: 11; Apoc. I: 7) there is an allusion to the Son of Man of Daniel. Divine beings are thus carried along and God Himself is "the rider of the clouds" (Ps. LXVII: 5; cf. Isa. XIX: 1), an expression also applied to the god Aliyan Baal in the Phoenician mythology that we know from Ugaritic texts.[2] The divine or at least transcendent character of the Son of

Man in Daniel also appears in the attribution of an eternal empire given him (Dan. VII: 14). Generally, the Book of Daniel (second century B.C.) is said to depend on Ezekiel (sixth century) and "the one who had the appearance of a man" of Ezek. I: 26 is presented as a counterpart of the first man created in God's image (Gen. I: 26). However, in describing his "Son of Man" as a divine being in human appearance, Daniel was thinking in paradoxical terms: old humanity derives from a man bearing divine likeness, the Messianic world rests on the divine glory concentrated in a human form.

According to the priestly tradition the "glory of the Lord" means the sensible presence of God, manifesting Himself in fire (Exod. XIII: 22) or dazzling light (XXXIV: 29). In Ezekiel this *glory* takes the form of one surrounded with splendor (cf. I: 26f.). Did the departure and return of the "glory of the Lord" described by the prophet (Ezek. XI: 22f.; XLIII: 1–9) prefigure the mysteries of the Ascension and *parousia* (cf. Acts I: 9ff.) which are also associated with the cloud of the theophanies (cf. Matt. XXIV: 30; I Thess. IV: 17)?

The Sapiential books also attributed to Wisdom a wish to appear in human form. Certainly, she dwells on high, borne on the *clouds* (Sir. XXIV: 4), and shares the throne of God (Wis. IX: 4), but she does not scorn to descend on earth, "in the holy Tent" (Sir. XXIV: 10) to find delight in the sons of men (Prov. VIII: 31). To Baruch's question about Wisdom, "Who has gone up to the heavens and taken her, or brought her down from the clouds?" (III: 29) the Gospel has an answer: "No one has ascended into heaven except him who has descended from heaven: *the Son of Man* who is in heaven" (John III: 13).

The Book of Henoch, of probably pre-Christian origin, collects a great variety of developments centered on this fundamental theme: the lot of the just and the wicked is linked to the eschatological role of *a Son of Man* who will judge the world and govern the just. The author of the Apocrypha also calls this Son of Man "Messiah," "Christ," "Anointed," "Just," "Chosen One," "Chosen of justice and faithfulness." The Lord of spirits (God) chose him, *kept him hidden*, and revealed him only to the saints and to the just (cf. Matt. XI: 25). The kings and the great will know him only on Judgment Day, which will mark the condemnation of the wicked and the inauguration of beatitude for the just:

> *And the righteous and elect shall be saved on that day,*
> *And they shall never thenceforward see the face*
>   *of the sinners and unrighteous.*
> *And the Lord of Spirits will abide over them,*
> *And with that Son of Man shall they eat*
> *And lie down and rise up for ever and ever.*
> *And the righteous and elect shall have risen from*
>   *the earth,*
> *And ceased to be of downcast countenance.*
> *And they shall have been clothed with garments*
>   *of glory,*
> *And these shall be the garments of life*
>   *from the Lord of Spirits:*
> *And your garments shall not grow old,*
> *Nor your glory pass away before the Lord of*
>   *Spirits.*   (Hen. LXII: 13–16.)[3]

The description of the Son of Man and his action in the *Book of Henoch* indeed illustrates one of the chief characteristics of the apocalyptic genre: the revelation of the divine mystery and of its *secrets*, containing God's plan for every creature and His saving design in all its amplitude. Such a revelation both rekindles hope and comforts in the face of trials; in that respect, the apocalypse has the same principal purpose as prophetic revelation: to show that earthly events, both small and great, do not depend on chance, but follow a pattern drawn up by God and by Him gradually fulfilled in the course of time. The great privilege of the just consists in this: these divine *secrets* were revealed to them with the knowledge of the Son of Man whose right it is to reveal "all the treasures of that which is hidden" (Hen. XLVI: 3; cf. Col. II: 3).[4]

The Son of Man is an individual figure who tends to become identified with *the heavenly community* which he governs. Well attested in Henoch, this characteristic is also found in Daniel: the Son of Man "received dominion, glory and kingship" (VII: 14); "The holy ones of the Most High shall receive the kingship, to possess it forever and ever" (VII: 18).[5] Jesus promised His disciples a similar preferment: "Do not be afraid, little flock, for it has pleased your Father to give you the kingdom" (Luke XII: 32). In Jewish thought it is possible for a collectivity to be personified, and to pass easily from the individual to the collective.[6] The notions of Son of Man and Servant adapt to this peculiarity which already distantly heralds the Christian reality of the Mystical Body in which without any admixture the prerogatives of the Head are somehow communicated to the members.

It is more difficult to answer the question, "Why is this heavenly being called *Son of Man*, an expression that usually means 'man' in Semitic languages (cf. Mark III: 28)?" The answer has been sought in those primitive speculations on a "first man" or divine prototype of humanity. In other *milieux* the concept of "the primordial soul" into which all other souls were believed to have been originally included, corresponds to that concept of "the primordial man." For Hindu religious speculation, primordial man is born again with every new age in the world. The biblical account (Gen. I: 26f.) rejects the mythological element in such speculations and describes the creation of the first man in God's image. As we shall see, this last concept is related to an important aspect of Pauline theology.

But *incarnation* is not contemplated for the Son of Man in Daniel and apocalyptic literature. That heavenly being is to *judge* the world, overcome the wicked, and reign forever with the upright; he belongs to a literary tradition that does not consider the idea of a Messiah who redeems the sinful world by his sacrifice. In Judaism this tendency to eliminate suffering from the role of the Messiah will become pronounced. An Aramaic commentary, the Targum, discovers the description of the glorious establishment of the Kingdom of Israel in the fourth Servant Song, and eliminates, at least in its written form, most of the statements on suffering. To avoid this deliberately tendentious type of exegesis and yet to affirm belief in a glorious Messiah, a rabbinic tradition of the same epoch will postulate the existence of *another* Messiah, the Messiah of Joseph or Ephraim, who would take on the role of an expiatory victim. Certain formal instances suggest a limited literary influence of the Servant Songs on the Context of Daniel's Son of Man. The *exaltation* of the Son of Man, for example, seems to prolong a current of thought that had inspired this passage: "See, my servant shall prosper, he shall be raised high and greatly exalted" (Isa. LII: 13).

JESUS, THE SON OF MAN

In His person, Jesus has united two missions: one the suffering of the Servant of the Lord, the other the glory of the Son of Man. This remarkable synthesis appears in several of Jesus' sayings: "For as the lightning when it lightens flashes from one end of the sky to the other, so will the Son of Man be in his day. But first he must suffer many things and be rejected by this generation" (Luke XVII: 24f.). "For the *Son of Man* also has not come to be served but *to serve, and to give his life as a ransom for many*" (Mark X: 45). The theology of John the Evangelist has recorded this double vocation of the Saviour in a series of enigmatic formulas that are intelligible to the believer. The Son of Man, come down from heaven upon earth, must return to heaven by passing through the cross (cf. III: 13). The "ascent" of the Son of Man upon the cross (VIII: 28; XII: 32) shall mark the hour of His glorification (XII: 23; XVII: 1); it shall constitute a decisive stage in His exaltation.[7] The Son of Man "lifted" upon the cross, like the brazen serpent (III: 14; cf. Num. XXI: 9), constitutes the salvific rallying sign (John XI: 51f.; XII: 32) that an Isaiah had foreseen under the figure of Mount Sion (II: 2), of the Davidic Messiah (XI: 10ff.), and of the ensign raised by God (XLIX: 22). Therefore, the *believer's glance* shall remain fixed on the Crucified for a long time (John XIX: 37; Luke XXIII: 49).

The particular appearance of the Son of Man was also drawn by Psalm VIII, which is certainly Messianic on several counts: the connection with the liturgy of the Feast of Tabernacles, the use by Jesus on Palm Sunday (Matt. XXI: 16), the citations of verse 7 by Paul (I Cor. XV: 27; Eph. I: 22) and by the author of the Epistle to the Hebrews (II: 6f.), to express and establish the Risen Christ's supremacy (cf. Phil. III: 21). In fact, *Son of Man* of the Psalm seems to designate the new man, the personified "Remnant" that presides at the Messianic inauguration:

O Lord, our Lord, how glorious is your name
  over all the earth!
You have exalted your majesty above the heavens.
Out of the mouths of babes and sucklings
you have fashioned praise because of your foes,
to silence the hostile and the vengeful.

When I behold your heavens, the work of your
  fingers,
the moon and the stars which you set in place—
What is man that you should be mindful of him,
or the son of man that you should care for him?

You have made him little less than the angels,
and crowned him with glory and honor.

> *You have given him rule over the works of your*
>   *hands,*
> *putting all things under his feet.*   (Ps. VIII.)

Other aspects of the Messianic scope of Psalm VIII are
linked with the Christological title "last Adam."

Jesus may also have called Himself "Son of Man" with
reference to the Book of Ezekiel, in which the title is
constantly used to designate the prophet (cf. II: 1–8). As a
matter of fact, Jesus the Son of Man presents Himself, like
Ezekiel (cf. XII: 6; XXIV: 24), as a *sign* for His generation
(Matt. XII: 39; XXIV: 30). For a certain time the prophet,
too, was burdened with the *sin* of the houses of Israel and
Juda (IV: 4ff.). Purification from sin is a central theme of
His preaching (cf. XVIII: 30f.): "For I have no pleasure in
the death of anyone who dies, says the Lord God. Return and
live!" (XVIII: 32; cf. Luke XIX: 10). The transformation
shall be the work of the Spirit (Ezek. XXXVI: 26); Ezekiel
received the power from God to release its strength: "Then
he said to me: Prophesy to the spirit, prophesy, son of man,
and say to the spirit: Thus says the Lord God: From the
four winds come, O spirit, and breathe into these slain that
they may come to life" (Ezek. XXXVII: 9). The Son of Man
and the Spirit work together for the renewal of creation.

The sign of Jonas (Matt. XII: 38ff.) also seems analogous
to the description of the Son of Man proper to the Fourth
Book of Esdras:

And it happened that after the seven days I saw a vision during
the night. And behold a violent wind arose on the sea so that it
stirred all its waves. And I saw that this wind sent something
like a man up from the depth of the sea, and I saw that *this man*
was flying even with the *clouds* of the sky. (XIII: 1–3.)

Perhaps Iranian in origin, this tradition makes the sea
the usual habitat of primordial man. But biblical tradition
places in the abyss the habitat of the powers of evil and
from it Daniel also has the four monsters climb in a context

(VII: 3) devoted precisely to the Son of Man (VII: 13). The submission of the waves illustrates Jesus' cosmic triumph (cf. Mark IV: 41; VI: 51); His resurrection marks Rahab's (Ps. LXXXVIII: 10–13), and Leviathan's defeat (Ps. LXXIII: 13–17; Apoc. XV: 2) even more than the passage of the Red Sea does (cf. I Cor. X: 1).

The *collective meaning* of Daniel's notion of the Son of Man is not missing from the title as Jesus used it Himself. Indeed in the Gospel texts it often recalls the intimate union of the Master and His disciples, of the Son of Man and His brothers on earth, of the Messiah and the community that He came to found. In Matthew we learn what the central aspect of the *judgment* confided to the Son of Man will be: "Amen I say to you, as long as you did it for one of these, the least of my brethren, you did it for me" (Matt. XXV: 40; cf. John XIII: 20). Luke has retained that saying of Jesus' which formulates the foundation of shared authority: "He who hears you, hears me, and he who rejects you, rejects me; and he who rejects me, rejects him who sent me" (Luke X: 16; cf. Matt. X: 40). The Johannine allegory of the vine (John XV: 1–6) is an attempt to describe the intimate, vital dependence of the Christian community on its Head. Already a pre-Christian, Greek version had suggested a parallelism between "the Son of Man" and "the vine" that is Israel:

> *Protect this* vineyard
> *which thy right hand hath planted,*
> *and this* son of man
> *whom thou hast made strong.*
> (Ps. LXXIX: 16, Greek.)

IN THE PAULINE WRITINGS

Although the title "Son of Man" is not found in St. Paul, the corresponding notion inspires several central texts in the Apostle's theology.[8] In the first place, there is this passage from the First Epistle to the Corinthians on the resurrection of the dead:

So also it is written, "The first man, Adam, became a living soul" [cf. Gen. II: 7]; the last Adam became a life-giving spirit. But it is not the spiritual that comes first, but the physical, and then the spiritual. The first man was of the earth, earthy; the second man is from heaven, heavenly. As was the earthy man, such also are the earthy; and as is the heavenly man, such also are the heavenly. Therefore, even as we have borne the likeness of the earthy, let us bear also the likeness of the heavenly. (XV: 44–59.)

Here Paul seems to want to propose a solution to an old problem: what relationship exists between the first man and the Son of Man? The fact of the first sin eliminated Adam as an explanation for the origin of the Son of Man, the ideal prototype of humanity. According to Philo, a Jewish philosopher and contemporary of Christ's, Genesis describes the creation of *two* "first men": one is the heavenly man created in God's image (Gen. I: 27), the other is sinning Adam, "formed out of the dust of the ground" (II: 7). This arbitrary speculation, however, is contradicted by Paul's teaching in I Cor. XV, where he evokes the figure of a first Adam, an earthy one, and of a *second Adam*, a heavenly one: *the true Son of Man*, the historical Jesus, become by His resurrection the "image of the Heavenly" in His body and soul, the exemplar and first fruit of all the risen.

This manner of calling Christ, "man" (I Cor. XV: 21, 47), to signify perhaps "Son of Man," is also found in another Pauline development that again contrasts the two works: the destructive one of Adam and the restoring one of the second Adam: "But not like the offense is the gift. For if by the offense of the one the many died, much more has the grace of God, and the gift in the grace of the one *man* Jesus Christ, abounded unto the many" (Rom. V: 15).

A passage from the hymn to Christ in the Epistle to the Philippians belongs, it seems, to a similar context:

Have this mind in you which was also in Christ Jesus, who though he was by nature God, did not consider being equal to God a thing to be clung to, but emptied himself, taking the nature of a slave and being made like unto men. And appearing in the form of man, he humbled himself, becoming obedient to death, even to death on a cross (II: 5–8).

The very Pauline idea that Christ is *the image of God* (cf. Col. I: 15; II Cor. IV: 4) that is, of the Father (cf. Rom. VIII: 29) is implied here. In contrast to Adam, who succumbed to the temptation of wanting to be like God (Gen. III: 5) and thus lost his resemblance to Him, Jesus, the "heavenly man," did not claim, at His first coming, the divine honors due to His rank, but obediently assumed the role of Servant, and through His sacrifice brought back to humanity that lost image. Through this faithfulness and abasement He merited for His entire incarnate being the divine title of Lord, with the functional role of universal sovereign (cf. Phil. II: 9–11). In the sacrificial passing of Jesus' humanity to God, in His death and resurrection, a new humanity began to exist: "If then any man is in Christ, he is a new creature: the former things have passed away; behold, they are made new!" (II Cor. V: 17).

Constantly Jesus rejected the political role of the Messiah-King (cf. John VI: 15). Perhaps a trace of this refusal remains in His answer to the High Priest (cf. p. 33, n. 2). As a matter of fact, Matt. XXVI: 64 can be interpreted that way: "Thou hast said it. Nevertheless, I say to you, hereafter you shall see *the Son of Man* sitting at the right hand of the Power and coming upon the clouds of heaven." According to John He answers Pilate: "My kingdom is not of this world . . . my kingdom is not from here" (XVIII: 36). Jesus' saying on the destiny of the Son of Man (Matt. XXVI: 64) means before all else that His accusers and judges shall soon see the appearance of signs that will enable them to discern the true one destined to the glorious advancement described by Dan. VII: and Ps. CIX: 1 "Sit at my right hand till I make your enemies your footstool."

During His earthly career Jesus, the Son of Man, made the expiatory vocation of the Servant His own, and by His sacrifice restored to humanity the divine image that the betrayal of its earthly ancestor had stolen from it.[9] The Evangelists were very much interested in the question that Jesus asked the man born blind: "Dost thou believe in the Son of Man?" (John IX: 35). Perhaps the different New Testament tendencies, especially those of John, to "inaugurate" the eschatology are partly linked to the designation of Jesus as the Son of Man, a title that calls up a figure of the last times.

NOTES ON 24

[1] Apart from two *logia* (Mark II: 27; Matt. XII: 31f.), which could be ambiguous, the expression "Son of Man" in the Gospels always designates Jesus.

[2] Ugaritic literature was at its height from the fifteenth to the thirteenth centuries B.C. The biblical authors seem to have had at least a fragmentary knowledge of these mythological poems rediscovered in 1929 at Ras Shamra, site of the ancient city of Ugarit on the Syrian coast, opposite the tip of Cyprus. Parallels of Isa. XIV: 12–15 and XXVII: 1 appear in these ancient texts (cf. also Isa. VII: 1), and the *Danel* of Ezek. XIV: 14; XXVIII: 3 could have been a Phoenician character. Furthermore, in the Phoenician ritual there exists a sacrificial nomenclature similar on several counts to that of the Jews. These profane writings transmitted by popular tradition may have been used by the biblical authors as a "poetic source."

[3] As translated in R. H. Charles, *The Apocrypha and Pseudepigrapha of the Old Testament, in English,* vol. II (Oxford, 1913), pp. 228f.

[4] On the apocalyptic genre, cf. p. 229.

[5] Cf. J. Coppens–L. Dequeker, *Le Fils de l'homme et les Saints du Très-Haut en Daniel VII, dans les Apocryphes et dans le Nouveau Testament* (Bruges, 1961). The problem of the "Son of Man" is one which is today foremost in biblical interest, also among Catholic scholars. Cf. E. Dhanis, "De Filio hominis in Vetere Testamento et in judaismo," *Gregorianum* (1964), pp. 5–59; J. R. Scheifler, "El hijo del hombre en Daniel," *Estudios eclesiasticos,* 1960 (Miscelanea Fernandez), pp. 789–804. In my *Rédemption Sacrificielle,* pp. 256–301, will be found an elaborate exposition of the title "Son of Man" as applied to Jesus.

[6] Already in 1911 H. W. Robinson had used the expression "corporate personality," which some authors would now prefer to call "incorporating

personality" (cf. *Revue Thomiste* [1961], p. 15, n.). On the notion, see J. de Fraine, "Adam and Christ as corporate personalities," *Theology Digest* (1962), pp. 99–102.

⁷ "The Johannine Christ willingly uses words to whose natural meaning (the only one understood by the listeners) it is possible to add another one, supernatural or figurative; cf. II: 20 (Temple); III: 4 (rebirth); IV: 15 (living water); VI: 34 (living bread); VII: 3 (set out); VIII: 33 (slavery); XI: 12 (to awake); XII: 34 (to lift up); XIII: 9 (to wash); XIII: 36f. (set out); XIV: 22 (to manifest oneself). Hence a misunderstanding which supplies Christ with an opportunity to expound His teaching (cf. III: 11)" (*Bible de Jérusalem* on John II: 19).

⁸ About I Thess. I: 10, "to await from heaven Jesus, his Son," J. Dupont writes: "At least the question could be asked whether, in what he says about the *Son of God*, Paul is not transposing a theme that spoke of *Son of Man*" (*Revue Biblique*, 1962, p. 58, n. 32). To some authors it would seem that outside the Gospels the title "Son of God," in its transcendent meaning, replaced that of Son of Man, become obsolete. Cf. A. Gelin, art. "Messianisme," in *DBS*, vol. V, c. 1209; J. Coppens, *L'Attente du Messie*, p. 143.

⁹ On the figures of the "Servant" and of the "Son of Man" as applied to Jesus, see also C. Larcher, *L'actualité chrétienne de l'Ancien Testament, d'après le Nouveau Testament* (Paris, 1962), pp. 119–98.

25

THE FIRSTBORN

THE LAST ADAM

THE ALPHA AND THE OMEGA

THESE three titles have one thing in common—they define Christ as related to creation: first rank in the cosmos; transcendence; priority in time, and object of all the finality of created beings. The treatments that follow specify the proper contribution of each of the titles.

THE FIRSTBORN

According to the New Testament, Christ is the Firstborn introduced by God into the world (Heb. I: 6), the Firstborn of every creature (Col. I: 15; cf. Apoc. III: 14), the Firstborn of a multitude of brothers (Rom. VIII: 29), the Firstborn from among the dead (Col. I: 18; Apoc. I: 5). The title πρωτότοκος is linked with the Old Testament by several ties which show that in Jesus the true, *the new Israel* is represented and the awaited Messiah personified. With respect to the Christological "Son of God," we shall treat "divine filiation as an extra-Christian notion." Here let us restrict ourselves to the texts that directly relate to the theme of "firstborn."

The oldest text and the chief one, too, occurs in the context of the birth of the chosen people. God gives the following instruction to Moses: "So you shall say to Pharao: Thus says the Lord: Israel is my son, my *firstborn*" (Exod. IV: 22). This image must be interpreted by the language of

the Bible, which frequently states that a son is somehow one
who has been created by the father on whom he truly
depends. Two contexts are evoked in a passage from the
Deutero-Isaiah, one the Yahwist account of creation (Gen.
II: 7) and the other the Exodus account: "Yet, O Lord, you
are our father; we are the clay and you the potter: we are
the work of your hands" (Isa. LXIV: 7; cf. LXIII: 16).

In the major section of a long development called "the
book of consolation," Jeremiah expresses to the Israel of the
North the hope that the exiles will return from Assyria to
the restored kingdom of David. Does God not say: "I am a
father to Israel, Ephraim is my *firstborn*" (XXXI: 9)?
Much later, on the eve of the national uprising of the
Maccabees, Jesus ben Sira expressed his trust in God thus:
"Show mercy to the people called by your name: Israel, whom
you named your *firstborn*" (Sir. XXXVI: 11). In Jewish law,
the eldest son *of the father*, "first fruits of his vigor," holds
the birthright (cf. Gen. XXV: 31–34) and can claim a double
share of his father's estate (Deut. XXI: 17). Every time
Israel is described as "the inheritance" of the Lord (Deut.
XXXII: 9) that privilege is remembered. And every firstborn male of *the mother* belongs to the Lord, for God said
to Moses: "Consecrate to me every firstborn that opens the
womb among the Israelites" (Exod. XIII: 2). Linked to the
prodigy of the paschal night (Exod. XIII: 15), this prescrip-
tion explains the origin of another formulation of Israel's
prerogatives: "For you are a people sacred to the Lord, your
God; he has chosen you from all the nations on the face of
the earth" (Deut. VII: 6).

With these metaphorical applications of the title "firstborn" to Israel vanished the idea of a priority over other
sons; the accent falls rather on *divine predilection*. The
Psalms of Solomon (apocrypha of the first century B.C.) tend
to identify "eldest son" and "only son" (XIII: 8; XVIII: 4).
This identity will be realized at the birth of the most famous
of the sons born of women, in Jesus: "And she brought forth

her firstborn son" (Luke II: 7). In the Fourth Book of Esdras (first century A.D.) the term "firstborn" is considered as synonymous with "only," "chosen," "privileged": "And we, thy people, whom thou hast called thy *firstborn*, thy only-begotten, thy beloved, we are given up into their hands" (VI: 58).

On several occasions God promises to make Israel once again superior (*elyôn*) to all nations, if it remains faithful to Him (Deut. XXVI: 19; XXVIII: 1). The divine name *elyôn*, the Most High, then in current use (cf. Ps. XLV: 5; LXXXII: 19) is applied once to the Messianic king in connection with the title "firstborn":

> *My faithfulness and my kindness shall be with him,*
> *and through my name shall his horn be exalted.*
> *I will set his hand upon the sea,*
> *his right hand upon the rivers.*
> *He shall say of me, "You are my father,*
> *my God, the Rock, my savior".*
> *And I will make him the firstborn,*
> *highest of the kings of the earth.*
> *Forever I will maintain my kindness toward him,*
> *and my covenant with him stands firm.*
> *I will make his posterity endure forever*
> *and his throne as the days of heaven.*
>
> (Ps. LXXXVIII: 25–30.)

*

*   *

Applied to Christ, the epithet "firstborn" is obviously filled with a meaning that the Old Testament hardly touched on. One such use of the title occurs twice in a "hymn to Christ," perhaps anterior even to the Epistle to the Colossians that records it:[1]

> *He is the image of the invisible God,*
> *the firstborn of every creature.*

For in him were created all things,
in the heavens and on the earth,
things visible and invisible,
whether Thrones or Dominations,
  or Principalities, or Powers;
all things have been created through and unto him,

And he is before all creatures,
  and in him all things hold together.
Again, he is the head of the body, the Church;

He is the beginning,
the firstborn *from the dead,*
that in all things he may have the first place.
For it has pleased God the Father
  that in him all his fullness should dwell,
and that through him he should
  reconcile to himself all things,
whether on the earth or in the heavens,
making peace through the blood of his cross.
                                    (Col. I: 15–20.)

This hymn honoring Christ, who is not named, is easily separated from its context: before and after the hymn Paul is addressing small groups of people determined by the pronouns "you" and "we." In their original meaning, mainly preserved, these strophes lauded Christ as "firstborn of every creature" and "firstborn from the dead." The literary structure of the hymn has been examined at the beginning of the section devoted to Christ "Head of the Body."

The title "Image of God" (Col. I: 15) defines the Son's relation to the Father; in apposition to that title, "firstborn of every creature" expresses the absolute pre-eminence of Christ over all creation. The typically Pauline conception, "Christ is the new Adam," reveals the context of the verse (Col. I: 15): created in God's image (Gen. I: 26f.), the first man received power to dominate inferior creatures (Gen. I:

28); the perfect image of God, Christ is "firstborn of every creature" because all things in heaven and on earth were created in Him (Col. I: 16).

In Christ, through Him and for Him, Paul says, everything was created; everything subsists in Him, who is before all things (Col. I: 15–17). These affirmations bring out the various aspects of a central truth: the absolute transcendence of Christ, who enjoys priority and supremacy of dignity over creatures. These statements suit "the *pre-existing* Christ but always considered in the unique historic person of the Son of God made man. It is that incarnate, concrete being who is the Image of God in so far as He reflects the image of the invisible God in a visible human nature (cf. Rom. VIII: 29), and it is He who can be called a creature, but firstborn in the order of creation, with a primacy of excellence and cause even more than of time" (*BJ*). St. Thomas Aquinas answers *yes* to the question, "Can we say that Christ as man is a creature?" But on the other hand we could not say that "Christ as *this* man is a creature," for then the person of Christ would be envisaged and no longer His nature. Nevertheless, the hymn clearly places Christ outside the series of creatures.[2]

A certain theory, dating back to Philo, made the *Logos* an intermediary inferior to God and an archetype of created things. To dispel any misunderstanding the hymn insists on the absolute transcendence and creative power of Christ. So too, if His supremacy over the different categories of angels is especially revealed, it is certainly to refute the false teachers of Colossae, who grossly exaggerated the role of these spiritual powers. The commentators interpret the statement "In him all things hold together" (v. 17) thus: For all beings Christ is a principle of cohesion and harmony; He makes a "cosmos," "an ordered universe" of the created world by giving to it a meaning and a value, by directing it to an end.[3]

The second strophe presents Christ as "firstborn from the dead," a somewhat unfamiliar formula meaning "first in the order of the resurrection of the dead." The creative Word and redeeming Jesus are one single person. This truth of the faith is clearly intended by the parallelism of the two strophes and by the attribution to the same subject of two distinctive, but closely linked, works: Creation and redemption. Besides, Creation was only a prelude to salvation history. In the Old Testament, deliverance from Egypt constitutes a far more important theme than Creation does. The Hebrews knew God first as Redeemer, then as Creator.

The description of Christ as "the firstborn from the dead" evokes the drama of death's presence in the world He created, but does not explain it. He too died, but He was the first to conquer death and as "prince of the risen" cleared the way toward an endless life: "Christ has risen from the dead, the first-fruits of those who have fallen asleep. . . . For as in Adam all die, so in Christ all will be made to live. But each in his own turn, Christ as first-fruits, then they who are Christ's, who have believed, at his coming" (I Cor. XV: 20–23). In the Epistle to the Romans St. Paul argues in the same way: in putting on us the image of Christ, body and soul, through grace and resurrection, God realized His saving plan: "For those whom he has foreknown he has also predestined to become conformed to the image of his Son, that he should be the firstborn among many brethren" (Rom. VIII: 29).

The Apocalypse also refers to the mystery of the resurrection in a text inspired by Psalm LXXXVIII cited above. There Jesus Christ is called "the faithful witness, *the first-born of the dead*, and the ruler of the kings of earth" (I: 5). In the foreground here is the sovereignty of Christ over "the dead," over "the Church of the firstborn ('εκκλησία πρωτοτόκων) who are enrolled in the heavens" (Heb. XII: 23).

THE LAST ADAM

In the First Epistle to the Corinthians we read: "the last Adam became a life-giving spirit" (XV: 45). No such express mention of the title "last Adam" is made elsewhere; the antithesis *Adam-Christ*, however, is a Pauline notion well known from Rom. V: 12–21. Before examining these texts, several aspects of a theme that Paul particularly stressed ought to be recalled: in the work of Christ a *new* humanity is *created*.

*

*   *

The symbolism of the garment is frequently used. "Put off the old man . . . put on the new man, which has been created according to God in justice and holiness of truth" (Eph. IV: 22f.). In Colossians Paul had likewise written:

Strip off the old man with his deeds and put on the new, one that is being renewed unto perfect knowledge "according to the image of his Creator." Here there is not "Gentile and Jew," "circumcised and uncircumcised," "barbarian and Scythian," "slave and freemen": but Christ is all things and in all. (III: 9–11.)

In the new order, distinctions of race, religion, culture, and social class, which had divided mankind since the Fall, disappear. The unity is restored in Christ (*BJ*). Such insistence on unity (cf. Gal. III: 28) is certainly reminiscent of mankind's state before the division brought by sin and symbolized by the failure of Babel (Gen. XI: 1–9). Furthermore, these two Pauline texts are interwoven with allusions that contrast the first and the last Adam. In the foreground is Adam's creation in the image of God. Several Church Fathers even go so far as to identify "the garments of skin" that clothed Adam after his sin (Gen. III: 21; cf. III: 7) with the old garment that the baptized strips off to follow Christ.

With sin Adam put on mortality; by His sacrificial death

Christ put aside His mortal, passible flesh which was like sinful flesh (VIII: 3). Brilliantly the Resurrection showed the Spirit's irruption into His entire being, and so Christ "was justified in the Spirit" (I Tim. III: 16). Once Jesus received circumcision as a symbol of that complete laying down of the fleshly body that His death and resurrection were to accomplish. At the Transfiguration, Jesus' garments become "white as snow," in a kind of anticipation of the glorious state of the risen. The white garment worn by the newly baptized also symbolizes the return to original justice and the paradisal state through incorporation to the new Adam: "All you who have been baptized into Christ, have put on Christ . . . you are all one in Christ Jesus" (Gal. III: 27f.). This "putting on" has nothing to do with Lutheran forensic justification; it does express a complete renewal of one's interior being.

*

* *

Let us now examine the central theological theme of the title "Last Adam": the restoration of the world wrought by Christ was *a new creative act*; regenerated humanity is a new creation. In this connection Père Benoit says felicitously: "Christ's humanity, His body and soul is like the crucible in which God recast His work, like the clay with which He has remoulded His new creature."[4] According to Col. I: 20, Christ's body was the place of reconciliation: "By sending his Son in the likeness of sinful flesh as a sin-offering, he has condemned sin in the flesh" (Rom. VIII: 3); "For our sakes he [God] made him to be sin [sacrifice for sin] who knew nothing of sin, so that in him we might become the justice of God" (II Cor. V: 21). The flesh of Christ, considered as mortal, bore the stamp of sin and represented the old humanity that will be destroyed by the sacrificial death of Jesus, and replaced in the Resurrection, by the new humanity. We, too, must "put on the new man," St. Paul writes, "which has been created according to God in justice and holiness of truth" (Eph. IV: 24; cf. Col. III: 9f.). At the end of the Epistle to the Galatians he traced "in large letters" this teaching: "For in Christ Jesus neither circumcision nor uncircumcision but a new creation is of any account" (Gal. VI: 15). About the same time he wrote to the Corinthians: "If then any man is in Christ, he is a new creature: the former things have passed away; behold, they are made new!" (II Cor. V: 17).

According to II Pet. III: 13 (cf. Apoc. XXI: 1ff.), a cosmic transformation will accompany man's renovation: "We look for new heavens and a new earth, according to his promises, wherein dwells justice" (cf. Isa. LXV: 17; LXVI: 22). The epithet "new" (καινός) belongs to the technical vocabulary of New Testament eschatology, and characterizes the condition of the last times in a multitude of expressions: new teaching (Mark I: 27), new wine (Mark II: 22; XIV: 25), new garment (Luke V: 36), new covenant (Mark XIV: 24; II Cor. III: 6), new commandment (John XIII: 34), new dough (I Cor. V: 7), newness of life (Rom. VI: 4), newness of spirit (Rom. VII: 6), new name (Apoc. II: 17), new canticle (Apoc. V: 9), new Jerusalem (Apoc. XXI: 2).

*

* *

The title "Last Adam" (I Cor. XV: 45) is intimately connected to these themes which present *the Messianic economy* as the creation of a new humanity. Let us restore the title to its context:

If there is a natural body, there is also a spiritual body. So also it is written, "The first man, Adam, became a living soul; the last Adam became a life-giving spirit. But it is not the spiritual that comes first, but the physical, and then the spiritual. The first man was of the earth, earthy; the second man is from heaven, heavenly. As was the earthy man, such also are the earthy; and as is the heavenly man, such also are the heavenly. Therefore, even as we have borne the likeness of the earthy, let us bear also the likeness of the heavenly. (I Cor. XV: 44–49.)

As we have already explained with regard to the title "Son of Man," Paul associates two figures: that of the "Last Adam," and that of the "Second Man," the heavenly one, the Son of Man. Let us insist here on the parallelism that opposes, as does Rom. V: 12–21, the two leaders, Adam and Christ: the first transmits his earthly, corruptible life to his descendants; the second powerfully vivifies His spiritual posterity. Our body must pass from the carnal state to the "spiritual" state; like Adam in the former state, it puts on, in the latter one, the state of the Risen Christ, "a life-giving spirit" (v. 45; cf. Rom. I: 4).

The Apostle focuses his attention on the body, for he treats of the resurrection in that section of the Epistle. He had said: "What is sown a natural body rises a spiritual body" (I Cor. XV: 44). Some authors prefer the translation "*supernatural* body," an expression that stresses more clearly the contrast with "natural body." The meaning is, however, clear and it has been rendered carefully (*BJ*): from "natural" or "psychic," the body becomes "pneumatic," incorruptible, immortal (I Cor. XV: 53), glorious (I Cor. XV: 43), freed from the laws of earthly matter (John XX: 19, 26) and from its appearances (Luke XXIV: 16).

*

* *

Redacted shortly after the First Epistle, the Epistle to the Romans takes up the Adamic typology in a development (Rom. V: 12–21) whose general meaning is obvious: the treacherous work of the first Adam has been more than abundantly repaired by the new head of the human race, Jesus Christ. In Genesis the name Adam designates man

according to a dual aspect: collective (II: 7) and individual
(IV: 25). The "representative" viewpoint is in the foreground of Paul's treatment but this is not the whole meaning, for the doctrine of original sin that underlies the
entire passage, implies the descendance of all men from a
single ancestor (cf. Acts XVII: 26; I Cor. XV: 21f.).

The reasoning that makes Adam the "type" of Christ, in
Rom. V: 12–21, has been interpreted thus: "To us it seems
rather that redemption is universal because sin had affected
all men. But for Paul, the new life of participation in
Christ's life is prior in God's intention. Since the life of
Christ was to affect the whole of the human race, the divine
plan made it necessary that one man should likewise be the
initiator of the state of sin, and that sin should spread to all
men because of him. Thus, in God's mind, there is a perfect
balance between the fall of man and his salvation. Adam is
then the 'type' of Christ (v. 14) and the fall is modelled on
salvation."[5]

For St. Paul Christ is the "Image of the Invisible God"
(Col. I: 15), "the Last Adam" and the "Heavenly Man"
(I Cor. XV: 45–47). Adam was then "the figure [τύπος] of
him who was to come" (Rom. V: 14); the imperfect
heralded the perfect. In creating Adam, God already had
Jesus Christ in sight, "the Firstborn of every creature." The
reign of death announces the reign of life. In God's plan the
solidarity of the redeemed in "the grace of the one man,
Jesus Christ" was to follow solidarity in evil with Adam
(Rom. V: 15). Death as mentioned throughout the contrast,
is not seen in its temporal aspect alone but also precisely as
a "privation of salvation," as a prelude to eternal death
(cf. Wis. II: 24), just as the life brought by Christ is seen as
eternal life (Rom. V: 17, 21). With original sin the first
Adam transmitted the evil of division to his descendants;
according to the "prophecy" of the high priest, the last
Adam was to die "to gather into one the children who were
scattered abroad" (John XI: 52).[6]

As we have seen in the treatment of the title "Prophet," the Gospel of Luke often presents Jesus as a new Elias. On the other hand, we know how persistently the third Evangelist offers Jesus as the model of Christians, as the first Christian: the one who teaches how to pray (Luke XI: 1f.), who Himself prays (V: 16; VI: 12), on His knees (XXII: 41; cf. Acts VII: 60); the one who forgives His enemies before His sacrifice (Luke XXIII: 34), as He had exhorted His disciples to do (Matt. V: 23f.) and as Stephen did (Acts VII: 60); especially the one who receives the Holy Spirit in the course of prayer (Luke III: 21f.; cf. Acts IV: 31).

The Pauline influence probably appears in the course of the genealogy that retraces Jesus' ancestors back to Adam (Luke III: 38), the head of humanity according to the flesh. This genealogy is immediately followed in Luke by an episode which seems to have ties with the figure of the first man, at least in Mark's account of it. Certainly, the *temptation in the desert* (Mark I: 12f.) clearly shows that in Jesus certain aspects of the religious experience of the chosen people, or of Moses himself, are reproduced (cf. Deut. VIII: 2; IX: 9; XXXIV: 1).[7] But allusions to Adam, who was also tempted by the devil, abound. Furthermore, there is in the temptation account a tendency found in Isaiah's Messianic prophecies (cf. XI: 6–9; LXV: 25); the description of the Messianic climate draws its features from paradisal themes: Jesus lives at peace with wild beasts (Mark I: 13; Hos. II: 20) and is served by angels.[8]

That original subjection of the inferior world to man, who was, in turn, perfectly submissive to God, reappears in Jesus' sovereignty over material creation: He walks on the waters (Mark VI: 45–52), as the Spirit hovered over the primitive abyss at the first creation (Gen. I: 2); He commands the turbulent sea (Mark IV: 41), imposing restrictions (cf. Gen. I: 9) and boundaries on it (cf. Job. XXXVIII: 8–11), clothed with power like God, whom the Psalmist praises: "You rule over the surging of the sea; you still the swelling of its waves" (Ps. LXXXVIII: 10). The disciples of the kingdom will also participate in that primordial mastery that preceded the fall and the dispersion of Babel:

And these signs shall attend those who believe: in my name they shall cast out devils; they shall speak in new tongues; they shall take up serpents; and if they drink any deadly thing, it shall not hurt them; they shall lay hands upon the sick and they shall get well. (Mark XVI: 17f.)

The power and the glory of the last Adam shall invade the entire kingdom. Conquered by Satan, the first is succeeded by a new head of humanity, the last Adam who had conquered the devil already on the mount of temptation, but especially at His Passion, which in Luke marks Satan's return (IV: 13; XXII: 3) and in John, his defeat (XII: 31).

Treating the title "Son of Man," we have indicated the Messianic character of Psalm VIII and noted the citations from it in the New Testament. That of the Epistle to the Ephesians deserves special attention in discussing the theological context related to the "Last Adam." Proclaiming the triumph and supremacy of Christ, Paul continues: "*And all things he made subject under his feet*" (Ps. VIII: 7), and "him he gave as head over all the Church, which indeed is his body, the completion of him who fills all with all" (Eph. I: 22f.). Brief as it is, the citation belongs to a text which refers to passages in Genesis devoted to the primitive couple. Just as Eve, taken from and "built" for Adam (Gen. II: 22), assures the first man of a descendance often compared to a building (cf. II Sam. VII: 11; Ps. LXXXVIII: 5), so too the Church, spouse of the last Adam (cf. Apoc. XXI: 2, 9), will be the collective personality issued from Christ that will constitute the grandiose edifice of the Messianic community (cf. Eph. V: 21–33), the central hearth from which the royalty of Christ Lord will extend over all mankind (also see the title "Bridegroom").

This conception of Paul's prolongs and refines the prophet's tendency to present the Messiah as a new Adam, king of a renewed creation (Isa. XI: 1–9), Son of Man, head of the saintly people of the Most High, to whom empire and domination are given (Dan. VII). The double typology, paradisal and Adamic, was gradually reduced to a single reality, the beatific person of Jesus, as it appears in the promise to the good thief: "Amen I say to thee, this day thou shalt be with me in paradise" (Luke XXIII: 43; cf. Phil. I: 23).

THE ALPHA AND THE OMEGA

The Apocalypse applies this title—composed of the first and last letter of the Greek alphabet—to God and to Christ to express in metaphor the divine infinity that is theirs. The title, however, probably does not come from Hellenic language, but rather is the result of a Jewish, rabbinic procedure transposed into Greek: the sign of the glorious presence, of the *schekinah*, was the syllable *aleph-tau*, the extreme letters of the Hebrew alphabet; by inserting *mem*, the word for "solidity" or "truth," the chief attribute of God, was obtained. Thus, the three phases of the infinite "duration"—beginning, middle, end—are represented.

Let us note in passing that the sign of the cross traced on Christian foreheads in ancient times was related to the mystery of Calvary only later on; in the beginning, it seemed to mean belonging to God, whose holy name (cf. Apoc. XXII: 4) was expressed by the *tau*, Ezekiel's sign (IX: 4), which the Essenes wore on their foreheads and which, in the time of Christ, was represented by the sign + or the sign ×. It was readily understood that this was also the sign of the Lord or the glorified Christ (cf. Apoc. XIV: 1) whose divinity was proclaimed. This conviction could have influenced Luke's formulation: "And he who does not *carry* his cross and follow me, cannot be my disciple" (XIV: 27; cf. Matt. X: 38). In Greek-speaking communities not familiar with Hebrew symbols, the sign of the cross was early associated with the glorious instrument of our redemption.[9]

In the oracles of the Deutero-Isaiah, *God* states in equivalent terms more than once that He is *the Alpha and the Omega*: "I, the Lord, am the first, and with the last I will also be" (XLI: 4); "I am the first and the last" (XLIV: 6). It is not surprising, then, to read in the Apocalypse: "I am the Alpha and the Omega, the beginning and the end, says the Lord God, 'who is and who was and who is coming, the Almighty" (I: 8). "It is done! I am the Alpha and the Omega, the beginning and the end" (XXI: 6). St. Paul had said it differently: "For from him and through him are all things." (Rom. XI: 36.)

The application of the title *Alpha and Omega* to Christ conforms to the New Testament principle verified on many occasions: those divine attributes that are not proper to the Father are applicable to Christ. The glorious Christ of the Apocalypse defines His divine being and authenticates His power as a judge by declaring "I am the Alpha and the Omega, the first and the last, the beginning and the end" (XXII: 13). Earlier, the Son of Man had attributed life to Himself in a way proper to God, in this saying addressed to the Seer: "Do not be afraid; I am the First and the Last, and *he who lives*" (Apoc. I: 17). Further on, the expression is used again in about the same sense: "And to the angel of the church at Smyrna write: Thus says the First and the Last, who was dead and is alive" (II: 8). Applied to Christ (or to God), the title *Alpha and Omega* affirms that He is eternal and immortal, the beginning and end of all things. In a polemic against the idols, St. Paul has formulated a short profession of faith that adequately defines the content of the title that we have just examined: "For us there is only one God, the Father, from whom are all things, and we unto him; and one Lord, Jesus Christ, through whom are all things, and we through him" (I Cor. VIII: 6).

NOTES ON 25

[1] L. Cerfaux observes: "Paul is here influenced by the style of the hymn writers, but we would not go so far as to say that in this letter he has copied a hymn known to the Colossians. Following one or more models, he composes what he has to say according to a set style, and in this case this may even be the same as expounding or building upon an underlying composition" (*Christ in the Theology of Saint Paul*, p. 398).

[2] Why does Paul seem to include Christ among the creatures although He proclaims His transcendence? The answer is given by Paul himself when he says that "in Him all things were created," which seems to mean that He is the exemplary cause in which God contemplated as in a mirror the universe to be created. That interpretation is confirmed by the teaching of Proverbs, Job and Ecclesiasticus concerning the association of Wisdom with the act of creation. Cf. A. Feuillet, "La Création de l'Univers *dans le Christ* d'après l'Épitre aux Colossiens," *NTS*, vol. XII (1965–66), pp. 1–9. See also below, the treatment of Jesus, Wisdom of God.

[3] See J. Huby, *Saint Paul: Les Épîtres de la Captivité*, p. 42. The author writes in a note: "Let us only recall to mind that, as an answer to the Arians who were misusing this text to make a creature of the Son of God, several Greek Fathers, such as St. Athanasius, St. Gregory of Nyssa, St. Cyril of Alexandria, applied the title "firstborn of every creature" to the Incarnate Word, considered as the beginning of the new, spiritual creation inaugurated by the Gospel. In open disagreement with the immediate context, their interpretation is abandoned today" (p. 39).

[4] P. Benoit, in *Lumière et Vie*, no. 31, p. 71. The themes of "new creature" and "new birth" are treated in *Évangile*, nos. 41, 43. On Christ the last Adam see also J. Daniélou, *From Shadows to Reality*, pp. 11–68. On "the new Adam and the Church," cf. L. Ligier, *Péché d'Adam et péché du monde*, vol. II, pp. 335–46. In *Dieu et l'homme selon le Nouveau Testament*, C. Spicq distinguishes "Adamic humanity" and "Christian humanity," composed of "two types of man represented by and in some way condensed in their respective ancestors: Adam and Christ" (p. 206). "The Christian is a new man precisely because he resembles Christ who by the Father's will became the exemplar and type of the regenerated man" (p. 193). On the rabbinic idea of Adam's shining garment and on connected themes, cf. *idem*, p. 192, n. 4. In Judaism the Messianic hope was often expressed in terms related to the lost Paradise (cf. Le Déaut, *La Nuit pascale*, pp. 117ff.).

[5] L. Cerfaux, *Christ in the Theology of Saint Paul*, p. 231. The controversial Rom. V: 12 is thus translated by Lyonnet in *BJ*: "Therefore as through one man sin entered into the world and through sin death, and thus death has passed unto all men *because of the fact* that all have sinned. . . ." By reading *in quo omnes peccaverunt*, "in whom [Adam] all have sinned," the *Vulgate* discovers an explicit, textual affirmation of the existence of original sin. Recent exegesis, however, denies that there is such an explicit affirmation, but hesitates in adopting a formulation. Cerfaux still follows, in a way, the old Latin interpretation by translating "because of him through whom all sinned." Those authors who interpret *omnes peccaverunt* as referring to personal, individual sins, do not deny that original sin is at least implicitly involved in the affirmation, since these sins ratified the Fall consciously. See J. Huby–S. Lyonnet, *Saint Paul: Épître aux Romains* (Paris, 1957), pp. 521–57. Also L. Ligier, *op. cit.*, vol. II, pp. 266–89, where naturally the

author insists on common culpability, the state of sin, and the universality of death that flows from sin. Cf. also J. Cambier, "Péchés des hommes et Péché d'Adam en Rom. V: 12", *NTS* (April, 1965), pp. 217–55; S. Lyonnet, "Original sin and Romans V: 12," *Theology Digest* (1957), pp. 54–57. J. Bonsirven observed that "in St. Paul original sin plays only an *episodic role*; when the requirements of the parallelism between Christ and Adam disappear, it is no longer mentioned" (*L'Évangile de Paul*, p. 114). On Sin as a power personified, cf. my *Rédemption Sacrificielle*, pp. 372ff.

[6] Rabbinic tradition often attributed a prophetic character to the role of the High Priest (cf. E. Bammel, in *Th. Lit. Zeitung*, 1954, pp. 351–6). Compare Exod. XXVIII: 30; Lev. VIII: 8; Ezra II: 63; Neh. VII: 65.

[7] As the Lord was tempted after His Baptism, so too the Christians, so too the Hebrews after crossing the Red Sea (cf. I Cor. X: 1–13, and J. Dupont, "Les tentations de Jésus dans le récit de Luc," in *Sc. Eccl.*, 1962, p. 27, n.). In this article Dupont also examines the characteristics that link Luke's account of the temptation to the drama of the Passion. On Matthew's account of the Temptation (Matt. IV: 1–11), cf. this same author's treatment in *Assemblées du Seigneur*, no. 26 (St. Andrew's Abbey, Bruges), pp. 37–53.

[8] According to the Talmud of Babylon, *the angels used to serve Adam* in the garden of Eden (cf. Sanh. 59b; Soncino ed., vol. I, p. 405).

[9] Cf. J. Daniélou, "The Taw Sign," in *Primitive Christian Symbols*, pp. 136–45; *Théologie du Judéo-Christianisme*, vol. I, pp. 206f.

26

THE JUDGE

IN the discourse that he delivered in Cornelius' home Peter recalled that the mission received by the Apostles from God was to attest that Christ is *"appointed by God to be judge of the living and the dead"* (Acts X: 42). The exercise of judgment is so central among the functions of the *Son of Man*, that Christ affirms of Himself: the Father "granted him power to render judgment because he is Son of Man" (John V: 27). Therefore, it is ideal to examine the title of Judge shortly after that of Son of Man.

THE IDEA OF JUDGMENT

Numerous biblical texts understand "judgment" as *divine intervention in history*: "Yet the Lord is waiting to *show you favor*, and he rises to pity you; for the Lord is a *God of justice;* blessed are all who wait for him!" (Isa. XXX: 18). An ancient tradition is particularly concerned with presenting God as judge of Israel. The Decalogue furnishes the occasion:

You shall not bow down before them (idols) or worship them. For I, the Lord, your God, am a jealous God, inflicting punishment for their father's wickedness on the children of those who hate me, down to the third and fourth generation but bestowing mercy down to the thousandth generation, on the children of those who love me and keep my commandments.

(Exod. XX: 5f.)

For it is especially in connection with the Covenant that Israel is submitted to judgment. Infidelity, then, could entail the annihilation of the people with the exception of the "Remnant" (Deut. IV: 26f.). Restrained punishment is not, however, excluded: it affects rebellious groups (cf. Num. XIV: 37) or individuals guilty of infractions of the Law (Gen. XXXVIII: 9; Lev. XXIV: 11–14). The pagan peoples are reproached especially for excessive pride in the exercise of their role as God's scourges in chastising Israel (cf. Judg. III: 7–11). The miraculous deliverance from Egyptian oppression will remain the typical event illustrating the double effect of an historic judgment of God: victory for Israel, ruin for its enemies (Exod. VII: 4). The first chapters of Genesis bring the idea of judgment back to the origins of humanity and thus universalize it. In Adam, God judges all men and allows them to glimpse salvation. The Deluge too is a judgment that chastises the whole of humanity and saves a "Remnant," in the person of Noah and his family.

Even more than the Law, *prophetic literature* exploits the idea of judgment, calling the time of judgment "the day of the Lord" or "that day": day of wrath (Zeph. I: 18), of vengeance (Isa. XXXIV: 8), of visitation (Hos. IX: 7; Jer. VI: 15), which is accompanied by darkness (Joel II: 2), anguish (Hab. III: 16), and distress (Neh. I: 7). In its popular sense, the day of the Lord was a day of crisis, when Yahweh would judge the enemies of Israel and save His people. However, for the prophets, the expression may also mean a day of chastisement for Israel. Amos reminds Israel that God did not commit Himself to saving an unfaithful people:

> *Woe to those who yearn for the day of the Lord!*
> *What will this day of the Lord mean for You?*
> *Darkness and not light!*
> *As if a man were to flee from a lion,*
> *and a bear should meet him;*

*Or as if on entering his house
he were to rest his hand against the wall,
and a snake should bite him.
Will not the day of the Lord be darkness
    and not light,
gloom without any brightness?*   (V: 18ff.)

In the role that they play as "conscience of their times" the prophets reproach Israel especially for its apostasy (Amos II), its prostitution with strange gods (Hos. II), the fundamental rift that calls this collective ruin: the catastrophe of 587. Earlier, Amos had used for the first time the expression "the day of the Lord" (V: 18) and announced that God was going to chastise Israel with the Assyrian invasion, a punishment especially deserved for those great riches that bore testimony to the exploitation of the poor (ch. VI). The malice of men can ruin the work of God: "What I have built, I am tearing down; what I have planted, I am uprooting" (Jer. XLV: 4). "The sword, famine and pestilence" represent the chief scourges of God; their mention hovers over the oracles of Jeremiah like a refrain (cf. XIV: 12; XXI: 9). The Lord ravages His own vineyard (Ez. XIX: 10–14).

Although they are pronounced in an absolute manner, the threats remain conditional (Book of Jonas): "But if that nation which I have threatened turns from its evil, I also repent of the evil which I have threatened to do" (Jer. XVIII: 8). The conception of the "Remnant" itself (see the title "Saviour") answered the theological necessity of assuring the transition between the inevitable misfortune and the final re-establishment. Furthermore, another form of judgment is going to save Israel: the restitution of its primitive state. The idea pervades Deutero-Isaiah with the theme of redemption (ge'ullâh). Yahweh said to Israel: "Fear not, I have redeemed you; I have called you by name: you are mine" (Isa. XLIII: 1). Even the "nations" are included in the salvific perspective: the Servant is deputed to them with his gospel of law (Isa. XLII: 1; XLIX: 6).

From national restoration the next step was to *the final re-establishment of all things*, the central point of the eschatological judgment.

The clarifications given by Jeremiah (XXXI: 29), Ezekiel (XIV: 12–23), and Deuteronomy (XXIV: 16) on individual responsibility (compare Exod. XX: 5) hastened the development of doctrines related to *personal judgment* and individual retribution. More interested in individuals than in groups, wisdom excels in that respect: "In the path of justice there is life, but the abominable way leads to death" (Prov. XII: 28). Several Psalms "beatify" the man who has chosen good (I: 1; CXI: 1). As clay in the potter's hand, men are in the hand of their Creator, who deals with them according to His justice (Sir. XXXIII: 13). Once Job had criticized current theories on evil; now Qoheleth undertakes questioning the popular conscience on good. His scepticism will favor belief in future retribution. On the subject of liberties to be permitted he himself forewarns the young man: "Yet understand that as regards all this God will bring you to judgment" (Qoh. XI: 9). Sapiential reflection on the inequality of conditions on earth also prepared the terrain for the clear formulation of the truth on the resurrection (see above).

In the Apocalypse the judgment of God receives special treatment. Expressing the reaction of the faith under the pagan persecution, these books question some ancient figure to whom a vision is thought to have revealed the secret key of history. The interplay of opposing forces does not concern only Israel, but *the whole world*, in which God wants to inaugurate his reign. Hostile empires incarnate *organized evil* and human history represents a visible repercussion of the intemporal struggle between God and Satan. Strict dualism is avoided, for God always remains master of the situation; He will show it at the end of history, at the advent of the true "day of the Lord." In this perspective, the Book of Daniel announces the inauguration of the world reign of God on the occasion of the Judgment (II: 44; XII: 1–4).

In the middle of the first century B.C., the Book of Wisdom stressed the sense of mercy in the divine economy of punishments (XII: 22; cf. II Macc. VI: 13). The salvific aspect of judgment came to the fore easily, when God's functions as Judge and Saviour were recognized: "Therefore as though upon unreasoning children, you sent your judgment on them as a mockery, but they who took no heed of punishment which was but child's play, were to experience a condemnation worthy of God" (Wis. XII: 25f.).

*

*　　*

The preaching of the Baptist announced the imminent coming of the Messianic and eschatological judgment (cf. Luke III: 1–18). Jesus' teaching on the Kingdom ties in with the idea of judgment (cf. Matt. XXV: 34) and recalls the imminence of the event and its moral aspect: "Repent, for the kingdom of God is at hand" (Matt. IV: 17; cf. Luke XIII: 3). Judgment eliminates undesirable elements from the community (Matt. XIII: 36–43) and definitely consecrates God's victory in the triumph of the Son of Man (cf. Matt. XXIV: 29ff.). Throughout the entire New Testament, the great day of Judgment is announced as certain, dazzling, and universal. This is not the place to consider individual, particular judgment, whose existence is at least implicitly affirmed in many texts. Let us instead focus our attention on the person of the judge, after having noted only that in the biblical conception "the delay of the *parousia* is a merciful delay" (D. Mollat).

THE JUDGE

Jesus often attributed the double function of judging and rewarding (Matt. XX: 23) to the Father, He Himself being

the witness: "Everyone who acknowledges me before men,
I also will acknowledge him before my Father in heaven"
(Matt. X: 32). More often Jesus offers Himself as the
arbiter of human destinies: those whom He does not know
are excluded from eternal happiness (Matt. VII: 23); the
"Day of the Lord" is the Day of the Son of Man (Luke XVII:
24.), to whom judgment is confided:

> But when the Son of Man shall come in his majesty, and all the
> angels with him, then he will sit on the throne of his glory; and
> before him will be gathered all the nations, and he will separate
> them one from another, as the shepherd separates the sheep from
> the goats; and he will set the sheep on his right hand, but the
> goats on the left. Then the king will say to those on his right
> hand, "Come, blessed of my Father, take possession of the
> kingdom prepared for you from the foundation of the world.
>
> (Matt. XXV: 31–34.)

On the mount of the *Transfiguration* Jesus appeared
clothed in the glory of the Ancient of the Days, the Judge
of Dan. VII: 9f. and assisted by Moses and Elias, His
assessors: a fleeting glimpse of the glory of His *parousia*
(cf. II Pet. I: 17f.). Man's attitude toward his fellow man
will be the determining factor at the Last Judgment (cf.
Matt. XXV: 35–46), for the Son of Man is mysteriously
present in each of the brethren in the human community.
Not content with merely announcing the Judgment and
the Reign, Jesus inaugurates them with a sort of "anticipated" or "actualized" eschatology,[1] a notion already
present in the Synoptics (cf. Matt. X: 23; Luke XI: 20) and
further developed in Johannine theology (cf. John V: 24.).
Rejection of Jesus or of the Gospel is already a judgment:

> And whatever town or village you enter, inquire who in it is
> worthy, and stay there until you leave. As you enter the house,
> salute it. If then that house be worthy, your peace will come upon
> it; but if it be not worthy, let your peace return to you. And
> whoever does not receive you, or listen to your words—go forth

outside that house or town, and shake off the dust from your feet. Amen I say to you, it will be more tolerable for the land of Sodom and Gomorrah in *the day of judgment* than for that town. (Matt. X: 11–15.)

The devils think themselves victims of an anticipated, definitive judgment: "What have we to do with thee, Son of God? Hast thou come here to torment us before the time?" (Matt. VIII: 29). The *hour* of the Passion and of darkness (Luke XXII: 53) recalls the *Day of the Lord* and would seem to indicate the imminence of the *parousia*: "Nevertheless, I say to you, hereafter you shall see the Son of Man sitting at the right hand of the Power and coming upon the clouds of heaven" (Matt. XXVI: 64). Eschatological signs accompany the death of Jesus: darkness, earthquake, tearing of the Temple's veil, coming to life of the just (cf. Matt. XXVII: 45–54). A new era has come; the future invades the present. As a matter of fact, every moment is charged with an eternal weight, for henceforth man meets the Son of Man in his neighbor and is brought to judgment (cf. Matt. XXV: 35–46).

The foundation of the Church, the glorious resurrection of Jesus, as well as the judgment of the year 70 on Jerusalem are implied in this statement: "Amen I say to you, there are some of those standing here who will not taste death, till they have seen the kingdom of God coming in power" (Mark VIII: 39). In its own way, even the governing of the Church anticipates the final judgment: "You will sit upon thrones, judging the twelve tribes of Israel" (Luke XXII: 30). The gathering of the "saints," in Pauline theology, is already realized by their election as members of this body called the Church (cf. I Pet. II: 9; Matt. XIII: 48). From this perspective the sacraments take an eschatological meaning. Like the Last Judgment, baptism both brings about a "rebirth" (Tit. III: 5) and saves (cf. I Pet. III: 21). The Eucharist, too, announces Jesus' return, produces a discernment, and is fulfilled in a climate of judgment

(I Cor. XI: 23–34). Sufferings and persecution also take an eschatological character for Christians: "In this there is a proof of the just judgment of God counting you worthy of the kingdom of God, for which also you suffer" (II Thess. I: 5).

Paul regularly attributes the judgment to God (Rom. II: 2; XIV: 12) or to the Lord (Eph. VI: 8; Col. III: 24); before God's (Rom. XIV: 10) or Christ's (II Cor. V: 10) tribunal all men shall appear. These two viewpoints are reconciled in the formula from the Epistle to the Romans: "According to my gospel, God will judge the hidden secrets of men through Jesus Christ" (II: 16). It is "Christ Jesus, who will judge the living and the dead" (II Tim. IV: 1; cf. I Pet. IV: 5).[2] In the allegory of the vine, judgment seems to be a privilege of the Father, who cuts off barren branches (John XV: 2). Nevertheless, "neither does the Father judge any man, but all judgment he has given to the Son" (John V: 22). The union of the Father and the Son (cf. John X: 30) explains the apparent antinomy. Let us note the New Testament insistence on clarifying the nature of the judgment and the personality of the judge whose anticipated presence aims at warding off any surprise.

JOHANNINE WRITINGS

The idea of judgment and the person of the Judge are among the key concepts of the Johannine writings. According to the Fourth Gospel, for example, Jesus brings about a division in humanity which is equivalent to a judgment. The opposition Light-Darkness, Truth-Lie is embodied by the existence of two groups: believers-unbelievers, the seeing-the blind, sheep of the fold-strange sheep, disciples or Jews (in John's sense). In Christ-Light eschatological discernment is already effected in the judgment that separates the just from the wicked. More than other New Testament authors, John tends to connect the decisive event of eschatology with the first coming of Christ and with His death.[3] The person of Jesus (John III: 19; IX: 39), His word (VIII: 37; XII: 48), His works (XII: 37; XV: 24) involve a discriminatory power that attests the truth of this statement: "Now is the judgment of the world; now will the prince of the world be cast out. And I, if I be lifted up from the earth, will draw all things to myself" (John XII: 31f.). The death of Jesus actually stamps a definitive character on the refusal of the Jews before the Light and on the opposite way of the true believers.

This great judicial debate that opposes Light to Darkness runs throughout the entire Fourth Gospel and reaches its climax in the trial of Jesus. Such a conception of Jesus' life develops and makes explicit the prophetic anxiety voiced at the Presentation:[4]

And Simeon blessed them and said to Mary his mother, "Behold, this child is destined for the fall and for the rise of many in Israel, and for a sign that shall be contradicted. And thy own soul a sword shall pierce, that the thoughts of many hearts may be revealed." (Luke II: 34f.)

This discernment appears in the course of the Public Life: "He who hears my word, and believes him who sent me, has life everlasting, and does not come to judgment, but *has passed* from death to life" (John V: 24; cf. III: 18f.). The healing of the man born blind provides the opportunity for a clarification: "For judgment have I come into this world, that they who do not see may see, and they who see may become blind" (John IX: 39). The present judgment anticipates that of the last day: "He who rejects me, and does not accept my words, has one to condemn him. The word that I have spoken will condemn him on the last day" (John XII: 48).

The Incarnation, however, represents a *merciful* and *saving* intervention: "For God did not send his Son into the world in order to judge the world, but that the world might be saved through him" (John III: 17). Jesus Himself admits this: "I have not come to judge the world, but to save the world" (XII: 47). Certainly, considered as Son of Man (V: 27), Jesus is a judge, but this Son of Man is *different* from the figure of that name whose essential role according to the Jewish apocalypses (cf. the Book of Henoch) consists in annihilating God's enemies on the last day. The presence of the Son of Man on earth is itself the result of God's salvific initiative (Luke XIX: 10). Once refused, the Truth reveals man's deceit and his malice, condemns the unbeliever, and deprives him of any further excuse (John XV: 22). Jesus' preaching anticipates the course of the Judgment (XII: 48) and entails the destiny of each one of us.

*

* *

The "judgment" aspect of Jesus' presence underlies every Johannine account of the Passion and is particularly dramatic in a passage that should be translated in this way: "[Pilate] *had* Jesus *sit down* on the judgment seat . . . and said to the Jews, Behold, your king!" (XIX: 13). With their answer, "Away with him! Crucify him!" the Jews pronounced their own condemnation. Jesus is their judge because they do not want Him as their king (cf. XIX: 21). This scene at the praetorium appears as the climax of the "great trial" that runs across the whole Fourth Gospel.[5] The episode of Gabbatha (= "the Height") anticipates that of Golgotha, where Jesus will be "lifted up," and His kingship and the judgment of the world will become a definitive reality. Before the episode just mentioned Pilate had presented Jesus to the crowd, saying: "Behold, the man!" (John XIX: 5), a statement that probably reminded the Evangelist of the title "Son of Man."

On what arguments is such an interpretation of the scene at the praetorium founded? The philological proof is more difficult to grasp. The Greek verb (ἐκάθισεν), usually translated "sat down," can carry a transitive sense meaning "to make sit." The sentence's movement confirms this meaning: Pilate *leads* Jesus to the platform and has him take the position and function of the judge. The solemn framework given to the scene creates an expectation that is not satisfied according to the traditional tone of the text, for Pilate does not pronounce the sentence expected. On the contrary, the drama of the King-Judge, seated on the judgment seat and "condemned" by the Jews, adds to and resolves the tension that has not ceased to build from the beginning of the Gospel.

The insistence in John's account of the Passion on the *royal dignity of Jesus* (cf. XVIII: 33–XIX: 22) is obvious. If Jesus is seated on some kind of throne, Pilate's "Behold, your king" (XIX: 14) takes on a startlingly dramatic strength. For John, as we know, Jesus' death on the throne of the cross is already a glorification, for Calvary is the great sign of contradiction and the stone of division that actualizes the Last Judgment. As the Last Supper anticipates the sacrifice of Calvary, the praetorium scene anticipates the judgment of the Cross. Already the postpaschal investiture is being played out on earth. St. Paul recalls what strength God "has wrought in Christ in raising him from the dead, and *seating him* at his right hand in heaven" (Eph. I: 20; cf. Ps. CIX: 1). It is the heavenly consummation (cf. Heb. I: 3) of a Messianic preferment described by Peter: David "knew that God had sworn to him with an oath that of the fruit of his loins, He would set upon his throne" (Acts II: 30).

*

*   *

All the prophetic imagery of the "day of the Lord" occurs in the descriptions that John's Apocalypse presents of God's victory, the triumph of the Lamb, and the eschatological judgment. It is a dramatic message addressed to the persecuted Christians, to reassure them on the outcome of the cosmic conflict that pits God against organized evil. After the letters to the Churches of Asia come the prophetic visions describing the salient points of "the great day" of God: the fall of Satan (ch. XII), the punishment of Babylon (chs. XVIIf.) and the extermination of the pagan nations (ch. XIX). Then comes the traditional setting for the Judgment:

> *And I saw a great white throne and the one*
> *who sat upon it; from his face*
> *the earth and heaven fled away,*
> *and there was found no place for them.*
> *And I saw the dead, the great and the small,*
> *standing before the throne, and scrolls were opened.*
> *And another scroll was opened, which is the book of*
> *life; and the dead were judged out of those things*
> *that were written in the scrolls, according to their*
> *works.*   (XX: 11f.)

Judgment is the privilege of God (cf. Apoc. XIV: 7; XIX: 2), but the *Son of Man* also exercises that function. From the beginning of the Apocalypse, he is presented with judicial attributes (cf. I: 12–18). Later on, there is mention of the power of the Lamb "to take the scroll and to open its seals" (V: 9; cf. XXI: 27). To the "Son of Man" also belongs the task of harvesting the ground with the scythe (XIV: 14ff.).

The *collective* aspect of the Judgment is stressed by the Apocalypse: "And I saw thrones, and men sat upon them and judgment was given to them" (XX: 4). The idea appears elsewhere in the New Testament. According to the First Epistle to the Corinthians, the Christian faithful share in the prerogatives of Christ, the sovereign judge of the world (VI: 2) and of the angels (VI: 3), reserved for that day (Jude 6; II Pet. II: 4). A biblical tradition accords to the just domination (or judgment) over the wicked (Ps. XLIX: 15), or over persecuting nations (Dan. VII: 22; Wis. III: 8). According to St. Paul, by their testimony the good "shall judge" the Law's transgressors (Rom. II: 27).

In the pericope of the cured paralytic (cf. Matt. IX: 1–8) Jesus connects *the power that He has to pardon sins* and to be the Sovereign Judge with His role as Son of Man (John V: 27; Matt. XXV: 31). The Apostles, too, share this double power (Matt. XVIII: 18; XIX: 28). Like Jesus and in His name, the Apostles will be able to anticipate or ward off the sentence of the last judgment.[6] A formulation proper to Matthew shows his interest in the powers conferred by Jesus on the apostles for the benefit of the Christian community: "But when the crowds saw it, they were struck with fear and glorified God who had given such power to *men*" (IX: 8).

Let us end with this exhortation of Saint Paul to the Christians: "Work out your salvation with fear and trembling" (Phil. II: 12). Although he considered the warning as applicable also to himself (I Cor. IX: 27), he felt in his heart an immense hope on the evening of his life:

As for me, I am already being poured out in sacrifice, and the time of my deliverance is at hand. I have fought the good fight, I have finished the course, I have kept the faith. For the rest, there is laid up for me a crown of justice, which the Lord, *the just Judge*, will give to me in that day; yet not to me only, but also to those who love his coming. (II Tim. IV: 6–8.)

NOTES ON 26

[1] Cf. D. Mollat, "Le jugement dans le Nouveau Testament," in *DBS*, vol. VI, c. 1350. This article and that of R. Pautrel (Old Testament) offer a good treatment of the Biblical theme of "judgment" (cc. 1321–1394). On the *parousia* see also *DBS*, vol. VI, cc. 1331–1419 (A. Feuillet).

[2] It is probable that the earliest baptismal *credo* ran as follows: "I believe in Christ, who died, who rose again, who is at the right hand of God, who is to judge the living and the dead"; cf. M. E. Boismard, *Quatre hymnes baptismales* . . . , p. 109 (proposed in connection with I Pet. III: 18–22).

3 Cf. D. Mollat–F. M. Braun, *L'Évangile et les Épîtres de saint Jean (BJ)*, pp. 21f. See also p. 102.

4 The words of Simeon "thy own soul a sword shall pierce" would apply to Mary, also as representing the chosen people and its destiny. Although this true and obedient "daughter of Sion" welcomes the Messiah with joy, she will be "rent apart" by the refusal of many. See P. Benoit, "Et toi-même, un glaive te transpercera l'âme!" (*CBQ* [1963], pp. 251–61).

5 See I. de la Potterie, "Jesus king and judge according to John XIX: 13," *Scripture* (1961), pp. 97–111; or the longer article of *Biblica* (1960), pp. 217–47; cf. 1962, p. 89. Two second-century writings, Justin's *Apology* (I: 35f.) and a fragment of the apocryphal *Gospel of Peter*, favor the proposed interpretation and illustrate its traditional character.

6 Cf. J. Dupont, "Le paralytique pardonné" (Matt. IX: 1–8), *NRT* (1960), pp. 940–58.

27

THE SON OF GOD,
THE BELOVED

THE titles "Son of God" and "Beloved" define Jesus'
relations to God or to the Father, while "Firstborn" accords
Him a pre-eminent and unique place with regard to
creation. Jesus is often called or calls Himself more suc-
cinctly "the Son," "His Son," "His Only Son," all so many
variants of one and the same title, "Son of God." The
biblical notion of sonship is very complex. Here let us
restrict ourselves to distinguishing and examining those
aspects the knowledge of which appears indispensable to
the understanding of the Messianic sonship of Jesus or of
His properly divine sonship.

DIVINE SONSHIP AS AN EXTRA-CHRISTIAN
NOTION

In ancient Eastern religions a divine origin was often
attributed to the kings, and the pharaohs were allegedly
sons of the solar God Râ. Later on, certain Roman emperors
assumed the title *divifilius*, "son of God." Hellenism contemporary to Christ admitted a still broader conception of
divine sonship and gave the title of Son of God to miracle-
workers and to all those "divine men" who were considered
as invested with divine forces. In mystery religions the
initiated of the "mystos" was thought to be a son of God.
Such acceptations of the title will no longer detain us, for
their relation to our title seems purely verbal or formal.

The use of the title "Son of God" in the Old Testament probably owes its origin to this saying of God's to Moses: "So you shall say to Pharaoh: Thus says the Lord: Israel is my son, my firstborn" (Exod. IV: 22, cf. Wis. XVIII: 13). *Israel is the Son of God*, because God has adopted it (Deut. XXXII: 10), chosen it as His people, consecrated it to Himself (Deut. VII: 6), and sustained it "as a man sustains his son all along the road" (Deut. I: 31) which led it to Palestine. *Hosea* foresaw that in better days "the children of Israel" would be called "sons of the living God" (II: 1); to this same prophet God had confided: "When Israel was a child, I loved it, and from Egypt I called my son" (XI: 1), a theme that will be taken up by Jeremiah (cf. II: 2) and Ezekiel (ch. XVI:). Emboldened by these oracles, the post-exilic Israelites shall say to God: "O Lord, hold not back [your pity] for *you are our Father*" (Isa. LXIII: 15f.).

Attributing certain privileges of the *angels* of the *heavenly court* (Job I: 6; Ps. LXXXVIII: 7) to the Israelite *judges*, the Old Testament also calls them "sons of God" (Ps. LXXXI: 6; cf. LVII: 2), a title that in Deuteronomy also designates the guardian angels of the nations (XXXII: 8). Individuals as such are called "Sons of God" only in the sapiential books. Ecclesiasticus applies the title to the charitable just man:

> *To the fatherless be as a father,*
> *and help their mother as a husband would;*
> *Thus will you be like* a son
> 　to the Most High,
> *and he will be more tender to you*
> 　*than a mother.*
> 　　　　　　　　　　　　(Sir. IV: 10.)

The Book of Wisdom records the sarcasms that the wicked proffer against the just, the faithful Jew:

> *He professes to have knowledge of God*
> *and styles himself* a child of God . . .

He calls blest the destiny of the just
and boasts that God is his Father . . .

For if the just one be the son of God,
he will defend him
and deliver him from the hand of his foes.
                              (II: 13, 16, 18.)

Careful to see in Jesus the new Israel (Matt. II: 15),
St. Matthew often applies the title "Son of God" to Him;
most likely he had in mind the sapiential passages when
narrating the episode of the insults hurled at the Crucified:

Now the passers-by were jeering at him, shaking their heads,
and saying, "Thou who destroyest the temple, and in three days
buildest it up again, save thyself! If thou art the Son of God,
come down from the cross!" In like manner, the chief priests
with the Scribes and the elders, mocking said: . . . "He trusted in
God; let him deliver him now, if he wants him; for he said,
'I am the Son of God.'" And the robbers also, who were crucified
with him, reproached him in the same way.

                              (XXVII: 39–44; cf. Ps. XXI: 9.)

In the death of Judas (Acts I: 18) Peter saw the accomplishment of the punishment reserved for the wicked
persecutors of the just man: "For he (the Lord) shall strike
them down speechless and prostrate" (Wis. IV: 19).[1] According to the Apostle Matthew's version, the traitor killed himself
by hanging (XXVII: 5).

The favor of election and the duty of obedience are
particularly associated with the title of Son of God in its
application to the representatives of the people, the *kings*.
God declares to David about his son Solomon: "I will be to
him *a father* and he shall be to me *a son*" (II Sam. VII: 14).
This text assumes a particular importance because after it
the title "Son of God" will be applied to the King-Messiah.
This transposition already appears in a parallel passage in
the Book of Chronicles, which "Messianizes" Nathan's
prophecy:

I will be to him a father, and he shall be to me a son: and I will not take my mercy away from him, as I took it from him that was before thee. But I will settle him in my kingdom *for ever:* and his throne shall be most firm *for ever*.

(I Chron. XVII: 13f.; cf. Luke I: 32f.)

A still more direct application of divine sonship to the Messianic king appears in this saying of his: "I will proclaim the decree of the Lord: The Lord said to me, *You are my son; this day I have begotten you*." (Ps. II: 7). In yet another oracle devoted to royal Messianism (Ps. LXXXIX: 20–38), Yahweh says of his anointed: "He shall say of me, You are *my father* my God, the Rock, my saviour" (v. 27).

JESUS AND THE TITLE "SON OF GOD"

We have already seen that the gospels mention the title "Son of Man" only when they record Jesus' sayings. The use of the title "Lord" belongs especially to the believing community. As for the title "Son of God," it appears in a great variety of texts that express Jesus' thought or the conviction of the enlightened disciples.

The title "Son of God" is remarkably rare in the Synoptic Gospels. Apart from a passage in the Annunciation to Mary (Luke I: 35) and the beginning of Mark (I: 1), the first application of the title to Jesus appears in the account of His Baptism: "And there came a voice from the heavens, *Thou art my beloved Son*, in thee I am well pleased" (Mark I: 11). As we have already said, this declaration recalls the inaugural vocation of the Servant of the Lord (Isa. XLII: 1). In Matthew it appears in *the third person*: "This is my beloved Son" (III: 17), a formula that already presents Jesus as the Doctor of the Nations, according to an interest especially dear to the First Evangelist and made explicit at the Transfiguration: "This is my beloved Son in whom I am well pleased; *hear him*" (Matt. XVII: 5). The word "beloved,"[2] as applied to Christ, is used only once in the

New Testament in Eph. I: 6 (cf. Col. I: 13), but John's frequent reminders of God's love for His Son (cf. John III: 35; V: 20) are equivalent to an implicit affirmation of the title.

The title "Son of God" is equally prominent in the account of the Temptation. Twice the devil begins with the phrase, "If thou art the Son of God" (cf. Matt. IV: 3, 6), inviting Jesus to reveal Himself as a triumphant Messiah. Why does He not claim the title "Son of God," which He received at baptism, to perform the startling actions of those miracle workers, also called "sons of God" because of the divine powers that allegedly invested them? At the third temptation which proposes an act of submission to the devil's power, the title is not invoked, for Jesus' divine sonship consecrated His submission to the Father's will and formulated the depth of His obedience. Matthew reports an isolated act of homage paid to the *power* of the Son of God: after the walking on the waters and the miraculous calm the witnesses fall down before Jesus and say: "Truly thou art the Son of God" (Matt. XIV: 33).

Two important Gospel passages seem to associate the title "Son of God" with that of "Messiah." To Jesus' question, "Who do you say that I am?" Peter answers: "Thou art the Christ, the Son of the Living God" (Matt. XVI: 15f.). According to Mark and Luke, Peter had said simply: "Thou art the Christ" (Mark VIII: 29; Luke IX: 20). Here Matthew has possibly combined two confessions of faith in one; the one that relates to the Son of God could have been pronounced on another occasion (perhaps at the multiplication of the loaves—cf. John VI: 67–69). To this testimony of faith *in the Son of God*, the declaration of Jesus should be related: "Blessed art thou, Simon Bar-Jona, for flesh and blood has not revealed this to thee, but my Father in heaven" (Matt. XVI: 17). As a matter of fact, we notice that the Synoptics often apply the title of Son of God to Jesus in association with the supernatural world: the

Father's voice at the Baptism, the revelation to Peter, the testimony of the devil (Matt. IV: 3, 6) or devils (Mark III: 11; V: 7). Several passages in which Jesus calls Himself Son of God (cf. Mark XIII: 32) also belong to this context: "No one knows the Son except the Father; nor does anyone know the Father except the Son, and him to whom the Son chooses to reveal Him" (Matt. XI: 27), a saying that has a Johannine tenor and is reported both in Luke and Matthew. The second passage for consideration concerns the question that Caiphas asked the Accused: "Art thou the Christ, the Son of the Blessed One?" (Mark XIV: 61). Here, as in Matthew (XXVI: 63), are linked two questions that were probably distinct at the interrogation (cf. Luke XXII: 67, 70).

The title "Son of God" does not suit Jesus nor was it appointed simply to be applied to Him as to a miracle worker (a Greek idea) or as to one appointed simply to carry out the divine plan (Old Testament). The Synoptics echo a tradition reflecting that stage of popular conviction that stopped at the *Messianity of Jesus*. Thus it does not seem that the affirmation of a superhuman dignity is implied, when Satan (Matt. IV: 3, 6), the possessed (Mark III: 11; V: 7), the centurion (Mark XV: 39), or even Peter (Matt. XIV: 33; XVI: 16) apply the title "Son of God" to Jesus. We are also justified in considering the theophany of the Baptism as the inauguration of the Messianic career of Jesus and to interpret the heavenly voice in this sense. At his investiture (Isa. XLII: 1), the Servant was also called "God's beloved," a designation that has affinities with that of only Son (μονογενής). The Father's "my Son" at Jesus' Baptism, however, took on a meaning which, beyond its immediate audience, reached the depth of the later revelations that Jesus Himself or His Spirit were going to communicate to believers. *A divine dignity* also seems implied in the Sanhedrin's scandalized exclamation that Luke reports: "Thou art then the Son of God!" (XXII: 70).[3] To pretend to the dignity of Messiah was not a crime.

Jesus' claim to divine sonship is not limited to the Fourth Gospel. In a few passages the Synoptics momentarily suspend their remarkable discretion to reveal a truth that Jesus seemed to prefer to keep as an intimate secret during His life on earth: the awareness of being truly the Son of God, the second Person of the Holy Trinity. Referring to the mysteries of the Kingdom in general (cf. Matt. XIII: 11), Jesus declares to the disciples:

I praise thee, Father, Lord of heaven and earth, that thou didst hide these things from the wise and prudent, and didst reveal them to little ones. Yes, Father, for such was thy good pleasure. All things have been delivered to me by my Father; and no one knows the Son except the Father; nor does anyone know the Father except the Son, and him to whom the Son chooses to reveal him. (Matt. XI: 25–27.)

This common knowledge of divine mysteries and this union of will surpass the prerogatives of divine sonship granted to God's envoys, to His representatives on earth, or to those who share in His holiness.

The saying to Mary Magdalene "I ascend to my Father and your Father" (John XX: 17) is often cited to illustrate the distinction that the Risen Christ established between His own sonship and that of His disciples. Already during His earthly existence Jesus had affirmed that distinction in the formulas: "*my* Father in heaven" and "*your* Father in heaven" (Matt. V: 16; VII: 21). The "*our* Father" of the Lord's Prayer does not contradict these assertions because the prayer taught the *disciples* how to pray (Matt. VI: 9; cf. Luke XI: 1f.). According to the Synoptics, Jesus often called God "my Father" (cf. Matt. X: 32; Luke XXII: 29), and Mark has kept the Aramaic formula in his account of the Agony: "And he said, *Abba* [Father]! All things are possible to thee. Remove this cup from me; yet not what I will, but what thou willest" (XIV: 36).

Yet rarely does Jesus call Himself "Son of God" in the

Synoptic Gospels. Apart from Matthew's text (XI: 25ff.), examined earlier (cf. Luke X: 21f.), can be cited the saying of the vineyard owner in the parable of the murderous vinedressers: "Now he still had one left, *a beloved son*" (Mark XII: 6). Another, more direct saying creates a problem[4] because it makes the Son unaware of the time of the *parousia*, although it states His pre-eminence above the angels: "But of that day or hour no one knows, neither the angels in heaven, *nor the Son*, but the Father only" (Mark XIII: 32). Erroneously basing themselves on that isolated statement, the Arian heretics affirmed the absolute inferiority of the Son. The text, however, refers to the Son as the Father's revealer: it is not part of his mission to make known the "times or dates which the Father has fixed by his own authority" (Acts I: 7). The Father too grants places of honor in the Kingdom (Matt. XX: 23).

The angel of the Annunciation said to Mary: "The Holy Spirit shall come upon thee and the power of the Most High shall overshadow thee; and therefore, the Holy one to be born shall be called *the Son of God*" (Luke I: 35). With regard to the name "Son of Mary," we recalled that this formulation of the Holy Spirit's role strongly suggests, together with other indications, the belief in the divine maternity of Mary. To "Son of God" should therefore be given here a higher sense than the purely Messianic meaning of the preceding verse: "Behold, thou shalt conceive in thy womb and shall bring forth a son; and thou shalt call his name Jesus. He shall be great, and shall be called *the Son of the Most High*; and the Lord God will give him the throne of David his father, and he shall be king over the house of Jacob forever; and of his kingdom there shall be no end" (Luke I: 31ff.; cf. John I: 49). Mary's subsequent question (Luke I: 34) furnished the occasion for an enrichment of the revelation: this successor of David, this "Son of the Most High" is "Son of God" in the strict sense. The divine maternity of Mary somewhat involves her virginal maternity that Matthew also stressed (I: 18–25): "for that which is begotten in her is of the Holy Spirit" (I: 20).

Like John, Mark limits himself to affirming the fact of Jesus' divine sonship. After entitling his Gospel "The beginning of the Gospel of Jesus Christ, *the Son of God*" (I: 1), he lets the facts speak and merely reports at the end the centurion's cry at Jesus' death: "Truly this man was the Son of God!" (XV: 39). John, besides, does not explain the human origin of Jesus but keeps saying that Christ *came forth from God* (cf. John VIII: 42). The Son's *pre-existence* before the Father is implied in the often repeated clarification that He has been *sent* by God to earth (cf. III: 16f.). In John (cf. John X: 10; XII: 46) and the Synoptics (Matt. X: 34; Luke XII: 49ff.) Jesus declares that He *has come* on earth, indicating a *personal* pre-existence that is clearly affirmed in the text: "Before Abraham came to be, I am" (John VIII: 58).

In the Fourth Gospel people like Nathanael (I: 49), Peter (VI: 69: *var.*), or Martha (XI: 27) associate the title "Son of God" with a purely Messianic dignity. Jesus Himself or John, his interpreter, seems to identify divine sonship with His role as God's envoy in several texts (X: 36; XVI: 27). But more often the divine sonship of Jesus is openly and definitely proclaimed as a truth (one among many) clarified by a postpaschal revelation: "Many things yet I have to say to you, but you cannot bear them now. But when he, the Spirit of truth, has come, he will teach you all the truth" (John XVI: 12f.). "But the Paraclete, the Holy Spirit, whom the Father will send in my name, he will teach you all things, and bring to your mind whatever I have said to you" (John XIV: 26). Expressing Himself through John in a postpaschal climate, Jesus repeatedly recalls the intimacy that unites Him to the Father: the Father knows Him as He knows the Father (John X: 15); everything that the Father has, the Son possesses too (John

XVI: 15; XVII: 10); the Father and the Son are one (John X: 30). Other clearer and more astonishing affirmations indicate that later theological clarifications in terms of "same nature" and of "equality" are already implicit in Johannine thought: "The Father is in me and I in the Father" (John X: 38; XIV: 11); "He who sees me sees also the Father" (John XIV: 9). John insists especially on the Father's love for the Son (cf. XV: 9f.; XVII: 23f.), to whom He has given *everything* (John III: 35). If the Son rarely states His love for the Father (only: John XIV: 31), He expressed that love by His obedience: "My food is to do the will of him who sent me, to accomplish his work" (John IV: 34).

THE TITLE "SON OF GOD" AND THE PRIMITIVE CHURCH

Now let us examine the chief testimonies of the New Testament writings outside the Gospels. The oldest *confessions of faith* seem to contain the formula "I believe that Jesus Christ is the Son of God." According to a very ancient gloss (Acts VIII: 37), the Ethiopian pronounced that formula inserted in the baptismal rite mainly because Jesus was proclaimed Son of God at His baptism. In the First Epistle of John we also read: "Whoever confesses that Jesus is the Son of God, God abides in him and he in God" (IV: 15). The Sonship of Christ is the exemplar and norm of the sonship of Christians:[5] If you do not believe in me, Jesus said, believe in my works, that you "may know and believe that the Father is in me and I in the Father" (John X: 38). To believe in the Son is to have access to the Father: "He who confesses the Son has the Father also" (I John II: 23). Other Scriptural references attest the inclusion of the title "Son of God" in the primitive *credo*. Let us cite this exhortation from the Epistle to the Hebrews: "Having therefore a great high priest who has passed into the heavens, Jesus, *the Son of God,* let us hold fast our confession" (Heb. IV: 14; cf. John XX: 31).

In the opening of the Epistle to the Romans (I: 1–7) St. Paul resumes the data of tradition and recalls God's *promises* "concerning his *Son* who was born to him, according to the flesh of the offspring of David, who was *foreordained Son of God* by an act of power in keeping with the holiness of his spirit, by resurrection from the dead, Jesus Christ our Lord . . ." (I: 3f.). The first mention of the Son considers Him in His pre-existence; according to the second, Christ's humanity was graced somehow with a new *Messianic* inthronisation by His Resurrection and "entered then into the enjoyment of the privileges of the Son of God." Paul had sketched that development in his inaugural discourse to the Jews (cf. *BJ*):

So we now bring you good news that the promise made to our fathers, God has fulfilled to our children in *raising up Jesus,* as also it is written in Psalm II: Thou art my son, this day have I begotten thee. (Acts XIII: 32f.)

Other Pauline uses of the title "Son of God" to designate Christ are perhaps connected with the tradition of the Gospels. The Greek term διδόναι, sacrificial in tone, is used by John to express the Father's generosity in the *gift* that He made to men (John III: 16). Paul also recalls the sacrifice that Abraham made of his *only son,* when he writes: "If God is for us, who is against us? He who has not spared even his own Son, but has delivered (διδόναι) him for us all, how can he fail to grant us also all things with him?" (Rom. VIII: 31f.). Christians, Paul writes elsewhere, have received "a spirit of adoption as sons, which urges them to cry out: Abba, Father" (Rom. VIII: 15), the very formula that Jesus used in Mark's account of Gethsemani (XIV: 36). After having recalled, as in the parable of the wicked vinedressers (Mark XII: 6f.), that a son is also the heir, Paul alludes once more to the suffering of Jesus: "We

suffer with him that we may also be glorified with him"
(Rom. VIII: 17). Equally deserving of citation is this
parallel from the Epistle to the Galatians: "And because you
are sons, God has sent the Spirit of his Son into our hearts,
crying Abba, Father" (IV: 6).

According to Paul also, Christ enjoys pre-existence, since
He has been *sent* (cf. Rom. VIII: 3; Gal. IV: 4). We have
redemption and forgiveness of sins in "the Beloved Son,"
who is "the Image of the invisible God, the Firstborn of
every creature." These affirmations (Col. I: 13ff.) resume
and develop an idea already exposed in the Epistle to the
Romans, on the saving plan of God: "For those whom he
has foreknown he has also predestined to be conformed to
the image of his *Son*, that he should be *the firstborn among
many brethren*" (Rom. VIII: 29; cf. Heb. II: 17).

It is remarkable that the title "Son of God" is *absent*
from several New Testament books: the Pastoral Epistles,
James, I Peter, II John, and Jude. The Second Epistle of
Peter cites the heavenly voice of the Transfiguration (I: 17).
The sole mention of the title in the Apocalypse is the
message addressed to the Angel of the Church at Thyatira:
"Thus says the *Son of God*, who has eyes like to a flame of
fire and whose feet are like fine brass" (II: 18).

A confession of faith already cited shows the interest for
the title "Son of God" held by the Epistle to the Hebrews
(IV: 14). Other passages in it are also significant. From the
beginning the Epistle's author grants the *Son* (I: 2) a
pre-eminent place and cites Ps. II: 7 to establish that
superiority (I: 5). Christ as Son surpasses Moses (III: 5f.).
The title links honor and service: "And he, Son though he
was, learned obedience from the things that he suffered"
(V: 8; cf. Phil. II: 6ff.). The miraculous origin and the
eternity of the priesthood of Jesus, Son of God and High
Priest, evoke the figure of Melchisedec, that "king of peace,
without father, without mother, without genealogy, having
neither beginning of days nor end of life, but likened to the

Son of God, he continues a priest forever" (Heb. VII: 2f.).

The fondness of the author of Hebrews for the title "Son of God" is another feature that ties this Epistle's theology to Johannine thought, where it is one of the major themes:

No one has at any time seen God. The *only-begotten Son* who is in the bosom of the Father, he has revealed him.

(John I: 18; cf. XVII: 26.)

Many other signs also Jesus worked in the sight of his disciples, which are not written in this book. But these are written that you may believe that Jesus is the Christ, *the Son of God*, and that believing you may have life in his name. (XX: 30f.)

The name of Jesus is Jesus Himself, for the *name* is a Semiticism to designate the person: to believe in the Son (John III: 16) is to believe in His name (III: 18); He who reveals the Father's name (John XVII: 26) affirms: "If you knew me, you would then know *my Father* also" (VIII: 19). To believe in the name of Jesus (John I: 12; II: 23), to recognize that He comes from God because of "the signs" (John III: 2), is the first step of a faith that will lead to belief "in the name of the only-begotten Son of God" (John III: 18; cf. I John V: 13) or "in the Son of God" (I John V: 10) and even to recognition of His divine sonship in the strict sense. Again, it is to commit oneself to follow Him, in the manner of the catechumens who, at their *baptism*, pronounced ritual formulas not unlikely dependent on John's expressions. Whoever believes that Jesus is the Son of God (I John V: 5) actually receives the *life* that is in Him (John VI: 40; XX: 31).

NOTES ON 27

[1] According to one possible interpretation of Acts I: 18, Judas is said to have *"fallen headlong"* and burst open in the middle (*RSV*), as the just man's persecutors in Wisdom IV: 19, whom the Lord will hurl *down headlong* ... (*BJ*). The problems relating to the double account of Judas' death have been discussed by P. Benoit: "La mort de Judas," in *Synoptische Studien* (*Wikenhauser Festschrift*) (1953), pp. 1–19.

² Here (Eph. I: 6): ἠγαπημένος while ἀγαπητός is also used alone in the citation adapted by Matt. XII: 18 (see p. 154).

³ By pretending that He would sit at the right hand of the Power, Jesus equivalently affirmed being equal to God and was accused of blasphemy (Matt. XXVI: 65 and par.; cf. Acts VII: 56ff.). Cf. P. Lamarche, "Le 'blasphème' de Jésus devant le Sanhédrin," *Rech. Sc. Rel.*, 1964, pp. 74–85.

⁴ The problem is reflected by the uncertainty of the manuscript tradition for Matt. XXIV: 36. Fr. Lagrange retains the variant, οὐδὲ ὁ υἱός, "nor the Son," for it is more probable that this passage in Matthew, a widely read Gospel, has been cut than that it was added, following Mark (*Évangile selon saint Matthieu*, 1923, p. 470). Even if the phrase is omitted, the addition "but the Father alone" maintains the statement as it appears in Mark.

⁵ On the sharing by Christians of the divine Sonship see L. Cerfaux, *Le chrétien dans la théologie paulinienne* (Paris, 1962), pp. 296–301. The use of the title "Son of God" in the Gospels has been treated recently: for Luke in *Revue Biblique*, 1965, 161–84, for John in *NTS*, X (1963–64), pp. 227ff.

28

THE LORD

THE title "the Lord (Κύριος)" applies *mainly* to the glorified
Christ, present in the Christian community, the Church,
as its Head, whom it invokes and who intercedes for it before
God. The name Κύριος was then associated quite early with
the liturgical life of the Church. Incorporated into the New
Testament, very ancient confessions of faith attest the
importance the title Κύριος held for the primitive community: "For if thou confess with thy mouth that Jesus is
the Lord, and believe in thy heart that God has raised him
from the dead, thou shalt be saved" (Rom. X: 9; cf. Acts
IV: 12). Here *eternal* salvation is in question, while faith
in the name of Jesus also gains temporal salvation (cf. Acts
III: 16).

In the ordinary, *profane language* of the Greeks, the
term Κύριος meant "master" or "owner" and generally
designated the subject of legitimate authority. It is more
important, however, to note that Κύριος was a synonym
for "god" in the eastern Hellenistic religions of the Roman
Empire:

For even if there are what are called gods, whether in heaven or
on earth (for indeed there are many gods, and many lords), yet
for us there is only one God, the Father from whom all things,
and we unto him; and one Lord, Jesus Christ, through whom
are all things, and we through him. (I Cor. VIII: 5f.)

By virtue of his political power the Roman emperor had

himself called Κύριος, a title that took on a religious character, when the Caesars received the honors of a cult. To adore Christ as the only Κύριος was, then, to reject two false cults: the one of the Hellenistic deities and the other of the emperor.

In the Septuagint the term Κύριος is currently used to translate the divine names *Adonai* and *Yahweh*. The application of the divine title Κύριος to Jesus seems to have had its start in a *liturgical* context, as the formula *maran atha*, "Our Lord comes" (*mar* = Κύριος) or rather *marana tha*, "Come, our Lord!" (I Cor. XVI: 22; cf. Apoc. XXII: 20) indicates. From its origin the eucharistic cult celebrated and drew Jesus' presence in the midst of His followers. His daily coming to the community anticipated His coming at the end of time, His *parousia*: "For as often as you shall eat this bread and drink this cup, you proclaim the death of the Lord *until he comes*" (I Cor. XI: 26). Had Jesus Himself not stressed the eschatological character of the Last Supper: "Amen I say to you, that I will drink no more of the fruit of the vine, until that day when I shall drink it new in the kingdom of God" (Mark XIV: 25). According to an ancient liturgical collection, the *Didache*, the prayer *marana tha* was said in the course of the eucharistic celebration. It belonged to a form of cultual worship proper to an Aramaic-speaking community. As such the Greek church received it from the Palestinian Church. This is equivalent to saying that there is no reason to attribute the origin of the Christological title Κύριος to a borrowing from the pagan Hellenistic cult.[1] The Church of Jerusalem was the first to use it to express its total faith in the glorified Christ.

The clearest and most numerous testimonies (more than a hundred) of the use of the divine title Κύριος are found in Paul's writings. An attentive examination of several of these testimonies shows that in the main they were transmitted to the Apostle from an older tradition voiced in the primitive confessions of faith. From this point of view, the following verse (already cited) is very significant: "For if thou *confess* with thy mouth that Jesus is the Lord and believe in thy heart that God has raised him from the dead, thou shalt be saved" (Rom. X: 9). A well-known passage from the Epistle to the Philippians seems to derive from an ancient hymn that is a veritable Christo-synthesis composed in honor of the Κύριος. Here are the last three strophes:

> *Therefore God also has exalted him*
> *and has bestowed upon him the name*
> *that is above every name,*
>
> *so that at the name of Jesus*
> *every knee should bend of those in heaven,*
> *on earth and under the earth,*
>
> *and every tongue shall confess*
> *that the* Lord *Jesus Christ*
> *is in the glory of God the Father.*
>
> (II: 9–11.)[2]

With the title Κύριος the name of God Himself was granted to Christ,[3] who henceforth shares in divine power and sovereignty. Through the mouth of Isaiah, God had pronounced an "unalterable word: to me every knee shall bend" (XLV: 23). Ever since the title of Κύριος was given to Jesus, all the attributes of God, except those which are proper to the Father, could be conferred on Him.

That sovereignty of the Lord Christ must be considered as underlying even in those texts that do not include the term Κύριος. Such is the case where it is said that Jesus "went into heaven, Angels, Powers and Virtues being made subject to him" (I Pet. III: 22). Here, as in the hymn of Philippians, the submission of invisible powers to the Κύριος is mentioned, for the glorified Christ is Head of the visible and invisible universe (cf. Eph. I: 10). This insistence on proclaiming the lordship of the Κύριος over extra-terrestrial powers probably derives from an interpretation of

one of the most frequently cited Messianic texts: "The
Lord said to my Lord: Sit at my right hand till I make your
enemies your footstool" (Ps. CIX: 1; cf. I Cor. XV: 25). For
the first Christians Israel's earthly enemies prefigured the
formidable resistance of Satan's world to the establishment
of the Kingdom of God.

The texts cited—and the list could go on—make it clear
that the title Κύριος, strictly defined, was applied to Jesus
by the Christian community only after the Resurrection.
Jesus Himself certainly was aware of being Κύριος; several
texts indicate that He suggested it to His audience. This
passage is such a case:

And while Jesus was teaching in the temple, he addressed them,
saying, "How do the Scribes say that the Christ is the Son of
David? For David himself says, by the Holy Spirit, *The Lord said
to my Lord: Sit thou at my right hand, till I make thy enemies thy
footstool. David himself, therefore, calls him 'Lord,' how, then, is
he his son?*" (Mark XII: 35–37.)

Earlier, Jesus had given His disciples the following
directive about the colt of an ass: "And if anyone say to you,
What are you doing? you shall say that *the Lord* has need
of it, and immediately he will send it here" (Mark XI: 3).
However, the name "Lord" cannot be understood in the
full sense in the text just cited, or in this one: "Not everyone
who says to me, *Lord, Lord,* shall enter the kingdom of
heaven; but he who does the will of my Father in heaven
shall enter the kingdom of heaven" (Matt. VII: 21). On the
other hand, in the *texts proper to Luke*, the frequent phrases
with Κύριος are not merely formulas of politeness due to
any famous rabbi.[4] The title is already used in the Infancy
accounts (Luke I: 43; II: 11, 26) and later, especially from
chapter VII on. At the sight of the widow of Naim *"the
Lord* had compassion on her, and said to her, 'Do not weep'"
(Luke VII: 13). The Third Evangelist has certainly in mind
a Greek-speaking community for which Jesus is the Κύριος.

The postpaschal formulation (cf. Luke XXIV: 34; Mark XVI: 19f.) is even more evident in the Fourth Gospel, where Κύριος is always used to designate the Risen Jesus (cf. chs. XX, XXI). Certainly a greater dignity than that of *rabbi* underlies the name "Lord" in this remark of Jesus' to His Apostles: "You call me Master and *Lord*, and you say well, for so I am" (John XIII: 13).[5] But several previous uses of the word Κύριος (cf. IV: 1; VI: 23) do not belong firmly to the primitive text. On the other hand, Thomas' confession in the Risen Jesus is inspired by a cultual veneration. As a matter of fact, the exclamation "My *Lord* and my God!" (John XX: 28) must be interpreted strictly: it expresses perfectly the faith of the primitive community for which Jesus of Nazareth is the glorified Christ and the divine Κύριος, sovereign of all created beings, visible and invisible. The continual use of Κύριος in the first part of the Book of Acts (chs. I–XV) attests this usage.

In his many studies devoted to the title "Lord," Msgr. Cerfaux is particularly interested in showing that the name Κύριος dates back to the primitive community and designates Jesus as the reigning Messiah. Let us examine briefly the relations between the title Κύριος and the royal dignity of Jesus.[6] The frequent use of the Hebrew *'adôn* (cf.II Kings XVIII: 27) or of the Aramaic *mārē* (cf. Dan. IV: 16, 21)[7] to designate sovereigns makes this title (Κύριος in Greek) a truly "royal epithet." Occasionally the conflict between the Roman Empire and Judaism was based on a refusal to grant the title Κύριος to the emperor. Two reasons were advanced for the refusal: the fear of seeming to approve the cult given to the emperor and the inaptitude of a pagan to be God's delegate. The Psalms of Solomon already protest against Pompey's claims: "He said: I shall be Lord (Κύριος) of the earth and sea, and he did not recognize that God alone is great, powerful, and truly strong" (II: 33).

Since royal dignity has always been considered, and rightly so, as the main attribute of the Messiah, "the royal epithet," Κύριος, was fittingly bestowed on him. The expression χριστὸς Κύριος, used once in the Septuagint (Lam. IV: 20), is found in the Psalms of Solomon, for example in this passage describing the reign of the Messiah, son of David: "He is a just king, instructed by God, placed over them; and during his days there is no iniquity among them; for all are holy, and their king is Christ the Lord (XVII: 36; cf. XVIII: 8).

As for the origin of the Christological title Κύριος, we have pointed out the influence of the prayer *marana tha*, "Come, our Lord!" related to the *parousia*. The epithet *marana*, according to Cerfaux, "is technically royal." "The first Christians," he adds, "pictured the Parousia for themselves under the light of a royal inthronisation of a triumphal entry of the heavenly ruler into his earthly kingdom."[8]

Traces of the tendency to connect the title Κύριος with the Messianic (royal) dignity and to the Reign of Christ are quite obvious in the Gospels. Sent to requisition the donkey for the triumphal entry into Jerusalem, the disciples say to the owner when they speak of Jesus: "*The Lord* has need of it" (Mark XI: 3). Now before all else the event of Palm Sunday was a Messianic manifestation whose sense Matthew defined: "Now this was done that what was spoken through the prophet might be fulfilled" (Zech. IX: 9; Isa. LXII: 11):

> *Tell the daughter of Sion:*
> *Behold, thy king comes to thee,*
> *Meek and seated upon an ass,*
> *and upon a colt, the foal of*
> *a beast of burden.*
>
> (Matt. XXI: 4 f.;
> cf. Mark XI: 10.)

Certain uses of the title Κύριος in Luke seem to reflect the primitive vocabulary of the Judaeo-Christians, who applied the title *Marana*-Κύριος to Jesus.[9] The Angel of the Lord announced to the shepherds that there was born in the (royal) city of David, a Saviour, Christ the *Lord* (Luke II: 11). Elizabeth's exclamation could be interpreted in the same sense: "And how have I deserved that the mother of my *Lord* should come to me?" (Luke I: 43). She addresses her sovereign's mother and recalls the dignity of the mother of the king, which was recognized in the Old Testament and in the Semitic world.

From the primitive community St. Paul received the faith expressed in the formula, "Jesus is Lord" (cf. Κύριος Ἰησοῦς, Rom. X: 9; I Cor. XII: 3). "There is normally," writes Msgr. Cerfaux, "a connection between Κύριος and the resurrection and *parousia*. The resurrection is the Messiah's enthronement as Christ or Messianic king. Christ exalted, and seated at God's right hand, is the sovereign whose solemn entrance we are awaiting."[10] The different applications that the notion of sovereignty lends itself to, made easy the passage from the Messianic (royal) sense of Κύριος to the properly divine meaning of the title. After the Resurrection, the sovereignty of Christ was understood as stretching across the entire range of Christian life (cf. Rom. XIV: 6ff.): "For to this end Christ died and rose again, that he might be Lord both of the dead and of the living" (Rom. XIV: 9). While the term "Christ" more particularly designates the (king) delegate of God, Κύριος tends to identify Christ with God. As we have said, such an identification was facilitated by the transfer of the attributes of the Lord Yahweh to Christ. The sovereignty of Christ the Lord was early seen in its cosmic dimensions, commanding respect "in heaven, on earth and under the earth" (Phil. II: 10).

According to Taylor, the origin of the application of the title Κύριος to Christ depended on many factors: the fact of the Resurrection; the waiting for the *parousia* (cf. I Thess. IV: 16); the memory of the parables in which the master (Κύριος) of the vineyard (Mark XII: 9) or of the servants (Matt. XXV: 19; Luke XII: 36) appears; Jesus' words on Ps. CIX: 1 (Mark XII: 35ff.);[11] the use of Κύριος in the Septuagint; finally and principally, the presence of Jesus experienced in the community's life of worship. Without denying the influence of these factors, we consider others to be yet more important: the implications of the superhuman personality of Jesus as manifested in His life and teaching; the revelations made to the Apostles and to Paul in particular; the directives of the Holy Spirit to the community: "He will teach you all the truth" (John XVI: 13).

NOTES ON 28

[1] On this question the theory of W. Bousset, expounded in his *Kyrios Christos* (Göttingen, 1913, 2nd ed.: 1921), is well known. "His thesis was very radical. He claimed that the religious title of *Kyrios*, being oriental in origin, was used especially to designate the gods who occupied the cultic foreground in 'mystic' circles. The little communities of Christians of Greek culture would then have treated Jesus as one of these gods before Saint Paul appeared on the scene. Paul would thus have received either from Antioch, Tarsus or Damascus, both the title *Kyrios* and the mystic basis of all his theology" (L. Cerfaux, *Christ in the Theology of Saint Paul*, New York, 1959, pp. 461–62). According to E. Lohmeyer, *Christuskult und Kaiserkult* (Göttingen, 1919), "the cult of Jesus would be the exact parallel of the cult of the emperors and the oriental kings" (L. Cerfaux, *op. cit.*, p. 462). Cerfaux (*ibid.*, pp. 462–79) pointed out the weak points of "these very adventurous theories" and exposed the true antecedents of the Christological title Κύριος. In the same direction, with an insistence on cultual influences: O. Cullmann, *Christology of the New Testament* (chapter on "The Lord"). The title Κύριος has been studied in its entirety by W. Foerster and G. Quell in *Theologisches Wörterbuch zum Neuen Testament*, vol. III (Stuttgart, 1938), pp. 1038–95: English translation (1958) in the series *Bible Key Words*. A monumental, posthumous work of W. W. Baudissin, *Kyrios als Gottesname im Judentum und seine Stelle in der Religionsgeschichte* (Giessen, 1929) "directed in the author's thought . . . against Bousset, applies to Judaism a theory more or less connected to that of the former. Here again the importance of Hellenism in the history of the title Kyrios is stressed" (L. Cerfaux, in *DBS*, vol. V, c. 201).

[2] On the ancient hymns incorporated into the New Testament, cf. M. E. Boismard, *Quatre hymnes baptismales dans la Première Épitre de Pierre* (Paris, 1961), pp. 7–14. The main part of the book analyzes I Pet. I: 3–5; II: 22–25; III: 18–22; V: 5–9.

[3] "At the moment of His Resurrection, Jesus entered a manner of being which is that of God Himself. He received the 'Name above every other name,' the proper name of God, an ineffable Name, as the Being of God is incomprehensible. In prolonging Jewish liturgical usage which substituted the title

Lord for the sacred tetragram, thereby making it a revelation of the
ineffable Name, we see the Christians giving the Risen Jesus the title 'Lord'
and attaching the same meaning to it" (J. Dupont, "Nom de Jesus," in
DBS, vol. VI, c. 540). L. Cerfaux has formulated clarifications on the subject
of Paul's use of the title for Christ: "Whenever he cites explicitly or
virtually, and especially when he clarifies and arranges his references
carefully, as in the Epistle to the Romans, where he indicates the exact
source that he is using, he keeps for Κύριος its value as a proper name for
God (the Father). There are few exceptions to this rule. Only when he is
no longer arguing from the text and is quoting it from memory does the
Christian 'rule' replace the exegetical rule" (*Recueil Lucien Cerfaux*, vol. I,
pp. 186f.). The "rule" admits other exceptions: "There are, nevertheless,
contexts where Saint Paul lets the Christian reading come into the Old
Testament . . . " (p. 187).

4 "It is not surprising that the use of this title should occasionally overlay
the gospel writers' reminiscences, to the extent that they speak of the 'Lord
Jesus' even when describing events of his earthly life. This we find particularly in Luke and John, in which the title simply denotes the Saviour as
Christians know him" (L. Cerfaux, *Christ in the Theology of Saint Paul*,
p. 466). Cf. p. 258.

5 Some have attempted to find in this passage a trace of the usage *mari* ("my
Lord") to designate Jesus during His public life. But an almost parallel
passage in Matthew hardly favors such a supposition: "But do not you be
called *Rabbi*; for one is your Master [διδάσκαλος], and all you are brothers"
(XXIII: 8).

6 Cf. L. Cerfaux, "Le titre Kyrios et la dignité royale de Jésus," in *Recueil
Lucien Cerfaux*, vol. I, pp. 3–63.

7 Applied to God to designate Him as Lord and sovereign, the word *'adôn*
adds the suffix to form *'adônî*, "my Lord," and is regularly used in the
(intensive) plural under the form *'adônāi*. The vowels of this expression
served as a perpetual *qeré* (for reading) to the sacred tetragram יהוה,
which was probably pronounced Yahweh, and certainly not Jehovah (cf. the
testimony of Clement of Alexandria: *Stromata*, V, ch. 6, n. 34). In place of
mārē', (with suffix: *mārî'*, "my Lord"), postbiblical Aramaic uses *mar* without
the terminal *aleph*.

8 L. Cerfaux, article "Kyrios," in *DBS*, vol. V, c. 216.

9 Cf. p. 256. The expressions "brethren of the Lord" (I Cor. IX: 5), and
"the brother of the Lord" (Gal. I: 19) certainly came to Paul from
Jerusalem (cf. L. Cerfaux, *art. cit.*: c. 221).

10 L. Cerfaux, *Christ in the Theology of Saint Paul*, p. 465.

11 Peter made a similar use of Psalm CIX in a discourse to the crowd. Having
recalled the fact of Christ's Resurrection with the help of Psalm XV he
continues:

> For David did not ascend into heaven, but he says himself: "The Lord
> said to my Lord: Sit thou at my right hand until I make thy enemies
> thy footstool. Therefore, let all the house of Israel know most
> assuredly that God has made both *Lord* and *Christ*, this Jesus whom you
> crucified." (Acts II: 34–36.)

By His Resurrection, Peter then concludes, Jesus was made the "Lord" of
which Psalm CIX speaks and the "Messiah" (Christ) to which Psalm XV
refers (cf. *BJ* and p. 54).

29

THE LOGOS

THERE is no exact equivalent for the Greek term Λόγος, used in the Prologue of the Fourth Gospel. "Word" may be used in English, *"Parole"* in French or *"Verbum"* in Latin, provided that they are understood to include all that is involved in the notion of Revelation. Some reliable authors believe that John incorporated in his Prologue a primitive Christian hymn dedicated to the Logos. It would even be possible to reconstruct the hymn with its four strophes, two with couplets and two with triplets:[1]

I. *In the beginning was the Word,*
    and the Word was with God;
    and the Word was God.

    All things were made through him
    and without him was made nothing
    that has been made.

II *In him was life*
    and the life was the light of men.

    He was the true light
    that enlightens every man.

III *He was in the world*
    and the world knew him not

    He came unto his own,
    and his own received him not.

IV   *And the Word was made flesh
       and dwelt among us,
       full of grace and truth.*

       *Of his fullness
       we have all received
       grace for grace.*

No other Christological title better underscores that *pre-existence* of Jesus (cf. John XVII: 5, 24) whose meaning later theology will clarify: three persons exist from all eternity in a single, divine substance; the second Person, the Word or the Son, took on flesh at a precise moment in history. Jesus, the incarnate Logos, is a divine person existing in two natures, human and divine. These formulas express the components of a reality that will never cease being a profound mystery for the human mind. Nevertheless the Johannine developments of the Logos are directly concerned with showing that the action of Christ did not begin with His earthly existence. From Creation on, He was at work, pre-existing as the Word. Although the truth about the Logos was given us by Revelation, we may seek out the influence that previous ideas could have exercised on its formulation.

Salvation history with Jesus as its center dates back to the beginning of time. Anxious to stress that, John has his Prologue recall the priestly account of the world's creation (Gen. I: 1–II: 4). Both texts open with the expression "in the beginning" and never stop insisting on the presence and activity of the *Word* in his relations with the light. In Hebrew, the word *dabar* means "event" and "history" (cf. Luke II: 15; Latin), just as well as "word." The divine word makes history. The economy of grace is a new creation; it is proclaimed by a new Genesis.

The Old Testament celebrates the creative word as an autonomous power: it made the heavens (Ps. XXXII: 6; cf. Ps. CXVIII: 89f.) and worked cures (Ps. CVI: 20); it runs rapidly, transmitting God's orders (Ps. CXLVI: 15); it does not return to Him until its mission is accomplished (Isa. LV: 11). The Wisdom writings will insist on the word's activity: by it all things were made (Sir. XLII: 15; Wis. IX: 1) and subsist (Sir. XLIII: 26); it executes divine judgments (Wis. XVIII: 14–16).

There is, however, a more direct biblical approach to the Johannine mystery of the Logos: that of *Wisdom personified.* The Synoptic Gospels (cf. Matt. XI: 19; Luke XI: 49)[2] and a few certain Pauline texts (cf. I Cor. I: 30) discreetly affirm that Jesus is Wisdom incarnate, an identification stressed by the Fourth Gospel, especially in the Prologue which applies to the Logos the same attributes that the Sapiential books attributed to Wisdom: from all eternity it dwells before God, presides at creation (Prov. VIII: 22–31), rules the universe (Wis. VIII: 1), and reflects eternal light (Wis. VII: 26). Sent on a mission to earth (Wis. IX: 10; Prov. VIII: 31), to "choose the spot for a tent" (Sir. XXIV: 8), it comes up against the opposition of men (Prov. I: 24ff.). In more recent writings, Wisdom is identified with the *Torah*, the Jewish Law (cf. Sir. XXIV: 23; Bar. IV: 1).[3] John suggests that henceforth Wisdom is the Logos, the incarnate Son of God. In John I: 17, however, a different antithesis is proposed: "For the Law was given through Moses; grace and truth came through Jesus Christ."

The philosopher Heraclitus in the sixth century B.C. and, later on, the Stoics used the term *Logos* to designate the divine principle that penetrates and governs the cosmos. Plato made the Logos the ideal archetype of things, and Philo considered it as the intelligible cosmos and the first creature of God. In Gnostic thought the Logos constituted, according to some authors, "an intermediary, mythological being between God and man." It cannot be repeated too often: the same words in John mean something totally different from those extrabiblical speculations which did not speak of an incarnate Logos who would save the world. Nevertheless, the expression did possibly enter the Christian language through a Hellenistic vocabulary. The use of the expression *Logos* could correspond to the primitive ideas of faith in the Lord, Creator of the world (cf. I Cor. VIII: 6; Col. I: 16), which were associated with the biblical prerogatives of Wisdom (which becomes the Logos in John). From Wisdom, which says of God the Creator "then was I beside him as his craftsman," it was a rather easy transition which led to the Logos, who was "with God, without whom nothing was made" (John I: 3).

In the Old Testament, Wisdom (*Hokmâh*) is present at creation rather like an exemplary idea (noetic aspect), while the Word (*dabar*) plays an active role, except in several texts where it is said to be present and unmoving at Yahweh's side: "Your word, O Lord, endures forever; it is firm as the heavens. Through all generations your truth endures; you have established the earth, and it stands firm" (Ps. CXVIII: 89f.; cf. John V: 17). Both functions are assumed in the Johannine Logos with whom, however, the concept of *life* is associated, rather than that of stability (a Greek idea).

*

*   *

By writing "the Word was made flesh," John wanted to dissipate every misunderstanding: the *Word* is not a philosophical abstraction of a divine being clothed in a human appearance, as the Docetists taught. For the evangelist, the Logos is the pre-existing, *personal* Christ, who at an historical moment assumed a human nature:

And the Word was made flesh and dwelt among us. And we saw his glory—glory as of the only-begotten of the Father—full of grace and of truth (I: 14.)

The notions of *light* and *glory* are correlative. After speaking of one at the beginning of the Prologue, John continues with the other to describe the Incarnation. A subsequent title will give us the occasion to treat the mystery of Jesus, "brightness of the glory of God" (Heb. I: 3), especially in relation to biblical Wisdom. Let us simply note here that a *Pauline* text testifies to the pre-Johannine use of the concept of glory to describe Christ: "For God, who *commanded light to shine out of darkness*, has shone in our hearts, to give enlightenment concerning the glory of God, shining on the face of Christ Jesus" (II Cor. IV: 6).

In the Prologue the main features of the figure of the Logos are linked to the idea of creation. But at the end of the literary unit, another theme comes forth, that of the Logos *revealer of God:* "No one has at any time seen God. The only-begotten Son, who is in the bosom of the Father, he has revealed him" (I: 18). Certainly, it can be objected that the *Son* is directly envisaged here. But, precisely, there is, in John's mind, identity also between the Logos and the Son. Furthermore, the "glory of God" also designated the sensible manifestation of God. The unity of all that appears in v. 14 cited above. St. Paul professed the same doctrine in his affirmations on Christ "image of the Invisible God" (Col. I: 15). Thus, v. 18, too, announces themes that will be taken up throughout the Fourth Gospel (cf. XV: 15; XVII: 6). For John, the Logos is not only God's thought *about the world*, it is also quite simply "God's thought."

*

*　　　*

A concern for anti-Docetist realism also appears in the first lines of the First Epistle of John, which on many counts, parallels those of the Gospel prologue:

I write of what was from the beginning, what we have heard, what we have seen with our eyes, what we have looked upon and our hands have handled: of *the Word of life.* And the Life was made known and we have seen, and now testify and announce to you, the life Eternal which was with the Father, and has appeared to us. (I: 1f.)

By admitting—and it seems that we must do so—the priority of the Prologue's underlying hymn to the epistle, we can easily explain the brusque, isolated expression "Word of Life." The author of the epistle has linked the qualifier "life" to a notion already known and accepted.

The formula "Word of Life" evokes a widespread biblical current, well represented in the Old Testament by *Deuteronomy*, which repeatedly insists that the Word of God (almost personified—cf. XXX: 14) is a source of life (XXXII: 45ff.). In the primitive Church the Gospel itself— the total reality of Jesus—is considered as the word of life (Acts V: 20; Phil. II: 16), "the good news" (Acts X: 36), as Christ Himself taught (cf. John V: 24f., 39f.). Nevertheless, it was the Prologue of the Fourth Gospel that bridged the gulf by identifying Jesus with the Logos. The theme "Word of Life" finds other echoes. Faithfulness to the directives of that word as contained in the Law conditioned the growth in Israel of the divine gift of life: "Not by bread alone does man live, but by every word that comes forth from the mouth of God" (Matt. IV: 4; Deut. VIII: 3; Wis. XVI: 26). The Synoptic parable of the sower (cf. Mark IV: 13–20) reveals the marvelous fruit that the word can produce for those who receive it.

In certain texts we are orientated toward the personification of the Word without completely attaining it. The word of the Lord is glorified (Acts XIII: 48f.); it grows (VI: 7; XII: 24) and the Apostles dedicate themselves to its service. The Captivity Epistles often have recourse to the theology of the Word: the mystery of the whole Christ, on the way to fulfillment in the Church, is designated by the term *Logos* twice (Col. I: 25; IV: 3); to Christians it is said: "Let the word of Christ dwell in you abundantly"

(Col. III: 16); the "brethren" grow bold in proclaiming the word (Phil. I: 14) and shine like luminous hearths in presenting "the word of life" to the world (II: 16).[4]

In the Fourth Gospel the word of Jesus is often presented as the very word of the Father (cf. XIV: 24; XVII: 14). There the term *Logos* does not ordinarily designate the entire message of Jesus, but "the living word full of the authority of the Master." The prophetic formula: "the Lord said to . . ." is not present here to authenticate the preaching of one whom a heavenly voice identified thus: "This is my beloved Son; hear him" (Mark IX: 6). "Because He *is* the Word, Jesus *does not speak* the Word."[5] Certain formulas that He uses let it be understood: "If you abide in my word, you shall be my disciples indeed" (John VIII: 31); "If you abide in me, and if my words abide in you, ask whatever you will and it shall be done to you" (XV: 7). But it was left to the Prologue of the Fourth Gospel to affirm clearly the personification or hypostasis of the Word. Even in the formula *mēmra' da' Adônaï* ("Word of the Lord") from the Targums, which may have suggested the Johannine Logos, the stage of poetic personification already begun in the Old Testament has not been surpassed.

*

*   *

According to the Epistle to the Hebrews the word of God reveals the intimate orientation of each one of us:

> For the word of God is living and efficient and keener than any two-edged sword and extending even to the division of soul and spirit, of joints also and of marrow, and a discerner of the thoughts and intentions of the heart. (IV: 12f.)

The Johannine Christ had proposed the same idea differently: "He who rejects me, and does not accept my words, has one to condemn him. The *word* that I have spoken will *condemn* him on the last day" (John XII: 48). Here as elsewhere in the Fourth Gospel there is a tendency to identify the word and the Judge (cf. III: 19–21). Since Jesus is "the way, the truth, the life in person" (XIV: 6), His words are "truth and life" for believers (VI: 51) and condemnation for the unbeliever (III: 18).

Thus one gets closer to the "Logos of God" of the Apocalypse. The knight who receives this name is *the exterminating Logos:* Christ in His eschatological function as judge at the end of time. The theme of the vengeful word of God received its most characteristic expression in this passage from the Book of Wisdom where the inspired author describes the execution of the divine will upon Egypt's firstborn:

For when peaceful stillness compassed everything and the night in its swift course was half spent, Your all-powerful word from heaven's royal throne bounded, a fierce warrior, into the doomed land bearing the sharp sword of your inexorable decree. And as he alighted, he filled every place with death; he still reached to heaven, while he stood upon the earth. (XVIII: 14ff.)

Several elements of the context (Apoc. XIX: 11–15) confirm that "the Word of God" is the exterminating Logos: "And he who sat upon it [a white horse] is called Faithful and True, and with justice he judges and wages war . . . he is clothed in a garment sprinkled with blood (of vengeance; cf. Isa. LXIII: 3) . . . *from his mouth goes forth a sharp sword* with which to smite the nations . . . he treads the wine press of the fierce wrath of God almighty." In the equipment necessary for the Christian's spiritual combat, St. Paul says, is "the sword of the spirit, that is, the word of God" (Eph. VI: 17). This could refer to particular, inspired words, useful at the moment of temptation (cf. Matt. IV: 4–10), or, more generally, to the revelation of God in Jesus Christ.

Is it not rather advisable not to limit the theological range of the expression "Logos of God" to the sense suggested (Apoc. XIX: 13)? Since the title is a *secret name* (Apoc. XIX: 12), would it not be, as the Logos of the Prologue, revelatory of God, its ineffable expression?

NOTES ON 29

[1] See R. Schnackenburg, "Logos-Hymnus und johanneischer Prolog" in *Biblische Zeitschrift* (1957), pp. 69–109.

[2] Cf. p. 279.

[3] Cf. p. 82. Compare Deut. XXX: 12 and Bar. III: 29.

[4] On the Pauline notion of the Word of God, cf. H. Schlier in *Littérature et théologie pauliniennes*, pp. 127–41. Also a book written in collaboration: *La parole de Dieu en Jésus-Christ* (Tournai, 1961).

[5] J. Starcky, art. *Logos*, in *DBS*, vol. V, c. 482. On *Logos*, cf. J. Dupont, *Essais sur la christologie de saint Jean* (Bruges, 1951), pp. 9–58; H. Schlier, *Le temps de l'Église* (Tournai, 1961), pp. 278–90; M. E. Boismard, *St. John's Prologue* (London, 1961); F. M. Braun, *Jean le Théologien*, vol. II (Paris, 1964), pp. 137–50; R. Schnackenburg, *New Testament Theology To-day* (New York, 1963), pp. 93f. He writes: "The *Logos* theme is an example of how John reveals that, while his roots were always in the Old Testament, he was also open to Hellenistic Judaism and to the spiritual currents of his time; but we must be careful not to reduce everything to this sort of pattern" (p. 94).

30

THE POWER AND THE WISDOM OF GOD

ACCORDING to St. Paul, two classes of men did not recognize God as they should have: the pagans, who knew Him and yet did not honor Him as God; the Jews, who by refusing the Gospel misunderstood the designs of Divine Providence. "But to those who are called, both Jews and Greeks, Christ, *the power of God and the wisdom of God.* For the foolishness of God is wiser than men, and the weakness of God is stronger than men" (I Cor. I: 24f.).[1] The pagans of the Graeco-Roman civilization considered the Cross an absurdity, and the Jews expected a Messiah invested with a spectacular power. Weakness in the eyes of the Jews and folly for the Greeks, Christ is actually the strength of God and the wisdom of God.

JESUS, POWER OF GOD

Power is one of the chief divine attributes. In the Old Testament the categories of Power, rather than those of being, serve in defining divinity. The divine name *El* (singular of Elohîm) probably means "powerful." At any rate, in Genesis there is mention of "the strength of the Mighty One of Jacob" (XLIX: 24; cf. Ps. CXXXI: 2) and Isaiah calls Yahweh, "the Mighty One of Israel" (I: 24) and "the Mighty One of Jacob" (XLIX: 26; LX: 16). God revealed His saving might in an exceptional manner at the Red Sea crossing; that might then, is the divine attribute most frequently mentioned in the famous song of victory that followed the miraculous event (Exod. XV: 1–18).

The *new economy* is the work of the power of God. The angel announces to Mary: "the Holy Spirit shall come upon thee and the *power* of the Most High shall overshadow thee" (Luke I: 35). Later on the Virgin was to declare: "He who is *mighty* has done great things for me" (Luke I: 49). Jesus Himself mentions divine power in a saying that perhaps respects the rabbinic refusal to pronounce God's name; He answers the High Priest: "And you shall see the Son of Man sitting at the right hand of *the Power* and coming with the clouds of heaven" (Mark XIV: 62).

In the *Pauline* perspective the Gospel "is the *power* (δύναμις) of God unto salvation to everyone who believes" (Rom. I: 16). The power of God particularly bursts forth in the mystery of the Resurrection: "Now God has raised up the Lord and will also raise us up by his *power*" (I Cor. VI: 14; cf. Col. II: 12). "What the exceeding greatness of his *power* towards us who believe. Its measure is the working of his mighty *power*, which he has wrought in Christ in raising him from the dead, and setting him at his right hand in heaven . . ." (Eph. I: 19f.). Christ's Resurrection is also attributed to "the glory of the Father" (Rom. VI: 4); yet more often to God Himself (I Thess. I: 10; I Cor. XV: 15), an indication that the Apostle does not envisage too precise an attribution. Towards the end of his life, St. Paul again proclaimed: To God "be honor and everlasting dominion" (I Tim. VI: 16).

The Gospels call the power of *Christ* ἐξουσία. He teaches (Matt. VII: 29) and acts with authority (ἐξουσία). More especially, Jesus has been invested with such power in virtue of his role as judge. The Father "granted him power (ἐξουσία) to render judgment, because he is the Son of Man" (John V: 27). Jesus began to exercise this judgment by the remission of sins. To show the Scribes "that the Son of Man has power on earth to forgive sins," He says to the paralytic: "Arise, take up thy pallet and go to thy house" (Matt. IX: 6). The crowds "glorified God who had given such power *to men*" (IX: 8).[2] To the Apostles Jesus "gave power (ἐξουσία) over unclean spirits, to cast them out, and to cure every kind of disease and infirmity" (Matt. X: 1). If they forgive sins, their decision must be ratified in heaven (Matt. XVIII: 18). This limitation is absent from Jesus' power. The insistence of the Gospels on the ἐξουσία of the Son of Man in His role as Judge certainly evokes this verse from Daniel, where the term ἐξουσία (in the LXX) affirms three times the power conferred on the Son of Man:

He received *dominion* [ἐξουσία], glory and kingship; nations and peoples of every language serve him. His dominion is an everlasting dominion that shall not be taken away, his kingship shall not be destroyed. (Dan. VII: 14.)

The power exercised by Jesus during His earthly life anticipated and announced the power that would invade Him at the moment of His Resurrection, and especially the eschatological power which would assure His victory over His enemies at the end of time. The Risen Christ declares to His Apostles: "All power in heaven and on earth has been given to me" (Matt. XXVIII: 18). Daniel's prophecy was fulfilled and Satan's alleged power (Luke IV: 6) is now conferred on the Son of Man, who bestows it on His Apostles: "Go, therefore, and make disciples of all nations, baptizing them in the name of the Father, and of the Son, and of the Holy Spirit" (Matt. XXVIII: 19). Jesus had foretold: "Amen I say to you, there are some of those standing here who will not taste death, till they have seen the kingdom of God coming *in power*" (Mark VIII: 39; cf. I Cor. IV: 20). During His life on earth, Jesus, according to Luke, was led by "the power of the Spirit" (IV: 14), a power at work since the Incarnation (I: 35) and particularly active at the birth of the Church (XXIV: 49; Acts I: 8).

At His Resurrection Jesus is proclaimed Son of God in a special manner (Acts XIII: 33) and is even "foreordained Son of God by an *act of power* in keeping with the holiness of his spirit, by resurrection from the dead" (Rom. I: 4).

For all *Christians* "the power of the Holy Spirit" begets hope (Rom. XV: 13; cf. I Cor. II: 4). This internal strength that characterizes the Kingdom was used discreetly, but surely, during Jesus' lifetime (cf. Mark IV: 26–32). At harvest time, on the last day, "when all things are made subject to him, then the Son himself will also be made subject to him who subjected all things to him, that God may be all in all" (I Cor. I: 24). The Power will then return to God who had sent it on a mission in the world. Thus ends our survey of a theme related to the title "Power of God" which St. Paul had recalled to the Corinthians (I Cor. I: 24).

JESUS, WISDOM OF GOD

In the same verse (I Cor. I: 24) St. Paul calls Jesus "Wisdom of God." Surprisingly enough, the title is nowhere else applied to Christ in the New Testament. One reason could be that the term σοφία, "wisdom," had become unusable because of its association with current gnostic conceptions. Numerous allusions, however, reveal, as we shall see, the conviction of New Testament authors: Jesus is the Wisdom of God.

The idea of wisdom is of current use in the Old Testament. Under a *first form*, it designates a natural quality that education and experience confer on man. Along with the priests, the prophets, and the military, exceptional subjects of this quality belonged to a ruling class (cf. Jer. XVIII: 18). Royal counselors before the Exile (cf. I Kings XII: 6), the Sages were later recruited among the Scribes trained in the Law of Moses (cf. Sir. XXXIX: 1–11). This natural wisdom, long identified with the art of happy living, was later to be animated by a religious spirit and inspired by a fundamental moral principle: "The fear of the Lord is the beginning of *wisdom*" (Greek: Prov. I: 7; cf. Sir. I: 11–20).

But there is *another* wisdom, superior and proper to the divinity. In itself this wisdom is an inaccessible mystery for man. After having described the various human activities, the Book of Job declares that for all his efforts man could not discover Wisdom or explain its origin:

> *Whence, then, comes wisdom, and where is*
> *the place of understanding?*
> *It is hid from the eyes of any living being,*
> *from the birds of the air it is concealed.*
> *God knows the way to it;*
> *it is he who is familiar with its place.*
> (XXVIII: 20–23.)

In view of a special mission, the gift of a wisdom reflecting that of God was granted to several privileged men. Daniel received it and celebrated it in a hymn that, like Paul's writing (I Cor. I: 24), associates it with power:

> *Blessed be the name of God forever and ever,*
> *for* wisdom *and* power *are his.*
> *He causes the changes of the times and seasons,*
> *makes kings and unmakes them.*
> *He gives* wisdom *to the wise*
> *and knowledge to those who understand.*
> *He reveals deep and hidden things*
> *and knows what is in the darkness,*
> *for the light dwells with him.*
> *To you, O God of my fathers,*
> *I give thanks and praise,*
> *because you have given me* wisdom *and* power.
> *Now you have shown me what we asked of you,*
> *you have made known to us the king's dream.*
> (Dan. II: 20–23.)

This wisdom accomplishes God's works, such as Creation (cf. Prov. III: 19) and tends to become identified with the divine Spirit (Wis. IX: 17; cf. VII: 22ff.). A well attested literary process (cf. Prov. I–IX) often presents Wisdom as a personal being, present everywhere, omniscient (Wis. VII: 21–8; VIII), capable of exhorting men (Prov. IX: 1–6), with whom it deigned to converse after its appearance on earth (Bar. III: 36ff.). "The idea of a personified wisdom, a simple literary device in Prov. XIV: 1, grew in Israel after the Exile when polytheism no longer threatened the true religion" (*BJ*: Prov. VIII: 22).

Wisdom is "an aura of the *might* of God and a pure effusion of the glory of the Almighty . . . the refulgence of eternal light, the spotless mirror of the power of God, the image of his goodness" (Wis. VIII: 25f.). If such a description glorifies the excellence of Wisdom, it nevertheless distinguishes it from God, as one of His attributes. This exact conception further announced and prepared the way for the Incarnation of the Son of God. Three sapiential books, Proverbs, Sirah, and Wisdom, betray literary contacts with Daniel that permit an association of the more or less hypostatized Wisdom and the figure of the *Son of Man* (through the mediation of "the glory of the Lord" as related to both concepts of divine manifestation).[3] In these three books (cf. p. 197), too, another idea is especially stressed: although Wisdom, a source of salvation (Wis. IX: 18), dwells on high, borne on the clouds (Sir. XXIV: 4; cf. Dan. VII: 13) and sharing the throne of God (Wis. IX: 4; Dan. VII: 9), it does not refuse to come down on earth, "in the holy Tent" (Sir. XXIV: 10), to visit the sons of men (Prov. VIII: 31). To Baruch's question about Wisdom, "Who has gone up to the heavens and taken her, or brought her down from the clouds?" (Bar. III: 29), the evangelist answers: "No one has ascended into heaven except him who has descended from heaven: the Son of Man who is in heaven" (John III: 13).

The identification of Jesus with Wisdom appears especially in the Fourth Gospel.[4] From the Prologue on, the description of the Word and His work is inspired by the attributes of Wisdom. The discourses of the Johannine Christ contain frequent allusions to Old Testament themes found in the Wisdom discourses. We think especially of the hospitable Wisdom:

> *Wisdom has built her house,*
> *she has set up her seven columns;*
> *She has dressed her meat, mixed her wine,*
> *yes, she has spread her table.*
> *She has sent out her maidens; she calls*
> *from the heights out over the city:*
> *"Let whoever is simple turn in here;"*
> *to him who lacks understanding, I say,*
> *"Come, eat my food,*
> *and drink of the wine I have mixed!*
> *Forsake foolishness that you may live;*
> *advance in the way of understanding."*
>
> (Prov. IX: 1–6.)

> *I spread my branches like a terebinth,*
> *my branches so bright and so graceful*
> *I bud forth delights like the vine,*
> *my blossoms become fruit fair and rich.*
> *Come to me, all you that yearn for me,*
> *and be filled with my fruits;*
> *You will remember me as sweeter than honey,*
> *better to have than the honeycomb.*
> *He who eats of me will hunger still,*
> *he who drinks of me will thirst for more;*
> *He who obeys me will not be put to shame,*
> *he who serves me will never fail.*
>
> (Sir. XXIV: 16–22.)

In the Fourth Gospel Jesus never tires of saying: "Come to me!" to me, "the light" (John III: 20f.), to me, "the life" (V: 40), "the bread of life" (VI: 35), "the living water"

(VII: 37; cf. Isa. LV: 1). To experience Wisdom is to vivify the desire to possess her (Sir. XXIV: 21). Jesus, however, grants more: "He who comes to me shall not hunger and he who believes in me shall never thirst" (John VI: 35; cf. IV: 14). The beneficiaries of this bounty are like those exiles in the Deutero-Isaiah, who "will no longer hunger or thirst" upon returning to their country (XLIX: 10). Christ is the vine that nourishes the branches and makes them *bear fruit* (John XV: 1–17). Like Wisdom, Jesus, the kindly master, invites all to taste the sweetness of His protection:

Come to me, all you who labor and are burdened,[5] and I will give you rest. Take my yoke unto you, and learn from me, for I am meek and humble of heart; and you will find rest for your souls. For my yoke is easy, and my burden light. (Matt. XI: 28ff.)

Other parallels can be proposed: they concern those who turn a deaf ear to the invitation. Wisdom forewarns the careless: "Then they call me, but I answer not; they seek me but find me not" (Prov. I: 28). A similar warning touches the Jews rebellious to the message of Jesus: "You will seek me and will not find me" (John VII: 34). The Deutero-Isaiah had already exhorted his contemporaries thus: "Seek the Lord, as long as he will be found; invoke him as long as he is near" (Isa. LV: 6; cf. Amos VIII: 11f.). Let us also remember that the "I am" formula, so frequent in the mouth of the Johannine Christ, offers affinities with the emphatic "I" of Wisdom.[6]

The mysterious character of Wisdom has already been pointed out: "None knows the way to her, nor has any understood her paths" (Bar. III: 31); "God knows the way to it; it is he who is familiar with its place" (Job XXVIII: 23). In popular belief the Messiah would remain concealed until his spectacular advent :"When Christ comes, no one will know where he is from" (John VII: 27). The pre-existence of Jesus blurs the facts of His origin: "I know where I came from and where I go. But you do not know where I came from or where I go" (John VIII: 14).

Other Gospel texts only faintly suggest that the title Wisdom of God belongs to Jesus. The following apostrophe is directed to the lawmakers: "For this reason also the *wisdom of God* has said, I will send them prophets and apostles; and some of them they will put to death and persecute . . ." (Luke XI: 49). For Matthew it is Jesus who pronounces the oracle: "Therefore, behold, I send you prophets, and wise men, and scribes; and some of them you will put to death . . ." (XXIII: 34). Some reliable authors think that the following aphorism refers to Jesus: "Yet wisdom is justified by her deeds" (Matt. XI: 19; *RSV*). A prudential axiom of this type was known to Ben Sirah: "Call no man happy before his death, for by how he ends, a man is known" (Sir. XI: 28). Did Jesus Himself not clearly reveal the presence of this Wisdom in a declaration transmitted by a source common to Luke and to Matthew: the queen of the South "came from the ends of the earth to hear the wisdom of Solomon, and behold, a greater than Solomon is here" (Luke XI: 31; Matt. XII: 42)?

*
* *

St. Paul does not condemn in itself that human wisdom which is the sum of the knowledge naturally accessible to the human mind. This wisdom prepared Moses for his role (Acts VII: 22), and it is not without prestige (I Cor. II: 1). However, when it is compared to the Wisdom of God (I Cor. I: 19), its inferiority becomes obvious. The revelation of the wisdom of God is gratuitous (cf. I Cor. II: 7), as is the fulfillment of *God's saving plan* whose secrets it possesses (II Cor. II: 11; cf. Rom. XI: 33). The folly of human wisdom consists in not knowing or in misunderstanding the divine salvation pattern and, in particular, the great saving act of the Cross (I Cor. I: 20–25). The wisdom of God, on the contrary, has become flesh in one who is going to realize His plan for salvation: "Christ Jesus, who has become for us God-given *wisdom*, and justice, and sanctification and redemption" (I Cor. I: 30). In unfolding His power God confided to Paul the grace "to announce among the Gentiles the good tidings of the unfathomable riches of Christ . . . in order that through the Church there be made known to the Principalities and the Powers in the heavens the manifold *wisdom* of God according to the eternal purpose which he accomplished in Christ Jesus our Lord" (Eph. III: 8–11).

This concrete *Wisdom* is an *object of knowledge:* "For I determined not to know anything among you, except Jesus Christ and him crucified" (I Cor. II: 2). The gift of wisdom enables Christians to come to "complete understanding, so as to know the mystery of God, the Father of Christ Jesus, in whom are hidden all the treasures of wisdom and knowledge" (Col. II: 2f.; cf. Eph. III: 9). The knowledge of Wisdom is one of God's prerogatives, as "the knowledge of good and evil" makes one like Elohîm (Gen. III: 5). The secrets of Wisdom are revealed, however, to those who, through faith, perceive the *unfolding of the plan of salvation* in God's saving interventions (cf. Heb. XI). The date of the last day will be revealed at its coming (cf. Matt. XXIV: 36). The "little ones" are more fit to receive the revelation of the mysteries of the kingdom than "the wise and prudent" (Luke X: 21).

We have seen above the use made of the Wisdom discourses in the hymn on the primacy of Christ (Col. I: 15–20). The same source of inspiration appears in the more abstract description of the Son of God as the refulgence of his glory and the effigy of his substance (Heb. I: 3). *The Wisdom of the Old Testament tends to become identified with the divine Spirit* (Wis. IX: 17; cf. VII: 22ff.). "But we all," St. Paul writes, "with faces unveiled, reflecting as in a mirror the glory of the Lord (Jesus), are being transformed into his very image from glory to glory, as through the *Spirit* of the Lord" (II Cor. III: 18). According to St. Cyril of Alexandria, the Lord, Jesus Christ, is Spirit, for in virtue of His Resurrection in the Holy Spirit (Rom. VIII: 11), "the last Adam became a life-giving spirit" (I Cor. XV: 45). The relation of Christ to the Spirit is clarified elsewhere when Paul writes about condition of Christians: "You, however, are not carnal but spiritual, if indeed the Spirit of God dwells in you. But if anyone does not have the Spirit of Christ," he does not belong to him (Rom. VIII: 9). The identity and the distinction which regulate the relationship between the Lord and the Spirit remain hidden from us like a profound mystery. A secret full of wisdom, long hidden in God, is, however, revealed in the coming of Jesus:

Now to him who is able to strengthen you in accordance with my gospel, and the preaching of Jesus Christ, according to the revelation of the mystery which has been kept in silence from eternal ages, which is manifested now through the writings of the prophets according to the precept of the eternal God, and made known to all the Gentiles to bring about obedience to faith—to the only wise God, through Jesus Christ, be honor forever and ever. Amen. (Rom. XVI: 25ff.)

NOTES ON 30

[1] Cf. L. A. Rood, "Le Christ comme δύναμις θεοῦ," in *Littérature et théologie pauliniennes*, pp. 93–108.

[2] Cf. p. 237.

[3] According to F.-M. Braun, the Son of Man of the Fourth Gospel is closer to Wisdom than to the glorious apocalyptic Man: *Jean le Théologien*, vol. II, p. 149.

[4] Cf. R. J. Dillon, "Wisdom Tradition and Sacramental Retrospect in the Cana Account (John II: 1–11)," *CBQ* (1962), pp. 268–96.

[5] By the burden of the Law and of the pharisaic observances which overload it even more. The "yoke of the Law" is a common rabbinic metaphor: cf. Sir. LI: 26; Lam. III: 27; Jer. II: 20; V: 5; Zeph. 3, 9 (Greek) and Isa. XIV: 25 (see *BJ* on Matt. XI: 28). Concerning the application of the title "Wisdom" to Christ, cf. also A. Feuillet, "Jésus et la Sagesse divine d'après les évangiles synoptiques" (*Revue Biblique*, 1955, pp. 161–96), where "the Johannine logion" of Matt. XI: 25ff. and Luke X: 21f. is especially treated.

[6] On *ego eimi* see pp. 6of, and H. Zimmermann, "Das absolute 'Εγώ εἰμι als die neutestamentliche Offenbarungsformel," *Bibl. Zeitschrift* (1960), pp. 54–69; 266–76.

31

THE IMAGE OF THE INVISIBLE GOD
THE EFFIGY OF HIS SUBSTANCE
THE REFULGENCE OF HIS GLORY

THESE three titles can be examined together, for they are close both in meaning and in formulation. The first appears in the Epistle to the Colossians (I: 15); the other two try to describe the Son of God at the beginning of the Epistle to the Hebrews (I: 3). Three main concepts are implied in these titles: image (effigy), light, glory. The relationship of these themes appears in two texts from the Second Epistle to the Corinthians:

And if our gospel also is veiled, it is veiled only to those who are perishing. In their case, the god of this world has blinded their unbelieving minds, that they should not see the *light* of the gospel of the *glory* of Christ, who is the *image* of God.

(IV: 3; cf. Wis. VII: 25f.)

But we all, with faces unveiled, *reflecting* as in a mirror the *glory* of the Lord, are being transformed into his very *image* from glory to glory, as through the Spirit of the Lord. (III: 18.)

A similar relationship underlies the following development from the Epistle to the Romans: those whom God has chosen beforehand have also been predestined to reproduce the *image* of His Son; He has called them, justified and *glorified* them (VIII: 29f.).

CHRIST, IMAGE OF GOD

The texts cited use the metaphor of the image in a double manner: they describe Christ in relation to God and man in relation to Christ. Such an association of ideas derives from a Pauline interpretation of the Messianic restoration: the Son of Man, or the heavenly man, has always been the perfect image of the Father; faithful and obedient to His vocation as Servant, He has restored humanity by His sacrifice to its original dignity, accomplishing the Father's will to make man conform to that divine image that is the Son.

Paul repeatedly affirms the dual fact of the original fall and of the rehabilitation: "For if by the offense of the one the many died, much more has the grace of God, and the gift in the grace of the *one man* Jesus Christ, abounded unto *the many*" (Rom. V: 15). In the same epistle he adds that the redeemed have been predestined by God "to become conformed to the image of his Son, that he should be the firstborn among many brethen" (Rom. VIII: 29). Since His pre-existence, "Image of the invisible God, Firstborn of every creature" (Col. I: 15) by His divine being, Christ has become the leader of all the redeemed by His work of reconciliation. According to the Genesis account, although man was created in God's image (I: 26f.; cf. Wis. II: 23), he lost that dignity by succumbing to the temptation offered: "You will be like God, knowing good and evil" (III: 6, 22). Paul certainly is thinking of that fall, when he writes:

Strip off the old man with his deeds and put on the new, one that is being renewed unto perfect knowledge "according to the image of his Creator." (Col. III: 9f.; cf. I John III: 2.)

This new creation (cf. II Cor. V: 17) took place at baptism in which we put on Christ (Rom. VI: 4). Progress in the interior life is described by St. Paul as a spiritual renovation which further conforms the baptized to the image of Christ (Rom. VIII: 29), the very image of God (II Cor. IV: 4; Col. I: 15). *The image of the second creation* surpasses the first in beauty; furthermore, its value grows with the Christian's interior progress: "But we all are being transformed into his very image, from glory to glory, as through the Spirit of the Lord" (II Cor. III: 18).

Paul suggests a new application of the notion of God's image, but always in the same context, that opposing the first and the last Adam. Here the transformation of bodies by the *resurrection* is in question:

The first man, Adam, became a living soul; the last Adam became a life-giving spirit. But it is not the spiritual that comes first, but the physical, and then the spiritual. The first man was of the earth, earthy; the second man is from heaven, heavenly. As was the earthy man, such also are the earthy; and as is the heavenly man, such are the heavenly. Therefore, even as we have borne the likeness of the earthy, let us bear also the likeness of the heavenly. (I Cor. XV: 45–49.)

It is not the human soul (ψυχή), the natural principle of life, that explains for St. Paul the resurrection of the bodies, but the Spirit (πνεύμα) which, through the soul, penetrates the body which it makes "pneumatic," in a certain sense "spiritual," like that of the Risen Christ: "But if the Spirit of him who raised Jesus from the dead dwells in you, then he who raised Jesus Christ from the dead will also bring to life your mortal bodies because of his Spirit who dwells in you" (Rom. VIII: 11). Elsewhere, this glorification of the bodies is attributed to Christ Himself, who has been "foreordained Son of God by an act of power in keeping with the holiness of his spirit, by resurrection from the dead" (Rom. I: 4):

But our citizenship is in heaven from which also we eagerly await a Saviour, our Lord Jesus Christ, who will refashion the body of our lowliness, conforming it to the body of his glory by exerting the power by which he is able also to subject all things to himself. (Phil. III: 20f.)

It is clear that "the predestined to become conformed to the image" of the Son of God (Rom. VIII: 29) are the future risen with Christ whose *glorified body* is also, in its way, an image of God (cf. I Cor. XV: 49; II Cor. III: 18).

"He is the Image of the Invisible God" (Col. I: 15). This basic assertion is set in a development (I: 15–20) whose rhythmic structure recalls the style of one of those primitive Christological hymns from the liturgy (cf. the title "The Firstborn"). At any rate, St. Paul accepts such a description of Christ, as is attested to by many uses that he makes of it. When he describes Christ as the image of God, the Apostle draws a theme he was fond of: Adam was the figure (τύπος) of him who was to come (Rom. V: 14). Created in the image of God, father of mankind according to the flesh, he announced Christ, the last Adam (I Cor. XV: 45), the *new head of the human race*, the Image in which God restored His creation (cf. Rom. VIII: 29). In Jesus Christ God sees humanity in His image, like the one he had planned to create. If the historic *person* of the Son of God made man can play such a role in "the history of salvation," it is that already in its pre-existence it was the perfect image of the Father.

In the language of the ancients, which the Pauline metaphor echoes, the image (εἰκών) of a being is not its resemblance but its expression: *the image is the thing itself expressed.* Pauline vocabulary finds a resonance in the accepted terminology. A few years before Paul a Jewish-born Greek philosopher, Philo, discussed the Logos, and found it an imperfect image of God. For the Apostle, however, the "image" of God that is Christ is so perfect that it equals the model: the Son differs from the Father, theology adds, solely because He is "begotten." The Son is also an image of God in His Incarnation; by it He becomes visible and manifests the Father (John I: 18).

Father Huby writes of Col. I: 15: "The word εἰκών (image) means resemblance and derivation. Resemblance alone is not enough, for there must be a relation between the image and the prototype from which it derives. The *image* can result from an artificial imitation: for example, a portrait or a photograph; it can be due to natural causes:

the son in relation to the father; but it always implies derivation from an archetype. Therefore, the glory of the image reflects on its exemplar."[1]

*

*   *

A still more exact expression from the Prologue to the Epistle to the Hebrews describes the Son as the perfect replica of the Father. The whole context deserves citing, for it affirms the divinity of the Son, first in His very being and then in His functions:

God who at sundry times and in divers manners spoke in times past to the fathers by the prophets, last of all in these days has spoken to us by his Son, whom he appointed heir of all things, by whom also he made the world; who, being the brightness of his glory and the image of his substance,[2] and upholding all things by the word of his power, has effected man's purgation from sin and taken his seat at the right hand of the Majesty on high, having become so much superior to the angels as he has inherited a more excellent name than they. (Heb. I: 1–4.)

The phrase "effigy of His substance" translates the Greek χαρακτήρ τῆς ὑποστάσεως αὐτοῦ which could be interpreted as "the expression of the divine being." The term "imprint" or "stamp" also translates the Greek χαρακτήρ well and underscores "the absolute likeness, the rigorous identity" between God and the Son, to whom the Father wholly communicates His divine nature. Even more so than εἰκών, an "image," capable of various definition, χαρακτήρ affirms that the Son is "the adequate expression of the Father's nature." The word ὑπόστασις does not mean "person," here as in the fourth century, but the substance or essence of a being. Here the emphasis is on the identity of nature, while the next expression, "the refulgence of His glory," clearly denotes the distinction of the persons. Philo fused Biblical thought and Platonism when he called the soul "figure and imprint of the divine power" and described the Logos as an effigy engraved on the seal of God and stamped on creatures. With similar language the Epistle to the Hebrews expresses some aspects of revealed truth, which will provide a basis for the later elaboration of Trinitarian theology.

THE REFULGENCE OF DIVINE GLORY

This subtitle is a formula from the Prologue to the Epistle to the Hebrews, cited above *in extenso*. It translates the Greek phrase ἀπαύγασμα τῆς δόξης which certainly depends on this Old Testament passage describing Wisdom:

For she is an aura of the might of God and a pure effusion of the glory [δόξης] of the Almighty; therefore nought that is sullied enters into her.

For she is the refulgence [ἀπαύγασμα] of eternal light, the spotless mirror of the power of God, the image [εἰκων] of his goodness. (Wis. VII: 25f.)

The term ἀπαύγασμα, "refulgence" or "reflection," can also be translated "radiation," an interpretation that more adequately suits the brightness derived from the glowing hearth. Sedulius Scotus wrote in the Middle Ages: "Just as radiation is not separated from the sun, so too the radiation of Paternal glory is inseparable from the Father." These words remind us how appropriate the metaphor of radiation is for the profound mystery of the Son's generation by the Father. Light, the most immaterial element known on earth, flows incessantly from the source from which it emanates and whose intensity it reflects. "*Lumen ex lumine*" will be the Nicaean Creed's clear expression of the Son's consubstantiality with the Father. Nevertheless the tradition is a *biblical one* that the author of Hebrews decided to use when he described the Son as "refulgence of divine glory."

THE GLORY OF THE LORD

In the Wisdom text just cited, the three concepts *glory*, *radiation*, and *image* are associated; the same is true of Paul's reproach to the unbelieving who do "not see the *light* of the gospel of the *glory* of Christ, who is the *image* of God" (II Cor. IV: 4). Rabbinic writings explain that the image of God, which illumined Adam's face, was a reflection of God's *glory*. The Fourth Book of Esdras, an extra-canonical Jewish work of the Christian era, teaches that the face of the blessed will shine with a brilliance greater than that of the stars (VII: 55). St. Paul remembers the biblical account of the Creation and sees the luminous glory shining on the face of Christ:

> For God, who commanded light to shine out of darkness, has shone in our hearts, to give enlightenment concerning the knowledge of the glory of God, shining on the face of Christ Jesus. (II Cor. IV: 6.)

According to its etymology, the Hebrew term *Kabôd*, "glory" (cf. I Sam. IV: 21), contains the idea of weightiness. In this sense, St. Paul can talk of "an eternal weight of glory" reserved for the chosen (II Cor. IV: 17). But the *glory of the Lord* is almost always associated with light, probably because it often took on the sensible aspect of luminous phenomena, since constant biblical usage associates light with the presence of God: the pillar of light guiding the Hebrews (Exod. XIII: 21f.), the descent of Yahweh under the form of fire at Sinai (Exod. XIX: 18), the divine power in the lightning (Ps. XVII: 14f.), the fire of eschatological judgment (Isa. LXVI: 16). In a poem that seems to belong to "the Messianic cycle of chapters IX and XI" (*BJ*), Isaiah describes the protection which God will provide to Jerusalem purified:

> *Then the Lord will create,*
> *over the whole site of Mount Sion*

and over her place of assembly,
A smoking cloud by day
and a light of flaming fire by night.
For over all, his glory
will be shelter and protection:
shade from the parching heat of day,
refuge and cover from storm and rain.

(IV: 5f.)

More directly, according to the priestly tradition, "the glory of Yahweh" is a "consuming fire" (Exod. XXIV: 17) and a dazzling light that will shine on the face of Moses (Exod. XXXIV: 29–35). Because of His transcendence the glory of Yahweh is inaccessible to man here below. Moses must be content to perceive its other side or reflection:

Then Moses said, "Do let me see your glory!" He answered, "I will make all my beauty pass before you, and in your presence I will pronounce my name, 'Lord'; I who show favors to whom I will, I who grant mercy to whom I will. But my face you cannot see, for no man sees me and still lives. Here," continued the Lord, "is a place near me where you shall station yourself on the rock. When my glory passes I will set you in the hollow of the rock and will cover you with my hand until I have passed by. Then I remove my hand, so that you may see my back; but my face is not to be seen." (Exod. XXXIII: 18–23; cf. Isa. VI: 3–5.)

In another tradition the "glory of Yahweh" accompanied the Hebrews of the Exodus *under the form of a cloud* (Exod. XVI: 10; cf. XIII: 21) and guided their march: "Then the cloud covered the Meeting Tent and the glory of the Lord filled the Dwelling . . . whenever the cloud rose from the Dwelling the Israelites would set out on their journey" (Exod. XL: 34–36). After having dwelled in the ark of the covenant (cf. Ps. XXIII: 7–10; I Sam. IV: 21) and in Solomon's temple (I Kings VIII: 11; cf. Ps. XXV: 8), the "glory of Yahweh" left Jerusalem in 587 to follow the exiles (cf. Ezek. X: 18–22), to be "their sanctuary" (Ezek. XI: 16), and then returned to be installed in a

purified, restored temple (Ezek. XLIII: 1–9). That sensible
and active presence of God in the cloud prefigured the
Incarnation, that descent of the glory of the Lord into Mary,
the new ark of the covenant (as we saw in the title "Son
of Mary"):

> *And the Word was made flesh,*
> *and dwelt among us.*
> *And we saw his glory—*
> *glory as of the only-begotten of the Father—*
> *full of grace and of truth.*
>
> (John I: 14.)

The oracle of Isaiah was fulfilled: "Then the glory of the
Lord shall be revealed and all flesh shall see it" (XL: 5).
Like the Prologue to the Fourth Gospel, the third part of
the Book of Isaiah associates the ideas of glory and light in a
prelude that heralds a glorious resurrection of Jerusalem in
Messianic times:

> *Rise up in splendor! Your light has come,*
> *the glory of the Lord shines upon you.*
> *See, darkness covers the earth,*
> *and thick clouds cover the peoples;*
>
> *But upon you the Lord shines*
> *and over you appears his glory.*
> *Nations shall walk by your light,*
> *and kings by your shining radiance.*
>
> (Isa. LX: 1–3.)

This prophet himself "saw the glory of Christ" (John
XII: 41) at the time of his vocation (cf. Isa. VI: 1–13). The
"father of believers" was also graced with a privileged
vision: upon learning that he will be father of a son whose
name would be Isaac (abridged form of *Yshq-El*, "God
smiled") he laughed. Jesus said, then, to the Jews: "Abraham your father *rejoiced* that he was to see my day. He
saw it and was glad" (John VIII: 56). After a brief examination of earlier New Testament writings we shall return to
the Johannine interpretation of the glory of Christ.

DOXOLOGIES AND ESCHATOLOGICAL GLORY

The Greek term δόξα translates the Hebrew *Kabôd* and enters into the composition of the expression "doxology," a formula, that is, which gives homage to God by proclaiming His glory. In classical Greek δόξα meant "opinion" (cf. "orthodoxy"), a meaning that, applied to the judgment given to others, favored the adoption of its derivatives: reputation, honor, and glory (cf. John XII: 43).

One of the first New Testament *doxologies* was sung, in Luke's telling, by the angels at Jesus' coming: "*Glory* to God in the highest, and on earth peace among men of good will" (II: 14). The Synoptic Gospels (cf. Mark II: 12; Matt. IX: 8) and in particular Luke (cf. VII: 16; XVII: 15) and Acts (cf. IV: 21) report that on many occasions the witnesses of the miraculous events "glorified God." Herod Agrippa I, on the other hand, refused to render *glory* to God, and rank himself as a creature, and so he died suddenly the death of persecutors (Acts XII: 22f.).

St. Paul himself formulated or transmitted *several doxologies* that are almost always addressed to God or to the Father, through the mediation of Christ: "To the only wise God, through Jesus Christ, be honor forever and ever. Amen" (Rom. XVI: 27). When Paul confides to the Corinthians that he is busy with a collection "for the glory of the *Lord*" (II Cor. VIII: 19), he seems to mean the glory of *Christ*, just as when he affirmed: if the princes of this world had known "the wisdom of God," they would not have crucified "the Lord of glory" (I Cor. II: 8).

Other writings clearly transfer to Christ formulas commonly addressed to God: "that in all things God may be honored through Jesus Christ, to whom are the glory and the dominion forever. Amen" (I Pet. IV: 11; cf. II Pet. III: 18). The author of the Epistle to the Hebrews prays to God for his readers: that He "fit you with every good thing to do his will, working in you that which is well pleasing

in his sight, through Jesus Christ, *to whom is glory* forever
and ever. Amen" (Heb. XIII: 21). Two doxologies from
the Apocalypse (I: 5f.; V: 12) are addressed to Christ also
and add that through them homage is given Him for His
redemptive work.

New Testament writings frequently present Christ's
Resurrection as a glorification (cf. Luke XXIV: 26)—often
with an implicit reference to the rehabilitation of the
Servant (cf. Acts III: 13; Isa. LIII: 11f.). This is hardly the
place tó insist on this aspect or on the glorification that is to
mark Christ's *parousia* (cf. Matt. XVI: 27). Paul describes
this *eschatological glory* in one of his epistles with features
that the prophets and the Psalmist applied to the coming
of Yahweh (cf. II Thess. I: 7–10). Such glory will also be
communicated to Christians (cf. Col. III: 4), particularly
at the resurrection of the dead (Phil. III: 20f.; cf. Matt.
XIII: 43). Desirous of encouraging the persecuted Christians,
Peter writes to them from Rome:

But rejoice, in as far as you are partakers of the sufferings of
Christ, that you may also rejoice with exultation in the revelation
of his glory. If you are upbraided for the name of Christ, blessed
will you be, because the honor, the glory and the power of God
and his Spirit rest upon you. (I Pet. IV: 13.)

The presence of the luminous cloud at the *Transfiguration* (cf. Matt. XVII: 5), the mention of the "glory" of
Jesus (Luke IX: 32), and of the brightness of His face and
person (Matt. XVII: 2)—all suggest that this theophanic
event anticipated the glory of the Resurrection and the
parousia and was the promise of it proclaimed by the Father.
The Second Epistle of Peter also proposes just such an
interpretation:

For we were not following fictitious tales when we made known
to you the power and coming of our Lord Jesus Christ, but we
had been eyewitnesses of his grandeur. For he received from
God the Father honor and glory, when from out the majestic

glory a voice came down to him, speaking thus: "This is my beloved Son in whom I am well pleased." And this voice we ourselves heard borne from heaven when we were with him on the holy mount. (I: 16ff.)

THE GLORY OF THE JOHANNINE CHRIST

Luke's mention of "the glory of Jesus" (IX: 2) in relation to His earthly existence constitutes an isolated testimony outside of the Fourth Gospel. *On the other hand, the evangelist John openly proclaims Jesus' divine sonship and also often affirms that a glory accompanied the person of the Son of God even during His life on earth.* The rabbis called the glorious presence of God *šekinâh*; the expression also occasionally designated God Himself, whose sacred name was not pronounced out of excessive respect (cf. II Pet. I: 17). John probably refers to the notion in the Prologue to his gospel (I: 14.).[3]

In the Synoptics the voice of the Father had proclaimed in favor of the transfigured Jesus: "This is *my beloved Son*; hear him" (Mark IX: 7). The Johannine Prologue affirms that the Word made flesh holds His glory from the Father whose *"only-Son"* He is (John I: 14.). The glory of the Father and that of the Son go hand in hand. About Lazarus, Jesus declares: "This sickness is not unto death, but for the glory of God, that through it the Son of God may be glorified" (John XI: 4). Another miracle, the one at Cana, performed by Jesus, "manifested His glory and His disciples believed in Him" (John II: 11). The glory of the Johannine Christ during His life on earth is not manifest, as it would be at the Transfiguration, by a luminous phenomenon; only faith allows us to perceive it (John XI: 40), for miracles glorify the Son of Man by attesting that He is the Son of God (cf. XI: 4).

The coming of the Son of God on earth appears in the Fourth Gospel as a sort of *parousia, an anticipated parousia,* which is the central idea in John's perspective of an actualized eschatology. The postpaschal, heavenly condition of Jesus somehow coexists with His earthly condition, especially on the last days of His Passion, for during His trial and on the Cross, Christ judges the "world" and conquers it (John XVI: 33; see also the title "Judge"). The titles "Son of God" and "Son of Man" are equally glorious; the prerogatives of the one are communicated to the other (cf. V: 25ff.). The hour of His death is for Jesus the hour of His glorification:

These things Jesus spoke; and raising his eyes to heaven, he said, "Father, the hour has come! Glorify thy Son, that thy Son may glorify thee, even as thou hast given him power over all flesh, in order that to all thou hast given him he may give everlasting life." (John XVII: 1f.)

One and the same hour includes the Passion and the Resurrection, for these are two aspects of one and the same mystery: the sacrificial passage to God. "Before the feast of the Passover, Jesus, knowing that the hour had come for him to pass out of this world to the Father, having loved his own who were in the world, loved them to the end" (John XIII: 1). Jesus' sacrifice accomplishes the Redemption and glorifies the Saviour: "The hour has come for the Son of Man to be glorified. Amen, amen, I say to you, unless the grain of wheat falls into the ground and dies, it remains alone. But if it dies, it brings forth much fruit" (John XII: 23f.; cf. XII: 32).

The Son asks the Father: "Glorify me with thyself, with the glory that I had with thee *before the world existed*" (John XVII: 5).[4] Addressing the Father again, He expresses the desire that the disciples rejoin Him: "in order that they may behold my glory, which thou hast given me, because thou hast loved me before the creation of the world" (v. 24). The formula "before the creation of the world" belongs to the Jewish apocalyptic desirous to link the eschatological event with the eternal design of God. The New Testament exploited this literary expression with profound realism. "Before the foundation of the world," the adoptive sons are chosen and predestined (Eph. I: 4; cf. Rom. VIII: 29f.) the Kingdom is prepared for the elect (Matt. XXV: 34), while the names of the wicked are not inscribed in the book of life (Apoc. XIII: 8; XVII: 8). Christ Himself was foreknown "before the foundation of the world" (I Pet. I: 20). In its obvious sense, John XVII: 24 affirms that, at the end of His life, Christ shall be reinstated in the glory that was His since the beginning (cf. Phil. II: 6) and which shall now be communicated to His humanity. The presence of this pre-existing glory had been perceived by Isaiah in the aforementioned texts.

A passage from the Second Epistle to the Corinthians will serve as our conclusion. Moses' forehead radiated with a reflection of divine glory after each conversation of the Prophet with God (Exod. XXXIV: 33ff.). According to Paul, the veil which covered his face concealed the gradual disappearance of the radiance (II Cor. III: 13). The opposite is true of the disciples of Jesus Christ for they reflect the glory of the Lord-God, with faces uncovered, in a permanent fashion, and with an increasing intensity that corresponds to the spiritual renewing of each one:

But we all, with faces unveiled, reflecting as in a mirror the glory of the Lord, are being transformed into his very image from glory to glory as through the spirit of the Lord. (II Cor. III: 18.)

NOTES ON 31

[1] J. Huby, *Saint Paul: Les Épitres de la Captivité*, p. 36. On "Man, image of God," cf. C. Spicq, *Dieu et l'homme selon le Nouveau Testament*, pp. 179–213. The function of the image is to show forth the original . . . The icon is the reality itself of the archetype as manifested. On these grounds in particular, the Son, radiating the entire glory of the Father, shall be the perfect image of the invisible God (II Cor. IV: 4; Col. I: 15) and His luminous copy (p. 204). "By becoming like Christ His disciples will realize their vocation as images and sons" (p. 210). Cf. *l'Épitre aux Hébreux*, vol. II, pp. 9f., 302, by the same author. On the subject of the notions in Heb. I: 3, J. Bonsirven believes that

they are first and perfectly verified in the Son contemplated in the bosom of the blessed Trinity; but, since the assuming of a human nature does not entail a lessening of divinity, all that can be said unreservedly about the Incarnate Son in whom the fullness of divinity resides (Col. II: 9): cf. *Saint Paul, Épître aux Hébreux* (coll. *Verbum Salutis*), p. 177. "Christ is then the mystery of God become visible," J. Coppens writes, "as the Church in turn makes the mystery of Christ visible" (*Littérature et théologie pauliniennes*, p. 157).

[2] This Confraternity translation is correct although it differs slightly from the one we have adopted for the titles in order to remain closer to the French edition of this book. *RSV* reads: "He reflects the glory of God and bears the stamp of his nature."

[3] See p. 129, n. 7. On "the glory of God," cf. *Christus*, No. XI (1956); on "the glory of Jesus" in St. John, cf. J. Mouroux, *The Mystery of Time* (New York, 1964).

[4] See also p. 263.

32

GOD

ALL the New Testament texts that affirm the divinity of Jesus cannot be examined here.[1] Our purpose is not to prove a thesis, but to reflect on the way the first Christians envisaged their faith. To set up a proof, for example, we should have to read all those passages from the Fourth Gospel that describe the very intimate relations between the Son and the Father, to show more clearly that the title "Lord" (Κύριος) implies the divinity of the one designated, recall other titles of Jesus, in particular those of the Logos and Son of God (cf. John V: 18), reread several formulas (cf. "I am") and finally study more closely those functions which appear in full light only if they are examined with faith in the divinity of Jesus. Our treatment will be hardly more than a commentary on the texts that designate Jesus as "God" or that apply Scriptural sayings originally addressed to God. Let us begin with the second category.

The facility with which the primitive community applies what was said of God to Christ is doubtlessly based on the example of Jesus Himself. The analysis of the title "Son of God" gave us some insight into the consciousness of the Johannine Christ to be able to speak of His relations with the Father in terms of equality, unity and reciprocal immanence. He also said to His disciples: "You believe in God, believe also in me" (John XIV: 1); "If you had known me, you would also have known my Father" (John XIV: 7); "He who sees me sees also the Father"

(XIV: 9). The Synoptics agree with John in citing and applying to Jesus' coming a saying from Deutero-Isaiah, which announced the Lord's intervention:

A voice cries out: In the desert prepare the way of the Lord! Make straight in the wasteland a highway for our God! (Isa. XL: 3.)

The return of the Babylonian exiles to Jerusalem was actually to be accomplished, as the first exodus across the desert, under the guidance of God Himself. In the gospels, the formulas "Make ready the way of the *Lord*" (Mark I: 3) or "Make straight the way of the *Lord*" (John I: 23) invite men to prepare in their hearts a way to the interior kingdom that the Lord Jesus is to come and establish.

Under the impulse of an extraordinary prophetic inspiration, about the year 400 B.C., Joel had foreseen the coming of the Day of the Lord as the inauguration of a new era, that this exclamation tried to describe: "*Then everyone shall be rescued who calls on the name of the Lord*" (III: 5). This assurance retains its full value in the Book of the Acts, where the One Invoked is God (II: 21) and in the Epistle to the Romans, where Christ is invoked: "For whoever calls upon the name of the Lord shall be saved" (X: 13). In Acts a similar transposition is current on the name "*Lord*": "the fear of the Lord" (IX: 42; XI: 17); "the turning [conversion] to the Lord" (IX: 35); "the ministering [service] of the Lord" (XIII: 2); "the saying [word] of the Lord" (VIII: 25); "the ways of the Lord" (XIII: 10; cf. Hos. XIV: 10). To be more precise, Paul received from the primitive community the formula designating Christians and the Church as "those who invoke the name of the Lord,"[2] a formula that transposes on Christ and Christians a way of defining the chosen people in relation to Yahweh.

The term Κύριος, "Lord," is the Septuagint translation for the sacred Old Testament words *Adonai* and *Yahweh*.[3] The primitive Church surely invoked Christ under the words *mar*, "Lord," *mari*, "my Lord," or *marana*, "our Lord" (cf. I Cor. XVI: 22). Corresponding to these Aramaic terms, the Greek Κύριος was soon applied to Jesus as is shown by three passages of the First Epistle to the Corinthians that "Christianize" Old Testament texts: "Who has known the mind of the *Lord*, that he might instruct him? But we have the mind of Christ" (II: 16; cf. Isa. XL: 13); "Neither let us tempt *the Lord* as some of them tempted, and perished by serpents" (X: 9; cf. Num. XXI: 6); "You cannot be partakers of the table of *the Lord* and of the table of devils" (X: 21; cf. Mal. I: 7, 12). To describe the glory of Christ, as we have seen under the title "Lord," St. Paul takes up (Phil. II: 10f.) the oracle of the Lord: "To me every knee shall bend; by me every tongue shall swear" (Isa. XLV: 23). The Epistle to the Hebrews (I: 10) follows the same procedure when it applies to Jesus this homage to the immutability of the Lord:

> In the beginning, O Lord, thou foundest the earth:
> and the heavens are the works of thy hands.
> They shall perish but thou remainest:
> and all of them shall grow old like a garment:
> and as a vesture, thou shalt change them,
> and they shall be changed. But thou art always
> the selfsame, and thy years shall not fail.
> (Ps. CI: 26ff.)

Other New Testament authors also make use of the same literary procedure to express the faith of primitive Christianity in the divinity of Christ. "Taste and see how good the Lord is," the Psalmist had said (XXXIII: 9). The author of the First Epistle of Peter recommends to his readers the desire for "spiritual milk," which assures growth, "if indeed, you have tasted that the Lord is sweet" (II: 3). The Apocalypse often applies to Christ images that the Old Testament used to speak of God. Therefore, in I: 14, Christ is represented under features drawn by Daniel (VII: 9) for the Ancient of days.

These peculiarities of primitive Christian language attest a deep faith: certainly Christ does not replace Yahweh, but the *same homages and the same prayers* are addressed to God and to the Lord Jesus; to the Son and to the Father are addressed the same confidence and the same love; one and the same cult venerates and worships both. There is no personal identification between Christ and Yahweh, but both have a unique and transcendent majesty. Nor is there any dispersion of the faith: "Yet for us there is only one God, the Father from whom all things, and we unto him; and one Lord, Jesus Christ, through whom are all things, and we through him" (I Cor. VIII: 6). The people of God are prolonged in the Church of God, the new Israel (I Cor. I: 2; X: 32). That explains why Paul speaks currently of the "Church of God" (Gal. I: 13; II Cor. I: 1) or of the "Churches of God" (I Thess. II: 14; II Thess. I: 4), while the expression "the Churches of Christ" is encountered only once in the New Testament (Rom. XVI: 16).

The current attribution of divine dignity to Christ is not contradicted by Paul's affirmation, that at the end "the Son himself will also be made subject to him who subjected all things to him" (I Cor. XV: 28). The meaning of the sentence is certainly the following: having recapitulated all humanity in Himself, Christ will do homage for it and Himself before God His Father. Nor let the objection be made against Christ's divinity, that He affirmed that the Father is greater than He (John XIV: 28). In the fourth century two acceptable interpretations were proposed to explain this declaration. The Son would be called "inferior" in so far as He proceeds from the Father. Nevertheless, the Son receives from the Father the sole divine nature and so is equal to the Father. The other interpretation, in greater conformity with Johannine thought, affirms that the Son is inferior to the Father in His humanity: "Equal to the Father according to divinity, inferior to the Father according to humanity" (Creed of St. Athanasius).[4] In His farewell discourse, the stress is placed on obedience to the Father. Considered as man, the Son has a will distinct from that of the Father. The Father is "greater" because He commands; the incarnate Son is inferior because He submits (cf. John VI: 38), especially at the moment when He is getting ready to accomplish His sacrifice (cf. John XIV: 31).

*

* *

Paul's thought provides an easy transition to the second development mentioned: *Christ called God*. For Paul, as we have seen, there is only one God, the Father . . . and one Lord, Jesus Christ (I Cor. VIII: 6). Christ is "the image of God," the "Son of God," the "Lord," titles that already imply divine dignity. "Paul's speculations carry him a step further in the letter to the Philippians II: 9–11. Here we find an express statement to the effect that the name given to Christ is the ineffable name which belonged to God in the Old Testament and manifested his power."[5]

Putting his habitual terminology aside, Paul probably gave Christ the name of God in a *doxology* that normally was to be addressed to the Father (cf. II Cor. XI: 31): following an enumeration of the privileges granted Israel, he names as last the patriarchs "from whom is the Christ according to the flesh, who is, over all things, *God* blessed forever, Amen" (Rom. IX: 5). In this case, if "God" refers to Christ,[6] it does not designate the divine Person of the Father, but rather the divinity, God's being (cf. John I: 1). Thus, for Paul, "in him [Christ] dwells all the fullness of the Godhead bodily" (Col. II: 9). Paul again hoped that the Colossians would come to "all the riches of complete understanding so as to know the mystery of God: Christ[7] in whom are hidden all the treasures of wisdom and knowledge" (II: 2f.). A third, even clearer text belongs to a *pastoral Epistle* and probably owes its precise redaction to a disciple secretary. In it the Apostle exhorts to live a moral life, "looking for the blessed hope and glorious coming of our great God and Savior, Jesus Christ . . ." (Tit. II: 13). A similar expression is found in the beginning of the Second Epistle of Peter:

Simon Peter, a servant and apostle of Jesus Christ, to those who have obtained an equal privilege of faith with ourselves through the justice of our *God* and Saviour Jesus Christ. May grace and peace be given you in abundance in the knowledge of our God. (II Pet. I: 1f.)

In His Johannine discourses Jesus repeatedly insists on the intimacy of the relations that unite Him to the Father. It is not surprising, then, that the Fourth Gospel is framed, so to speak, by two declarations that attribute the title Θεός, "God," to Christ. At the very beginning John said of the pre-existing Logos, identical to the Incarnate Logos: "In the beginning was the Word, and the Word was with God; and *the Word was God*" (I: 1). An impressive confession is recorded toward the end of the Gospel. Thomas, the unbeliever turned believer, addresses this cry of faith in the Risen One, whom he knew in His wounds: "My Lord and my God" (John XX: 28), a formula related to the rather frequent Old Testament expression: "The Lord is my God" (Zech. XIII: 9: Κύριος ὁ Θεός μου). Another passage from the Prologue must be cited according to a widely accepted variant reading: "No one has at any time seen God. The only-begotten Son [μονογενὴς Θεός], who is in the bosom of the Father, he has revealed him" (I: 18). By using the term *monogenes* in this context, St. John means that Jesus is the absolutely perfect expression of God: as the only-begotten Son He is not only the sole one to reflect the glory of His Father (cf. Heb. I: 2f.), but He possesses it without shadow or limit, adequately, in a total fullness."[8] Christians in turn share that immanence but do so in a different way: "We may know the true God and may be in His true Son. He is *the true God* and eternal life" (I John V: 20).

Lastly, let us cite the testimony of the Epistle to the Hebrews, which is also partly Johannine in character. In a context (cf. I: 3) that expresses the identity of nature between the Father and the Son as well as the distinction of persons (*BJ*), the vocative "God" designates the Son twice:

But of the *Son*, God says, Thy throne, *O God*, is forever and ever, and a sceptre of equity is the sceptre of thy kingdom. Thou hast loved justice and hated iniquity; therefore *God*, thy God, has anointed thee with the oil of gladness above thy fellows. (I: 8f.)

The *divinity* which here Psalm XLV (Greek) attributes hyberbolically (in the Oriental style) to the King-Messiah is understood in its strict sense (see v. 3). To Christ-God belongs an eternal kingdom (*BJ*).

NOTES ON 32

[1] Cf. J. Lebreton, *Histoire du dogme de la Trinité*, vol. I (Paris, 1927), pp. 253–652.

[2] Cf. I Cor. I: 2; II Tim. II: 22; Acts IX: 14, 16, 21, 22. On the expression "those who invoke the Name of the Lord," see J. Dupont in *DBS*, vol. VI, cc. 520–25. "In Christian language, *to invoke the name of the Lord* means practically: give to Jesus the name Lord, acknowledge his divine Lordship" (c. 522).

[3] See p. 261, n. 7.

[4] The so-called Athanasius Creed was not written by the great bishop of Alexandria. Redacted in Latin, owing much to Latin theology, it was worked out about the end of the fifth century in an Augustinian milieu (see: G. Dumeige, *La Foi Catholique*, p. 29).

[5] L. Cerfaux, *Christ in the Theology of St. Paul*, p. 477. On the application of the title Θεός, "God," to the Son, see K. Rahner, *Theological Investigations*, vol. I (London, 1961), pp. 135–48. There are six complete texts (Rom. IX: 5; John I: 1–18; XX: 28; I John V: 20; Tit. II: 13), writes Rahner, "in which Θεός is used to speak of the Second Person of the Trinity, but still in a hesitant and obviously restricted way (the restriction is concerned of course not with the reality but with the use of the word)" (p. 143). The purpose of Rahner's argumentation appears in the following passage: "These findings are sufficient in themselves to justify the assertion that when the New Testament speaks of ὁ Θεός, it is (with the exception of the six texts mentioned) the Father as First Person of the Trinity who is signified. Ὁ Θεός signifies him and does not merely stand suppositionally for him . . ." (p. 143f.). He had previously made the observation that in none of the six texts "is Θεός alone, without the addition of modifying clauses but with the article used to speak of Christ" (p. 136). Also on the application of the name "God" to Christ see a note in *Ephem. Th. Lovan.* (1962), p. 366. Cf. *CBQ*, 1965, pp. 545–73.

6 The commentators of Rom. IX: 5f. belong to two main groups. Some read the verse as we did and attribute to Christ the last words. Others believe it to be a doxology intended for God the Father and read: "... to them belong the patriarchs, and of their race, according to the flesh, is the Christ. God who is over all be blessed for ever. Amen" (*RSV*). The first interpretation has for it arguments "drawn from the structure of the passage and from its doctrinal context" (J. Huby, *Saint Paul, Épître aux Romains*, Paris, 1940), pp. 326–29).

7 "The mystery of God, Christ . . ." Variants read differently: "of God," "of Christ," "of God in Christ," "of God, the Father of Christ," "of God the Father and of Christ," etc. But these readings seem secondary and derived from the text proposed in the *BJ* translation, which we have adopted, and which is supported by the Beatty papyrus, the Codex Vaticanus and St. Hilaire of Poitiers (see P. Benoit in *Épître aux Colossiens* . . . , Paris, 1949, p. 58).

8 C. Spicq, *Dieu et l'homme selon le Nouveau Testament*, p. 91. The author reads John I: 18 thus: "A *Monogene*, God, who is in the Father's bosom" (p. 92). He adds: "Here the title *Father* is a substitute for God." Spicq believes it is a misconception to draw, as many modern authors do, from the use of *yahid* (μονογενής-ἀγαπητός) in the Old Testament (cf. Gen. XXII: 2) and to understand: Jesus is morally son, considered as son, as the elect particularly loved by God (p. 91, n. 3).

33

THE AMEN

THE expression "Amen" (Greek: ἀμήν) is used once as a properly Christological title: "And to the angel of the church at Laodicea write: Thus says *the Amen*, the faithful and true witness, who is the beginning of the creation of God" (Apoc. III: 14). Greek and Latin have taken up the Hebrew word just as it was. In this passage from an eschatological discourse of the Deutero-Isaiah the word is applied to God as an epithet: "He will be blessed on whom a blessing is invoked in the land (cf. Gen. XIV: 19); he who takes an oath in the land shall swear by the God of *truth* (litt.: by Elohîm *Amen*), for the hardships of the past shall be forgotten, and hidden from my eyes" (LXV: 16). The Seer of the Apocalypse[1] was thinking not only of this text but of the Old Testament and Judaism, when he attributed his message to the *Amen* and immediately explained it as "the faithful and true witness who is the beginning of the creation of God" (III: 14). Examining some biblical texts associated with the notion of *Amen* will be the best way to arrive at the meaning of the corresponding title.

The primitive sense of the Hebrew root of *Amen* was "to bear or carry" in the physical sense that led to the idea of "security," "steadfastness," "certainty," especially in relation to the fidelity of God: "Understand, then, that the Lord, your God, is God indeed, the *faithful* God who keeps his merciful covenant down to the thousandth generation toward those who love him and keep his commandments"

(Deut. VII: 9). In a *Messianic* context devoted to "the Servant" the fidelity of God is again recalled by the use of a word similar to *Amen*: "When kings see you, they shall stand up and princes shall prostrate themselves because of the Lord who is *faithful*, the Holy one of Israel who has chosen you" (Isa. XLIX: 7). The same terminology reappears in an oracle associated with the new covenant: "I will renew with you the everlasting covenant, the benefits assured to David" (Isa. LV: 3). It is not surprising, then, that the causative form of the root of *Amen* means "to believe": "Abram *believed* the Lord, who credited the act to him as justice" (Gen. XV: 6).

Other Old Testament uses of "Amen" deserve consideration. Banaias, David's chief guard, answers the king who tells him of his intention to name Solomon king: "Amen: so says the Lord the God of my lord the king" (I Kings I: 36). In a deuteronomic passage attributed to Jeremiah, the prophet answers "*Amen*, Lord", to the divine proposal (Jer. XI: 5). To the prophet Hananya Jeremiah will again answer: "*Amen*! thus may the Lord do! May he fulfill the things you have prophesied" (XXVIII: 6).

In its *liturgical* use, *Amen* is a community response proclaiming its complete adherence to what has just been said and wishing its fulfillment. The doxological "Amens" that end the three books of the *Psalms* (XL: 14; LXXI: 19; LXXXVIII: 52) attest that liturgical use, as does the First Book of Chronicles: "Blessed be the Lord the God of Israel from eternity to eternity: and let all the people say *Amen*" (XVI: 36).

The frequent New Testament mention of *Amen* at the end of the doxologies (cf. Rom. I: 25; Heb. XIII: 21) shows its ancient use in the Christian community as a *liturgical response*. In the course of a clarification on the use of the gift of tongues, St. Paul asks this question: "Else if thou givest praise with the spirit alone, how shall he who fills the place of the uninstructed say 'Amen' to thy thanksgiving? For he does not know what thou sayest?" (I Cor. XIV: 16). In the Apocalypse the *Amen* often concludes the heavenly hymns (cf. I: 7, V: 14) presumably modeled on earthly acclamations. St. Jerome records that the faithful of Rome used to answer "Amen" so loudly and in such great numbers that it resembled the rumbling of thunder.

The importance of the Christian *Amen* flows from its connection with the person of Jesus Christ. St. Paul said so in an astonishingly deep theological statement: "For all the promises of God find their 'Yes' (ναί in Greek) in him; and therefore through him also rises the 'Amen' to the glory of God" (II Cor. I: 20). The person of Jesus and His work are, in fact, the ground of our certitude in the fulfillment of the divine promises proclaimed by the liturgical responses "Amen." For that reason the Catholic liturgy ordinarily has the faithful's *Amen* follow the formula "through Jesus Christ Our Lord."

The term ναί from II Cor. I: 20 translated "yes" is practically synonymous with "Amen." In the beginning of the Apocalypse, the two terms are linked: ναί, αμήν (I: 7). So too in the Gospels, "*Amen*, I say to you" is often replaced by "ναί, I say to you" (Matt. XI: 9; Luke VII: 26). The use that Jesus made of the formula "Amen I say to you" (cf. Mark III: 28) is very unusual: in the Old Testament, "Amen" approves what precedes; in Jesus' mouth, it stresses what follows. The Son speaks with the authority (Mark I: 27) of one whom God "appointed heir of all things" (Heb. I: 2) and in whom promises are fulfilled (Rom. XV: 8; Gal. III: 16). In the Synoptics the *Amen* is never doubled while it always is in the Fourth Gospel where it is equivalent to a superlative and is found more than twenty times in different words of Jesus': "*Amen, amen*, I say to you, you shall see heaven opened and the angels of God ascending and descending upon the Son of Man" (John I: 51). A similar duplication is found in the Old Testament both in a rite of imprecation (Num. V: 22) and in a doxological response: "And

Esdras blessed the Lord the great God: and all the people answered, *Amen, amen* lifting up their hands: and they bowed down and adored God with their faces to the ground" (Neh. VIII: 6).[2]

This review of connected themes allows us to appreciate the entire range of the unique Apocalypse affirmation: "Thus says the *Amen*, the faithful and true witness, who is the beginning of the creation of God" (III: 14). Here three titles are united, the last two explaining the first whose origin is complex: Jesus' frequent use of the formula "*Amen (amen)* I say unto you," the text of Deutero-Isaiah explained above (LXV: 16); Paul's teaching in II Cor. I: 20; the final realization of the divine promises in Jesus: God kept His word, in Jesus, for the Word was made flesh (John I: 14). The title "Beginning of the creation of God" (Apoc. III: 14) reminds us of the Christological title "Firstborn of every creature" (Col. I: 15, 18). The affinity is not too surprising, for the Christological *Amen* is recalled (Apoc. III: 14) by the angel of the Church at Laodicea, a community associated by Paul with that of the Colossians (cf. Col. IV: 16). Perhaps the author of Apoc. III: 14 knew the Epistle to the Colossians.

The *glorified* Christ is the one that the Apocalypse calls the *Amen*, for this title belongs to one who has finished His work or rather to one whose presence in heaven as the immolated lamb (V: 6) testifies to the perfect fulfillment of the saving plan of God. This shall be the subject of eternal praise by the elect and in this sense Augustine was right to affirm that the occupation of the blessed in heaven consists in saying unendingly: *Amen! Alleluia!*

NOTES ON 33

[1] The *genus litterarium* of an apocalypse is well explained by A. Gelin in *La Sainte Bible* (Pirot-Clamer), vol. XII, pp. 588f. Also see p. 198; on Apoc. III: 14 see a critical note in *JBL* (1963), pp. 213–15.

[2] In the ritual prayers recited at Qûmran for admittance to the Covenant a *redoubled Amen* is also said (cf. *Manual of Discipline* I: 15 to II: 18).

CONCLUSION

ABOUT fifty names and titles of Jesus have been examined. Some are well known to the Christian people; another twenty or so have either lasted or passed into oblivion for various reasons. Certain names proved inadequate to express the person and work of Jesus as they gradually became better known by the Church. Those less fortunate words, however, also deserve the attention of the faithful, for they recall secondary or provisional aspects of the mystery of Jesus; in meditating upon them certain people will doubt-lessly find lights and consolations that the usual names no longer evoke.[1]

A historical study of the use of the names of Jesus across the Christian ages could usefully fill a life of research. In many respects its conclusions would doubtlessly touch upon those of the history of dogma, for the fate of these names is often bound to the tendencies of piety and theology. From that viewpoint, the half century that followed the public advent of Jesus witnessed a manifold orientation, the pattern of which has been briefly described by Vincent Taylor (*The Names of Jesus*, pp. 169ff.). From him we borrow some considerations.

The epoch in question includes three periods which can be defined easily enough: (I) the years of the public ministry; (II) the thirty years that followed the death of Jesus and are marked by the first evangelization and the first writings: St. Paul's Epistles, the Gospels, the Acts of the

Apostles; (III) a period of less definite length, comprising the two or three decades that separate the year 65 from the composition of the last canonical book. The following schema divides the names and titles of Jesus according to their use during one or another of the three periods; the *titles repeated are italicized*:

I Jesus, the Son of Mary, the Son of Joseph, Rabbi, the Master, Prophet, the Christ, the Son of David, the Son of Man, the Son of God, the Son, my Beloved Son, the King, He-Who-Comes, the Holy One of God, the Bridegroom, the Shepherd.

II (*a*) Common titles: *Jesus, the Christ, the Son* (etc.,) the Prophet, the Servant, the Lord, the Just One, the Judge, the Stone, the Head of the Body, the Beloved (Eph. I: 6).

(*b*) Pauline titles: the Image of God, the Power and Wisdom of God, the Firstborn, the Last Adam.

III (*a*) Common titles: *Jesus, the Christ, the Son* (etc.) *the King, the Bridegroom, the Shepherd, the Prophet, the Lord, the Judge, the Stone* (the Rock), *the Image, the Firstborn*, the Saviour (see pp. 133f.), ("God").

(*b*) From the Epistle to the Hebrews: the Head or Author, the Refulgence of His glory, the Mediator, the High Priest.

(*c*) From the Fourth Gospel and the First Epistle of St. John: the Bread of life, the Light of the world, the Door, the Good Shepherd, the Resurrection, the Vine, "the Way, the Truth, and the Life," the Lamb of God, the Word, the Paraclete, the Expiation.

(*d*) From the Apocalypse: the Lion of the tribe of Juda, the Shoot of the race of David, the radiant Morning Star, the Lamb (ἀρνίον), the Alpha and the Omega, the Amen.

This dry enumeration does not do justice to Taylor's

analysis, which notes the exceptions, qualifies the attribu-
tions, and recalls, for example, the influence that cult
and devotion exercised on the origin and frequent use
of a good number of titles applied to Christ. Some titles
such as *Lamb* or *Saviour* often took on new meanings from
one period to another due to the influence of their milieu.
Other words, such as *Son*, first understood in a Messianic
sense, served afterwards to express the richer idea of the
person of Jesus as it came to be discerned and gradually
linked to the cult. "Of all the Christological titles," E.
Stauffer writes, "the richest for the relationships that it
implies, is that of Κύριος. Its history is a *compendium* as well
as a *repetitorium* of New Testament Christology. In fact it
runs successively across the whole range of Christological
titles and unfolds before our eyes the way that leads from
the doctrinal and royal dignity of Jesus to His divine
dignity."[2] The way the names of Jesus were admitted
reveals what traits of His mysterious being held the
attention of the primitive Christian community. The first
fruits of this theological reflection fixed the pattern which
was to guide the Christology of all ages to come.

Few extrabiblical names for designating the Saviour are
in current use. That of *Redeemer* comes to mind, for it is
not found in the New Testament as a title of Christ; its
evident biblical ties, however, were examined above:
Jesus is the one who redeemed us (numerous texts) and
whom Paul even designates as "the Redemption" (I Cor.
I: 30). We could reason in the same way for the name *Sacred
Heart of Jesus*, a very popular name with Catholics since the
seventeenth century. The encyclical *Haurietis Aquas*, of
May 15, 1956, offers a magistral treatment of the basis of
the cult to the Sacred Heart of Jesus according to Bible and
Tradition.[3] Let us quote this development by Pius XII:

> There is nothing, then, which forbids us to adore the Most
> Sacred Heart of Jesus, since it participates in and is the natural
> and most expressive symbol of that inexhaustible love with which

Our Divine Redeemer still loves mankind. That Heart indeed, even if it is no longer liable to the disturbances of this mortal life, still lives and beats. It is now inseparably joined with the Person of the Divine Word, and in it and through it with His divine will.

Wherefore, since the Heart of Christ overflows with divine and human love, and since it is abundantly rich with treasures of all graces which Our Redeemer acquired by His life and His sufferings, it is truly the unfailing fountain of that love which His Spirit pours forth in all the members of His Mystical Body.

Therefore the Heart of Our Saviour certainly expresses the image of the Divine Person of the Word and His twofold nature, human and divine. In it we can contemplate not only the symbol, but also, as it were, *the sum of the whole mystery of our redemption.*

When we adore the Most Sacred Heart of Jesus Christ we adore in it and through it both the uncreated love of the Divine Word and His human love and all His other affections and virtues. This is so because both loves moved Our Redeemer to sacrifice Himself for us and for the whole Church, His Spouse.

As the Apostle says: "Christ also loved the Church and delivered Himself up for her, that He might sanctify her, cleansing in the bath of water by means of the Word, in order that He might present to Himself the Church in all her glory, not having spot or wrinkle or any such thing, but that she might be holy and without blemish."

Under the word "Sacred Heart" the *love*, evoked by St. Paul in a prayer to the Father, is honored: "That he may grant you from his glorious riches to be strengthened with power through his Spirit unto the progress of the inner man; and to have Christ dwelling through faith in your hearts: so that, being rooted and grounded in love, you may be able to comprehend with all the saints what is the breadth and length and height and depth, and to know *Christ's love* which surpasses knowledge, in order that you may be filled unto all the fullness of God" (Eph. III: 16–19).

The number and the variety of the names and titles applied to Jesus by the Christian community bear witness, better than abstract speculations, to the ontological richness of the Incarnate Word—a richness that John of the Cross expressed so felicitously in his reflection on these words of the Prologue to the Epistle to the Hebrews. "God who at sundry times and in divers manners spoke in times past to the fathers by the prophets, last of all in these days has spoken to us by his Son":

Herein the Apostle declares that God has become, as it were, dumb, and has no more to say, since that which He spoke aforetime, in part to the prophets, He has now spoken altogether in Him, giving us the All, which is His Son.

Wherefore he that would now enquire of God or seek any vision or revelation, would not only be acting foolishly, but would be committing an offence against God, by not setting his eyes altogether upon Christ, and seeking no new thing or aught beside. And God might answer him after this manner, saying: If I have spoken all things to thee in my Word, Which is My Son, and I have no other word, what answer can I now make to thee, or what can I reveal to thee which is greater than this?

Set thine eyes on Him alone, for in Him I have spoken and revealed to thee all things, and in Him thou shalt find yet more than that which thou askest and desirest. For thou askest locutions and revelations, which are the part; but if thou set thine eyes upon Him, thou shalt find the whole; for He is My complete locution and answer, and He is all My vision and all My revelation; so that I have spoken to thee, answered thee, declared to thee and revealed to thee in giving Him to thee as thy brother, companion and master, as ransom and prize.[4]

NOTES ON CONCLUSION

[1] I. Hauscherr writes: "Everything in Christian spirituality is invocation of the Name" (*Noms du Christ et voies d'oraison*, Rome, 1960, p. 285). The effects that accompany the recitation of the "Prayer to Jesus" by the Russian pilgrim would seem to be equally attributable to the invocation of the names of Jesus: "In the spirit: one feels the sweetness of the love of God, interior peace, ecstasy of the spirit, purity of thought, a beautifying attention to God;—in the sensibility: a pleasant warmth of the heart; all the limbs filled with sweetness, joyous heartbeats, lightness and freshness; life becomes sensibly pleasant as sickness and sorrow no longer hurt; finally, revelations: illumination of the

intelligence, insight into the Scriptures; one understands the Spirit of creation, becomes detached from the tumult of the earth, recognizes the sweetness of the interior life, is as sure of the nearness of God as of His love for us" (*ibid.*, p. 20).

2 E. Stauffer, *Die Theologie des Neuen Testaments* (Gütersloh, 1948), p. 94, cited by C. Spicq, *Dieu et l'homme selon le Nouveau Testament*, p. 88.

3 Cf. *Cor Jesu, commentationes in litteras encyclicas Pii PP. XII "Haurietis Aquas"* (Rome, 1959), two volumes.

4 St. John of the Cross, *Ascent of Mount Carmel*, translated by E. Allison Peers (New York, 1958), II, 22, p. 202.

APPENDIX

In 1907 Father Diekamp published *Doctrina Patrum de Incarnatione Verbi* (Münster in Westf.), a Greek florilegium redacted about the end of the seventh century. At Chapter 38 of the work there is a list of scriptural names of the Saviour, apparently collected by the anonymous author of the *Doctrina*. We thought that it would prove useful and have reproduced it here, adding Scriptural references for the less well known names.[1] Some of these appellations are, as the compiler noted, taken in the figurative (τροπικῶς) or metaphorical sense. Generally we have respected his omission of the definite article.

1. Wisdom (I Cor. I: 30)
2. Word (Λόγος)
3. Son of God
4. God Word
5. Light of the world
6. True Light
7. Resurrection
8. Way
9. Truth
10. Life
11. Door
12. Shepherd
13. Messiah
14. Christ
15. Jesus
16. Lord
17. Master (Διδάσκαλος)
18. Word (Ῥῆμα: cf. I Pet. I: 25)
19. King
20. Just One
21. True Vine
22. Bread of life
23. The First and the Last (Apoc. I: 17)
24. The One Living, and become dead[2]
25. The Alpha and the Omega, the Beginning and the End (Apoc. XXI: 6)
26. He-Who-Is (Apoc. I: 8)
27. He-Who-Was (Apoc. I: 8)
28. He-Who-Comes
29. The Faithful One (Apoc. XIX: 11)
30. The True One (Apoc. XIX: 11)
31. Chosen Arrow (Isa. XLIX: 2)
32. Servant of God
33. Light of the nations (Isa. XLIX: 6)
34. Lamb without malice (Jer. XI: 19)
35. Lamb of God
36. The Man (Ἀνήρ: Zech. VI: 12)
37. Advocate (I John II: 1)

38. Expiation ('Ιλασμός)
39. Power of God
40. Wisdom of God
41. Means of Expiation ('Ιλαστήριον: Rom. III: 25)
42. Consuming Fire (Heb. XII: 29)
43. Sanctification (I Cor. I: 30)
44. Redemption (I Cor. I: 30)
45. Justice (I Cor. I: 30)
46. High Priest
47. Judah (Gen. XLIX: 9)
48. Lion Cub (Gen. XLIX: 9)
49. Lion (Gen. XLIX: 9)
52. David (cf. Jer. XXX: 9)
53. Holy One
54. Root (Isa. XI: 1)
55. Sprout (Isa. XI: 1)
56. Flower ("Ανθος: Isa. XI: 1)
57. Bud (Βλαστός: Ezek. XVII: 23)
58. Stone (Λίθος; cf. Luke XX: 17)
59. Rock (Πέτρα: I Cor X: 14)
60. Unicorn (Ps. LXX; LXXVI: 69; XCI: 10)
61. Star (Num. XXIV: 17)
62. Prophet
63. Prince of the host (Dan. VIII: 11)
64. Priest
65. Sacrifice (Eph. V: 2)
66. Altar (Heb. XIII: 10)
67. Beloved like the young of unicorn (Ps. XXVIII: 66 [LXX])
68. Redeemer (cf. Acts VII: 35; Ps. LXXVII: 35 [LXX])
69. A man ("Ανθρωπος: Num. XXIV: 17 [LXX])
70. Most High (Ps. LXXVII: 35)
71. A worm (Ps. XXI: 7)
72. Name of the Lord (Ps. XX: 8)
73. Poor youth (Qoh. IV: 13)
74. A poor wise man (Qoh. IX: 15)
75. Bridegroom
76. Panther (Hos. V: 14)
77. Leader ('Ηγούμενος: Dan. IX: 25; Matt. II: 6)
78. Leader ("Αρχων: Mic. V: 2)
79. Master of All (Παντοκράτωρ: Apoc. I: 8)
80. Hand (I Pet. V: 6)
81. The Right Hand (Ps. XCVII: 1; CIX: 1)
82. Arm (Ps. XCVII: 1; CIX: 1)

85. Name of God (Ps. XIX: 6)
86. Messenger or Angel (Mal. III: 1)
87. Sun of Justice (Mal. IV: 2)
88. Lamb (Πρόβατον: Isa. LIII: 7)
89. Cloud of Justice (Isa. XLV: 8)
90. "Rising Sun" is his name (Zech. VI: 12)[3]
91. Son of Man
92. Law (Isa. LI: 4)
93. Just Judge (II Tim. IV: 8)
94. Emmanuel (Isa. VII: 14; Matt. I: 23)
95. Wonderful Counselor (Isa. IX: 6)
96. Marvelous (Isa. IX: 6)
97. Counselor (Isa. IX: 6)
98. Mighty God (Isa. IX: 6)
99. Master ('Εξουσιαστής: Isa. IX: 6)
100. Prince of Peace (Isa. IX: 6)
101. Father of the world to come (Isa. IX: 6)
102. Cloud (cf. no. 89 and I Cor. X: 2)
103. Beloved (Matt. XII: 18)
104. Witness (Apoc. I: 5)
105. Salvation (Isa. XLVI: 13)
106. Justice (Isa. XLVI: 13)
107. Glory of the Lord (Isa. XXXV: 2)
108. Majesty of God (Isa. XXXV: 2)
109. Salvation (Luke II: 30)
110. Covenant of the people (Isa. XLII: 6)
111. Servant whom I have chosen (Isa. XLI: 8)
112. God of Israel (Isa. XLV: 3)
113. Saviour
114. Exultation ('Αγαλλίαμα: Isa. LXI: 11)
115. Image of God
116. Form (Phil. II: 6)
117. Brightness (Heb. I: 3)
118. Effigy (Heb. I: 3)
119. Firstborn
121. Beloved ('Αδελφιδός: Cant. I: 13)
122. Nard (Cant. I: 12)
123. Sachet of myrrh (Cant. I: 13)
124. Flower of the plain (Cant. II: 1)
125. Lily (Cant. II: 1)
126. Apple tree (Cant. II: 3)

127. Gazelle (Cant. II: 9)
128. Stag (Cant. II: 9)
130. Solomon (Cant. III: 11)
131. Shepherd (Zech. XIII: 7)
132. Cluster of henna (Cant. I: 14)
133. Palm tree (Cant. VII: 7)
134. Tree of life (Isa. LXV: 22)
135. Apostle (Heb. III: 1)
136. Good (Luke XVIII: 18)
137. Beloved Son (Mark XII: 6)
138. The Child (Matt. II: 11)
139. Newborn (Luke II: 12)
140. Stumbling stone (Rom. IX: 33)
141. Rock of scandal (Rom. IX: 33)
142. Peace (Eph. II: 14)
145. Only Son (John I: 18)
146. Bread (John VI: 51)

147. Drink (I Cor. X: 4)
148. Source (Ps. XXXV: 9; Apoc. XXI: 6)
151. Light
155. Offering (Eph. V: 2)
156. Ransom (Matt. XX: 28)
171. Heir (Heb. I: 2)
173. Meek (Zech. IX: 9; Matt. XI: 29)
175. Humble (Matt. XI: 29)
178. Curse (Gal. III: 13)
179. Blessing (Gal. III: 14)
183. Fall and Rise (Luke II: 34)
185. Intercessor (Rom. VIII: 34)
186. Spirit (cf. John IV: 24; II Cor. III: 17)
187. Water of Life (Apoc. XXII: 17)

NOTES ON APPENDIX

[1] Our translation is from the Greek text of Diekamp (*op. cit.*, pp. 286–90). Several names are found only in the *Codex Alexandrinus* of the Septuagint used by the compiler. The names which he uselessly repeats, and the apocryphal names (as numbers 50, 158–69, 182), we have not listed.

[2] By transcribing Ὁ ζῶν καὶ γενόμενος νεκρός the compiler has not followed the *textus receptus* of Apoc. I: 18 (cf. *Revue Biblique*, 1923, p. 616).

[3] In place of the Messianic name "Bud" (Hebrew reading), the Greek has "Rising Sun" (Ἀνατολή) in Jer. XXIII: 5; Zech. III: 8; VI: 12; cf. Luke I: 78.

INDEX OF BIBLICAL TEXTS